ORCHARD

NUT WALK

TEA
SHED

BAMBOO

THE
WOOD

PAMPAS

GRASS

HAY MEADOW

# A FENLAND
# GARDEN

**Francis Pryor** is one of Britain's most distinguished living archaeologists, the excavator of Flag Fen and a sheep farmer. He is the author of seventeen books, including *The Fens* (a Radio 4 Book of the Week), *Stonehenge*, *Flag Fen*, *Britain BC*, *Britain AD*, *The Making of the British Landscape* and *Scenes from Prehistoric Life*. Francis lives in the South Lincolnshire fens.

Also by Francis Pryor

*Britain BC*
*Britain AD*
*The Making of the British Landscape*
*Stonehenge*
*The Fens*
*Scenes from Prehistoric Life*

# A FENLAND GARDEN

## Creating a haven for people, plants & wildlife

# FRANCIS PRYOR

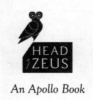

An Apollo Book

First published in the UK in 2023 by Head of Zeus Ltd,
part of Bloomsbury Publishing Plc

9 7 5 3 1 2 4 6 8

A catalogue record for this book is available from the British Library.

ISBN (HB): 9781801101608
ISBN (E): 9781801101622

Garden map @ Jamie Whyte, based on a drawing by Maisie Pryor

*The images used in the book are the author's own, with the exception of the following:*
Pages xii-xiii: aerial photograph of Inley Drove Farm, Robin Davis, Pride Magazines
Page 33: aerial photograph of roddons, from M. Waller, 'The Fenland Project,
Number 9: Flandrian Environmental Change in Fenland', plate vi, p.45 East Anglian
Archaeology Report No. 70, 1994 (Cambridge).
Page 34: plan of roddons and stream courses, from David Hall, 'The Fenland Project,
Number 10: Cambridgeshire Survey, Isle of Ely and Wisbech', fig. 93, p.168.
© Cambridgeshire Archaeological Committee.

Printed and bound in Great Britain by
CPI Group (UK) Ltd, Croydon CR0 4YY

Head of Zeus Ltd
5–8 Hardwick Street
London EC1R 4RG

WWW.HEADOFZEUS.COM

For Maisie, who helped me write
this one-sided version

# Contents

Timeline     XV

Introduction     I

## PART I

### *A Tale of Two Gardens*
### *From Limetree Farmhouse to Inley Drove Farm* (1980–92)

1. Finding the Fens     5

2. The Wisbech Fens, 1981:
   Our First Fenland Garden     29

3. The Move to Lincolnshire     55

## PART II

### *Inley Drove Farm:*
### *Planning and Planting the Basic Structure*

4. Creating the Wood     77

5. The Hay Meadow     99

6. The Orchard and the Nut Walk     123

7. The Vegetable Garden     145

8. Between the House and the Barn     171

9. The Front Garden     191

# PART III

*Inley Drove Farm: The Garden Grows*

10. The Long Border                             213

11. The Birch Grove                             233

12. Paths for Play and Reflection               253

13. Rooms and Cells                             267

14. Walking the Walk                            283

15. People and Gardens                          299


Acknowledgements                               317

Endnotes                                       319

Index                                          325

# A FENLAND
# GARDEN

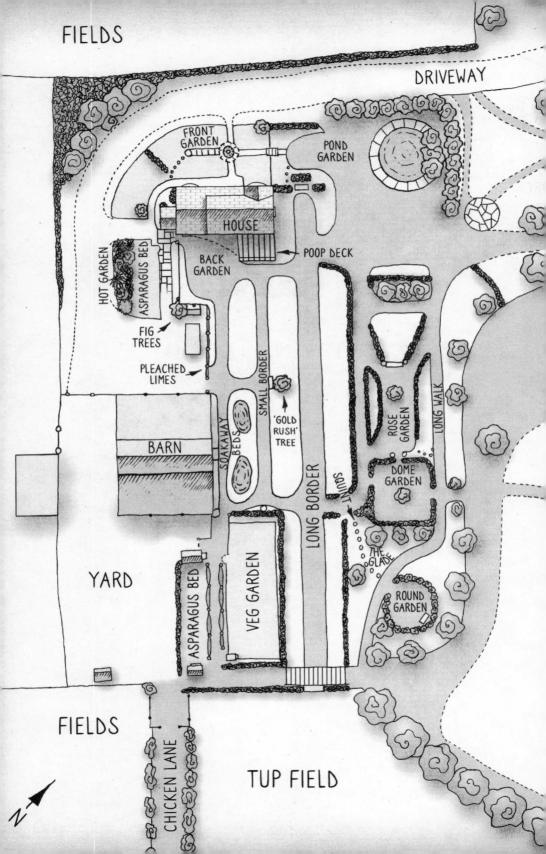

FIELDS

DRIVEWAY

FRONT GARDEN

POND GARDEN

HOUSE

POOP DECK

HOT GARDEN

ASPARAGUS BED

BACK GARDEN

FIG TREES

PLEACHED LIMES

SOAKAWAY BEDS

SMALL BORDER

'GOLD RUSH' TREE

LONG BORDER

STUMP

ROSE GARDEN

LONG WALK

DOME GARDEN

THE GLADE

BARN

ROUND GARDEN

YARD

VEG GARDEN

ASPARAGUS BED

FIELDS

CHICKEN LANE

TUP FIELD

N

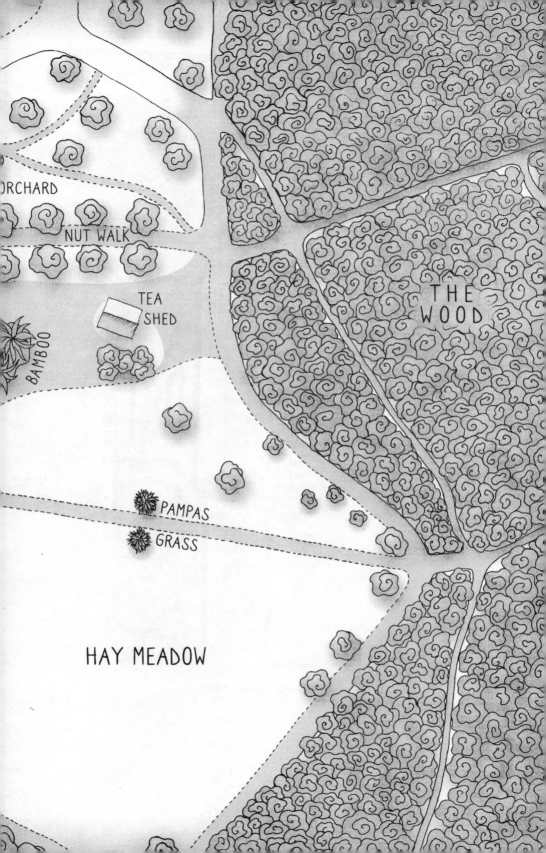

# Timeline

1981    *12 May*: Moved into Limetree Farmhouse, Wisbech fens.

1982    *November*: Flag Fen Bronze Age site discovered.

1987    *Summer*: Flag Fen Mere constructed. Flag Fen opens to the public.

1989    *Spring*: Apple orchard felled opposite Limetree Farm.

1989/90 *Winter*: Flag Fen Bronze Age landscape laid out.

1992    *Autumn*: Took possession of Inley Drove Farm; marked out borders of wood and planted grass in area that will become hay meadow.

*December 1992–January 1993*: constructed driveway into Inley Drove Farm.

1993    *Late winter–early spring*: Woodland planted.

*Late spring*: Planted Nut Walk.

*Late spring*: Started planting orchard.

*Spring/summer*: Barn constructed.

*Autumn*: Laid out vegetable garden.

1994    *Winter–spring*: Strong gales; continued planting orchard.

*Spring*: Limetree Farmhouse sold.

*Early summer*: Building work on Inley Drove Farmhouse begins.

*June*: Moved into the new barn at Inley Drove Farm.

*End of autumn*: Brick walls between house and barn completed by now.

*Christmas Eve*: Moved out of barn into Inley Drove Farmhouse.

1995    *Early winter*: Planted black poplar cuttings around the Tup Field and along the Black Poplar Walk.

*Spring*: Began landscaping around house and barn.

1996    *Summer*: Long border well established by now; pergola constructed at end of long border.

1997    *22 June*: Inley Drove Farm opened for National Garden Scheme (NGS) for first time.

1998    *April and July*: Serious floods.

1999    *Winter*: Land drains jetted out (cleared of blockages).

*Late winter*: Raised the soil level of the vegetable garden.

2000    *June*: exceptionally heavy rain leads to flooding of much of garden; NGS openings suspended pending improvements to drainage

*Autumn*: First large crop of apples from the orchard.

2001    Completed the Serpentine Walk.

2005    Wirework dome positioned in Dome Garden.

2010    Wirework dome moved from Dome Garden to Front Garden; by now, buttercups in meadow have formed a carpet.

2016    *17/18 September*: Opened the Inley Drove Garden for the NGS.

2020    *March*: First raid on snowdrops in wood.

*September*: Covid-19 pandemic fails to prevent Inley Drove Garden opening for the NGS.

2022    *28 July*: Coningsby in Lincolnshire (25 miles north of Inley Drove) records British record temperature of 40.3 °C (104.5 °F).

# Introduction

*A Fenland Garden* tells the story of how – and why – my wife Maisie and I created a large garden in the silt Fens of south Lincolnshire, some ten miles inland from the Wash. It's a challenging and fragile landscape with a long past, but – sadly – an uncertain future. Maisie and I are both field archaeologists with decades of experience excavating and researching ancient farms, settlements and burials in and around the Fens. In so doing, we have acquired unique knowledge not just of individual sites and finds, but also – by working with specialists in ancient soils, pollen and plant remains, all of which are superbly preserved in the waterlogged subsoils of the Fens – an understanding of the changing economies and environments of the communities they are investigating. This collaborative research has given us a long-term view of Fenland history and prehistory, which has been a major influence on the way we planned, created and modified our garden and its surroundings. It has also profoundly affected both how we laid out the garden and the way we planted it. The hundreds of trees in our wood, for example, are all native British species, as are the hedges and the grasses in the lawns and meadow. They provide a harmonious but restrained background to the sumptuous roses and exotic flowers that bloom in the various beds and borders.

Creating the garden hasn't been easy or straightforward. Indeed, it has been a challenging journey of discovery, with plenty of disasters large and small and sharp U-turns along the way, which I will describe in some detail. But it has also been a profoundly rewarding experience that has taught Maisie and myself much about horticulture, but also about ourselves and each other. Gardening is about far more than just growing (and eating!) plants.

Despite the many bumps in the road as we attempted to transform an over-fertilised wheat field into a flourishing and well-stocked garden, we have no regrets about the task we took on: the garden's existence is its own justification.

Gardeners have to garden: that's all there is to it. What I wanted to capture in this book is some of the excitement we felt as our new garden started to take shape. However, it also quite often proved to be a lonely experience, the two of us working on our own in a large tract of open fen. We now understand why farmers in their tractors, ploughing or tilling their vast Fenland fields, always wave back if a passing motorist waves or flashes their headlights in greeting. We would never fail to return the compliment if a neighbour, driving his or her tractor along the road, gave us a wave of greeting when we were out working on our land, planting hedges, edging a border or digging manure into the vegetable garden.

But now it's time to start our journey by turning the clock back some three decades, to an autumn day in 1992.

# PART I

## *A Tale of Two Gardens: From Limetree Farmhouse to Inley Drove Farm (1980–92)*

# I

# Finding the Fens

*Buying the Land • Structural Timbers •*
*The Flag Fen Reconstruction • Roddons*

We were standing in a gap in an old hawthorn hedge, staring across a large open field whose crop had been harvested six months earlier. You could see the rows of dried stalks where the wheat had once been growing, but by now weeds were also starting to poke through. They didn't look particularly healthy, either: a bit thin and undernourished. In fact, the entire scene should have looked bleak and cheerless, with a cool north-easterly breeze, weak sunshine and passing clouds blowing in from off the Wash. But that was not how it seemed to us.

We had just taken possession of the land and had driven straight to it from the estate agent's offices in Wisbech. I got Maisie to stand in the field entranceway and snapped a photo. It was taken around noon on an early autumn day in 1992. That picture is still very special to both of us. It shows the land where we were to build our house and establish our small sheep farm and large garden. We could picture them in our mind's eye and they looked nothing like the flat, rather cheerless field before us.

A view into our new garden from the gap in the hawthorn hedge
that later became the main gateway to the house and garden. This
photo was taken in September 1992, on the day we took official
possession of the land. A few weeks earlier we had persuaded a local
farmer to sow it with grass seed, following our plans, which clearly
marked the area we wanted to plant with trees. In this photo, the
un-seeded and un-tilled soil that would later be woodland shows up
darker and can be seen to the left of centre, in the middle distance,
just level with Maisie's shoulders. (See also page 126.)

We had been looking for somewhere to build a house and
establish a small farm for at least a year and it had been a
very hectic time for us. When we weren't working, we drove
around the Fens between Wisbech, Spalding and Boston,
looking for somewhere suitable. But there always seemed to be
problems: ground too wet, a busy road or a noisy vegetable-
packing station. Sometime in January 1992 we had attended
the auction of a field outside the Lincolnshire Fenland village
of Holbeach St Johns. Rather to our surprise, it was to prove
an excellent potential site: not too far away from electricity and

water and accessed by a well made-up farm track. It was also next to a small wood and there were some old brick-built farm buildings that could easily have been restored. At the time, we had had the idea of setting up a small sheep farm and those old buildings would have been ideal. But, sadly, the price the land went for was way out of our league. Later, we learnt it had been bought by a large commercial potato grower. His bid had caused something of a sensation among the many local farmers who attended the auction. Like us, they were amazed by the price he was prepared to pay.

We had attended the auction in the company of a friendly local estate agent who knew we wanted to buy land to build a house but was also very aware that we had never actually done any bidding. So he took us under his wing and accompanied us to the auction. He immediately spotted the rich potato farmer and didn't bid. Just as well: I'd probably have got carried away and spent a fortune. Even so, we both felt a bit down. The land had been perfect and now it was just going to grow yet more potatoes. We drove home in silence.

Next day, the phone rang. It was the nice estate agent who had taken us to the auction, and he sounded very enthusiastic as he told us that a farmer from a village near Holbeach St Johns had approached him after yesterday's sale. He had seen that we were interested in buying land. It just so happened that he had a field for sale, which he would be prepared to sell to us 'by private arrangement' through our friendly estate agent. The estate agent then gave us the farmer's phone number, which we rang immediately. In retrospect, I suppose we should have delayed that call for a day or two, so as not to appear *too* interested. But of course that's not what we did. Because we *were* keen. Very keen. So I phoned him immediately.

The call was answered by his wife, a charming lady, whom we later got to know very well. Sadly, she died a few years ago. Her husband – we shall call him Fred – had just finished breakfast. I could hear the sound of a chair being pushed back, then Fred took the receiver. He said he'd be happy to show us the field he had in mind, but not until the afternoon. This morning he had to finish drilling another field on the farm with spring barley, as rain was forecast later in the day. In late January, you have to seize every opportunity Mother Nature offers you.

Like all Fen farmers, Fred's ability to forecast the weather was spot-on; it started to rain just as we were following his battered Vauxhall estate out of the yard behind his house and onto the main village street. We drove past the medieval church with its fine limestone tower and well-stocked graveyard. It had clearly been a prosperous place in the late Middle Ages. We headed south-west out of the village in the general direction of Holbeach St Johns, but then turned rather abruptly right. We'd recced this part of the Holbeach and Sutton Fens quite closely, but somehow hadn't spotted this narrow droveway. It was very roughly paved and only just wide enough for a single vehicle; it also lacked those carefully arranged passing places that are such a welcome feature of narrow rural roads in more populated parts of the country; here, muddy field entranceways would have to suffice. After a couple of hundred yards, the thick, overgrown hawthorn hedge that ran along the right-hand side of the droveway stopped. Fred had stopped too. And so did we. I noted that Fred hadn't pulled off the road, so we left our Land Rover also blocking the road and joined him. He was standing in the field entranceway, which was a short causeway of dumped builders' rubble across a deep dyke. It didn't look very secure. I determined to strengthen it – if, that is, we eventually bought the land. Fred was surprisingly chatty and told us all about the various crops he had gown on its 17 acres, which mostly consisted of oilseed rape, wheat and barley. He also talked a bit about the pheasants and partridges that were attracted by the hawthorn hedge. He hinted broadly that he'd like to shoot across the land, if we did decide to buy it. I smiled encouragingly, but didn't agree to anything. Then he drove off and I went for a rapid walk with Maisie.

We beat the bounds. Each side of the field was about 250 yards long and it was bounded on its northern and western sides by old hawthorn hedges, which I reckoned had been planted sometime in the nineteenth century. The other two sides ran along drainage dykes that looked very like Internal Drainage Board drains. They were wide, deep and very well maintained, with mown sides and cleanly cut profiles. They would have been cut and scraped every autumn, before the high water levels of winter. Otherwise, the field was completely open and seemingly featureless, although Maisie and I could both discern the gentle and very distinctive rise and fall of old tidal creeks, known in the Fens as roddons.* The low mounds and lighter silty soils found in roddons make them ideal sites for houses and other buildings – and we could both see at least one likely spot for our hoped-for new house. The slightly coarser silts of roddon soils drain well and are very nutritious; plants – especially vegetables – love them. I shall have more to say about roddons in the next chapter.

That first walk had taken about half an hour. It was starting to get cold as the feeble sun set behind the rain clouds and a thick mist started to spread towards us from the east. But we didn't care: we were both smiling broadly as we trowelled the mud from the soles of our wet wellies and clambered aboard the Land Rover. We both knew that Fred's field would be the perfect place. All we had to do now was buy it.

I cannot honestly pretend that I can remember all the details of the negotiations that followed, but eventually the

---

* The Fenland term for fossilised watercourses, perhaps ultimately derived from the Celtic river name 'Roden', meaning 'swift river'.

estate agent agreed a price with Fred. And yes, it was slightly more than we had expected to pay, but I can now confess that we'd probably have gone even higher, if we'd had to: we both wanted that field very much. For various reasons, the actual purchase was quite an extended process, but eventually it was complete. Eight months later, we took possession and when we had signed all the various papers and deeds, we drove away from the agent's smart Georgian office in Wisbech (which, I must add, does smart Georgian offices better than almost anywhere else in Britain) and headed straight off to our new land. And that is how we found ourselves standing by the gateway into the field, staring out into the open acres, on that autumn day, back in 1992. It may have looked bleak, barren and empty to anyone else – but it was now *our* field. All we could see was its amazing potential, which was why we had become so very fond of it. I know it might appear to some people to be just another lonely, exposed Fenland field, but that wasn't how we viewed it. We could see it was lonely, but that was what we were after: we didn't want close neighbours. Yes, we were both keen to create a refuge for wildlife, but more important than that, we needed to fashion a haven for ourselves. Looking back on those times, I now appreciate that starting a garden was an emotional journey. It was about feelings, affection and security. These things were far more important than the urge to design and create something original or spectacular.

Neither Maisie nor I was born and raised in the Fens. Maisie's family came from Surrey and Scotland, mine from Hertfordshire and Ireland. And yet we both found ourselves living and working in a very different region with distinctive landscapes and communities, both of which we were – and are still – becoming increasingly attached to. So how and why did our lives change: was it by accident or design? I wish there was a simple answer to that question – but profound changes certainly happened, for both of us.

\*

Projects like building a house and laying out a garden rapidly acquire timetables of their own. I think I imagined we'd first build the house and then, as we furnished it, we would start to plan the garden. But the real world didn't share my fond imaginings: it proved a bit harder than we had thought to sell our old house in the Wisbech fens, just across the county boundary in Cambridgeshire, about eight miles to the south of the new field, because the property market had hit a rough patch and prices everywhere were falling.

Eventually, in the spring of 1994, Limetree Farmhouse, the house in the Wisbech fens where we had lived since 1981, was sold. This delay meant that we couldn't start to fund a builder until the early summer of 1994 and didn't move into the (unfurnished) house until Christmas Eve of that same year. While all this was happening, we needed to establish a presence on the new land: gardens aren't laid out from tents; you need somewhere dry and secure to store tools and wheelbarrows. A supply of water and power would also be useful. We managed to acquire planning permission for the project because we were establishing a self-sustaining sheep-keeping enterprise, which would require, among many other things, a barn where the ewes could produce their lambs every winter and early spring. Neither of us fancied one of the steel and concrete system buildings that were becoming popular at that time. But then we happened to stumble upon English Brothers, a timber importer based in Wisbech (whose inland port is one of England's furthest from the sea). And it turned out that English Brothers also ran a firm of builders – in timber, of course.

After a visit to their depot, we phoned their rep, a charming local man called Terry, who came to take a look at our rather bleak field. In no time, he had painted a picture in our mind's eye of a lovely, snug timber barn populated by snoring, slumbering ewes. And I have to confess, Terry's barn has proved a huge success. It was built by just two highly proficient carpenters with a supporting army of different-sized ladders. Shortly before it was to be erected, Maisie and I decided that we both needed workshops. Hers would be used to study ancient timbers, but mine was to be more conventional, with a bench, a vice and racks of tools. We decided that both workshops should have exterior double doors and concrete floors, which added a lot to the cost. The barn was finished early in 1993. About a year later, we sold Limetree Farmhouse and had to move out.

The enlarged new barn had cleared us out financially, so we decided against renting a temporary flat and instead bought a redundant old holiday caravan. It was here that we slept, together with countless mice. Early in June 1994, we parked the caravan directly outside the new barn. This allowed us easy access to Maisie's workshop, where we would cook, wash up and eat our meals. The main building of the barn was our sitting room, complete with straw-bale tables and armchairs. Meanwhile, a friendly local plumber fixed up a temporary shower cubicle in my workshop. The workshops' double doors opened onto the wide surrounding fen. I have happy memories of stepping out of the shower, stark naked, as Maisie handed me a towel, still warm from the sunshine on the washing line, and a glass of medium-dry sherry. As I took the glass from her hand, in the distance I could just see a few Dinky Toy-sized cars driving down the road as people returned home in the afternoon 'rush hour', such as it is in our remote part of the fen. I raised my glass to them.

The timber framework of the barn, with Maisie and our
black Labrador Major, standing on the recently dumped
bricks of the new stockyard.

I had told Terry about our plans to build a house when we commissioned the barn, and he understood that work on it couldn't start until we'd sold Limetree Farm. I had lived in timber-frame houses in Canada through the cold winters of the 1970s and I knew they were well insulated and very warm. Maisie was a specialist in prehistoric woodworking and was delighted when I suggested we go for a timber-frame building. Everything about them was somehow more relaxed: because they don't rely on heavy steelwork or quantities of concrete breeze-blocks, they don't need heavy-duty foundations. This is ideal for the soil in our area, since its load-bearing capacity is poor.

Although it is now more than twenty-five years old, the house we built still has far better insulated walls than the block-built houses that are appearing on new estates in local towns. We not only liked timber, we also grew to like the craftsmen who carried out the work. We would bring them cups of tea, listen to their talk and watch fascinated as they connected beam joints or worked on more delicate tasks, such as erecting the staircase or assembling the huge numbers of bookshelves that Maisie and I required. In those days, we were both deeply interested in prehistoric carpentry, as Maisie was writing the detailed report on the many hundreds of worked timbers we had excavated at Flag Fen. By the time the carpenters had completed work on the house, they had given me the confidence to build several smaller bookshelves myself, and to my delight they haven't bent, distorted or collapsed, despite being made to carry at least twice as many books as I had originally planned.

The building of the house was completed early in 1995. Because it had been timber-framed (and didn't require large quantities of bricks or stonework), its construction had not produced too much lorry and digger disturbance to the ground immediately around it. This meant that we were able to press ahead with our plans for the new garden while the house

A view of the house during construction in the summer of 1995.
The timber framework has been completed and the walls have been
clad with a black damp-proof membrane. Work on the roof has yet
to start. Note the completed barn to the left of the picture. Maisie is
observing the two bog-garden soakaway beds that take run-off
water from the barn roof.

was being built. We had been able to make some important
decisions, such as precisely where we were to position the
vegetable garden, as early as the winter of 1992–3. So, with key
elements of the garden's overall framework already established,
we had the confidence to start shaping individual beds and
plantings, away from the house-building works.

We began work on the new garden that winter, following the
purchase of the 17-acre arable field. I have to confess that it felt
somewhat strange to be laying out a small border that would
provide a pleasant view from the house – when the house itself
had yet to be built. It came as quite a relief when work on
the house began at the end of summer 1994. It was good to

have something to 'garden around' – a focus – even if it was just a timber frame and damp-proof cladding that made weird sounds when the wind got up.

We had chosen the land carefully to avoid doing any archaeological damage, but in the process of creating the garden we also made one or two unexpected discoveries. We knew in advance that the field had the kind of silty soil we were looking for and the water table was quite high; both would encourage rapid plant growth. But it wasn't to prove as simple as that.

I can remember the moment when I first inserted a spade into the ground of what was shortly to become our new garden. I was well aware that the silty soils of the land surrounding the Wash were some of the most fertile not just in Britain, but in the whole of Europe. So I was surprised that some of the weeds weren't as big as they were in our Limetree Farm garden: the dandelion roots were small and wispy; even the groundsel looked a bit thin, sad and undernourished. This was distinctly odd and not at all what I had expected.

So I did a bit more digging and was astounded to discover that my spade hadn't encountered – let alone cut in half – a single earthworm. I knelt down and took a handful of freshly turned-over soil. In those days, I had recently been prescribed my first pair of reading glasses, which I pulled from my pocket. I looked at the soil again, more closely: nothing whatsoever was moving in it. It was dead, it even felt dead: odourless, more akin to Plasticine than the organic-rich silty soil in the Limetree Farm vegetable garden. It was also impossible to crumble. Then it slowly dawned on me: the lack of earthworms would account for the absence of molehills, which I had noticed, but couldn't explain. Moles find their food in the soil and are very fond of earthworms. It was now obvious to me what had happened: nearly half a century of post-war intensive arable cultivation, with chemical sprays and artificial fertilisers, had killed off most signs of life below the surface. I laid my spade down, as a strange cold feeling began to take hold of me: we were going to have a *huge* amount of work to do.

We both knew that if we wanted to grow healthy plants, we would have to revitalise the soil – and the sooner the better. This was to prove one of our biggest challenges. But other complicating factors were also at play. We were aware that the layout of the new garden was not going to be simple. We wanted it to be very wildlife-friendly but also to reflect our shared attitude to the development of the landscape and the importance we both attached to Fenland history and archaeology. Today, people are becoming increasingly aware of the region's long and rich past, but perceptions were very different in the early 1990s. Maisie and I began to appreciate just how remarkable the ancient Fens were when we first worked there in the early to mid-1970s. But we only began to appreciate the challenges of actually earning a living in this landscape when we started to construct a visitor attraction at Flag Fen, just outside Peterborough, in 1987. The lessons we learnt there have been fundamental to the way we established both our Fenland gardens, first at Limetree and then at Inley Drove Farm. It is time for a brief diversion, about 25 miles south-west of our new field, to the ancient cathedral city of Peterborough.

\*

In November 1982, I had the great good fortune to discover the superbly preserved waterlogged site at Flag Fen. By the mid-1980s, I was absolutely convinced that we should make the effort to bring our archaeological work in and around Flag Fen to a wider audience, as I was becoming increasingly aware that what we were discovering was too important to be confined to a small audience of academics, archaeologists and our enthusiastic volunteer supporters alone. A decade later I was lucky enough to be involved in national television, through the highly popular Channel 4 series *Time Team*, but back in the late 1970s and 80s I was less ambitious: I had my eyes set on a local audience because I had seen the enthusiasm of our many visitors when we held open days during the excavations. I could feel their excitement as they gazed over the dig and the eagerness – almost breathlessness – of their many questions when the tours were over.

I knew from talking to visitors to our excavations that people understood very little indeed about life in pre-Roman Britain. It wasn't taught at school and most books on the subject were pitched at university students, rather than the general reader. Indeed, prehistory has only recently been introduced into the National Curriculum (sadly for primary schoolchildren only).[1] So these were some of the reasons why we encouraged family groups to attend our excavation's open days. I know of several youngsters who came along with their parents and then found they had developed an interest in archaeology for themselves.[2] Many went on to study it at university.

In the mid-1980s, we decided to do something about raising our public profile. The first step was to generate a bit of income by opening Flag Fen to the paying public on a more permanent basis than the occasional open day. It was immediately apparent to me that the dig alone might have inspired enthusiasts, but it wasn't enough on its own to attract the wider audience of regular visitors that we needed to raise a meaningful regular income. This new income stream had to be sufficient to support a shop and maybe a full-time manager too. So I had to decide what we could do to broaden our appeal, beyond the excavation. It was apparent to all of us that somehow we had to bring the Bronze Age to life

– and the only way to do this would be by recreating what we had so painstakingly excavated: namely, fields and farms. I wasn't aware of it at the time, but we were about to design a landscape garden.

I was determined that our recreation of the Bronze Age landscape at Flag Fen should stimulate visitors to use their imaginations, so we based it very closely on the results of our excavations over the previous fifteen or so years. I wanted to create a 'typical' tract of Fen-edge landscape, as it might have looked around or just after 1500 BC. This set me thinking about what makes any particular landscape 'typical' and what it was about that landscape that would have appealed to the communities that inhabited it. And it wasn't just a matter of crude economics. My study of anthropology at university had taught me that the different social groups living in a particular area had to co-operate. Tribal and family structures provide the cohesion needed to help people survive in hard times – and this requirement to meet regularly and exchange views, gifts and goods had to be reflected in the layout of the landscape. I wanted our visitors to be able to identify with their prehistoric forebears: this wasn't to be a zoo, where people observe from afar.

I knew from my own experience of growing up as part of a farming family that farms are not like factories; they cannot exist independently. Neighbours are important – indeed, they are essential. Small-scale trade and exchange is constantly happening as part of the day-to-day running of a farm or smallholding; very often your neighbours are also cousins or other relatives. Indeed, I strongly suspected that such ties would have been even more important in prehistory. Somehow, I had to get this across to an audience that was becoming increasingly urban, as the old market town of Peterborough evolved rapidly into the New Town.

Our first challenge was to acquire the land we needed for the new development. Happily, this came about without the major expense of our actually having to buy it. When I told the neighbouring landowner, which happened to be the local water provider, Anglian Water, about our future plans, they approved of them thoroughly and leased us about ten acres of land. I think they were able to justify this generous decision to their shareholders because the Trust we had set up to run Flag Fen was a registered charity. Having successfully acquired the extra land, I then found myself confronting a new reality: local media had publicised the land transfer, and considerable public interest was starting to be aroused. To be honest, I found it all slightly scary. I would frequently lie awake at night, wondering how our small team of half a dozen people would cope the next morning. Looking back on those times, I now realise that although I had thought the principal problem I faced was that of recreating a piece of prehistoric landscape, there were many more that would have to be addressed. For a start, ancient fields and farms had evolved to accommodate a local population of at most a hundred people. We, on the other hand, were expecting thousands of visitors. Historical garden designers must frequently have found themselves in similar situations.

I'm a huge fan of English country gardens. I acquired this interest when I was still a child, in the course of family visits to nearby stately homes such as Wrest Park or Knebworth House. Today, these places and others like them have many more visitors than they did back in the 1950s, yet their gardens can still cope with large crowds – and with a minimum of intrusive measures. This suggests that their layout had originally been intended to manage significant volumes of people, if only on special occasions. Early garden and landscape designers, such as Humphry Repton and Lancelot 'Capability' Brown, are famed for their lovely views and sweeping panoramas, but they also clearly understood how people moved through a landscape and how they could be accommodated in large numbers without the garden appearing to 'fill up' with people. This was precisely what I wanted to achieve in our reconstructed landscape at Flag Fen.

I didn't realise that I was reinventing the wheel, but I soon discovered what men like Brown and Repton had long known, which was that parks and gardens need to be effectively, but never intrusively, partitioned. Take people on walks in small parties; focus their attention on their immediate surroundings before confronting them with wider views. As I pondered the challenges (and opportunities) that lay ahead of us, I realised that I needed some principles to structure – to discipline – my imagination. I had seen too many supposedly 'historical' reconstructions where historical truth had been sacrificed in order to tell a good story. So I determined never knowingly to depart from the form and structure of the landscapes revealed in our excavations. I was also aware that I would somehow have to accommodate a pre-existing lake, visitor centre, car park and access road. The site was also crossed by a Roman road and access had to be allowed for regular dyke maintenance. I had no idea how I could possibly reconcile these seemingly conflicting goals. It was very worrying. I was suffering a version of something that's only too familiar to many people, including authors, at the outset of a new project. It was a sort of writer's block. I didn't know where to start.

*

It wasn't long before my mental block was pushed aside in a most unexpected fashion: by a large, tracked excavator, known as a Hy-Mac 580C. I've already mentioned that the land at

Flag Fen had been rented to us by the local water and sewage company, for a tiny amount, because we were a charity. But more was to come. Shortly before we began work – at a point where I still lacked a clear plan of what we were going to do – their generous offer was extended to include the loan of a tracked excavator. The Hy-Mac 580C had been *the* state-of-the-art digger earlier in the 1980s, when Britain led the world in excavator design and construction.[3] JCBs, of course, are still with us and thriving, but Hy-Macs have been largely forgotten – although I know of a few battered and mud-spattered examples lurking behind the barns of remote cattle farms, where they are still used to muck out the yards when the cows have been put out to their springtime grazing.

I remember the chilly winter morning in early 1990 when the low-loader arrived on site with the freshly serviced Hy-Mac aboard. The lorry driver unloaded the digger and then handed over about a dozen jerrycans of diesel and a small drum of grease. After a short guided tour of the machine, he gave me a cheery wave and headed off down the muddy access track. I was on my own now.

I suppose I should have felt rather alarmed. It was a bleak scene: I was standing alongside the digger near the edge of a large open field that had been ploughed about six months earlier and now sustained a ragged crop of patchy weeds, with couch grass and stinging nettles starting to encroach from the nearby dykeside. There was also quite a strong smell of sewage from the treatment works immediately upwind. But instead of leaving me at a loss what to do next, the digger had given me something to think about; like an old friend, I found it strangely comforting. I may even have given its old and slightly battered bodywork a reassuring pat.

The engine was still ticking over and I caught a slight hint of diesel fumes from the exhaust pipe above my head on the other side of the machine. I opened the cab door, and again there was the familiar smell of lubricant, engine oil and diesel, mingled with aromas of old sandwich bags and chocolate-bar wrappers stuffed behind the seat. I threw my knapsack into the back of the cab and climbed aboard. I looked around me at the various dials and levers. All seemed familiar. I'd been driving Hy-Macs since the early 1980s, when we used to clear large areas of topsoil in advance of our excavations, and this one looked to be in very good condition. I realised I was raring to go, but where was I to start? I knew we were only being loaned the digger for a few days, so I had to get going. Suddenly, my mental block had gone, and it was obvious to me what I needed to do: I would head over to the large tract of empty land between the lake and the winding old dyke that formed the eastern boundary of our land. It was the ideal 'blank canvas'. With the help of the Hy-Mac, I would recreate the long, straight, parallel banks and ditches that bounded each side of the large Bronze Age farm droveway, which we had first exposed back in 1974. It would prove to be the right decision.

Those twin ditches were to give structure to the entire park. For some reason, I found it much easier to plan the new site actually out there, on the ground. Maps and digital sketches are fine insofar as they go, but they don't say anything about the atmosphere of a place and they make no allowance for the passing of time or for changes in light and temperature. We were designing as we went along, which is something you are not supposed to do in the modern world, but I found it both effective and enjoyable – and it certainly gave me greater confidence. Low sunlight on the ditch sides and banks dramatically increased their presence and changed subtly with the passing of each hour, cloud or shower. I could imagine how people would respond as they walked through the park, not just along Bronze Age droveways, but past muddy hollows and patches of reeds, populated by croaking frogs and waddling ducklings. Reconstructed prehistoric houses and farms could be positioned correctly in their landscape setting. As we worked, I was soon able to visualise exactly where our planned new visitor centre could be located and how it would lead naturally out into the landscape park – in a way that didn't interfere with the prehistoric landscape. These buildings would come into their own on chilly midwinter afternoons, when visitors could settle down after their walk in the park to enjoy a well-earned mug of tea or coffee.

It took me slightly longer than I had expected to survey in, to excavate and then to carefully shape the reconstructed Bronze Age droveway, together with the various fields and yards that it would originally have linked together and serviced. I wanted to get it absolutely right, so we spent much time working from the plans we had published in the excavation report, measuring in the precise relative position of everything.[4] My copy of that report is still spattered in mud from the many hours when it lay open, precariously balanced on my lap, while my arms and legs pushed and pulled the levers and pedals in the cab of the Hy-Mac. It was while I was working so closely with the precise layout of the prehistoric droveway, field and yard ditches that I began to appreciate just how carefully they had been arranged. We knew from their excavation a few years earlier that the system had taken several centuries to build up, but everything followed the original broad structure and its orientation: new ditches, for example, rarely veered to one side. It was clear to me that they were working from a plan, but one that was not written down or drawn. The key points would have been out there, in the landscape: piles of stones, wooden posts or maybe planted shrubs – even old trees that happened to be growing in the correct spot. These locations would have been recognised and agreed by senior members of the various clans, families and communities living in the area.

I suspect the regular, even arrangement of the Bronze Age fields and farmhouses at Flag Fen would have facilitated communication and contact between different members of the closely knit communities. So these 3,500-year-old fields have something in common with the domestic gardens of more recent eras, where the layout often recalls the state of society at the time. Tudor gardens are highly structured and compartmentalised – rather like the clothes of the contemporary aristocracy. Georgian gardens are hierarchical and structured too, but they also include wide, sweeping views that reflect the broadening scope of people's perception. Victorian gardens are more tightly controlled and often reflect the romantic vision of writers such as Walter Scott. But for me, the most socially evocative gardens of all are those inspired by the Arts and Crafts movement in the late nineteenth and early twentieth centuries. Adherents of the movement, which saw itself as reacting against a decline in standards of design and decoration (arising from the advent of mechanised factory production), favoured traditional craftsmanship and medieval and folk styles of decoration. The movement also represented a gentle, but often passionate, departure from the strict middle-class values of late Victorian Britain. Arts and Crafts gardens exude openness, charm and romance and they continued to be very influential until the rise of modernist minimalism in the post-war decades.

It would be true to say that all of these gardens have had an influence on the approach Maisie and I have taken at Inley Drove. Essentially, we have cherry-picked, taking ideas for beds and borders from gardens we have admired and then reworking elements of them into our own garden. If there is an overarching philosophy behind the garden, it is that by and large we try to avoid over-organisation and tight structure.

The accurate layout and the subsequent maintenance of the hedges and ditches that gave structure to the prehistoric landscape at Flag Fen would have been crucially important to those early family farms (*c.* 1500 BC). It seems very likely that several of them would have provided access to the main droveways that linked the flood-free winter grazing of the Fen-edge (now mostly beneath Peterborough's industrial areas) to the more open, shared or common grazing of the lower-lying wetland pastures, immediately to the east. But when you share a droveway with neighbouring farms, you don't want their bulls mating with your cows, or their sheep wandering across your fields of wheat and barley, so the system has to be carefully laid out to avoid such problems arising in the first place. Entrances into fields belonging to different farms or families never lined up, thereby preventing animals from bolting through them. Every ditch had a purpose.

The main Bronze Age droveway (*c.* 1500 BC) as recreated at Flag Fen. This photo was taken in October 2007, almost two decades after its initial construction.

As I looked back from the cab of the Hy-Mac at what I had already completed, I was pleasantly surprised. It didn't appear to be quite the mess I had feared. In fact, it had a structure and a coherence that was strangely pleasing. It was as if those people so very long ago had shared something with me that mattered. On reflection, of course, they *had*. The way their lives and their societies were organised had found physical expression, which we had started to recreate, nearly four thousand years later. The landscape in which those Bronze Age farming families lived out their daily lives had a balance and a harmony, born of shared purpose. This gave it humanity and dignity, both of which are fundamental to the design of a good garden.

*

As we worked on large-scale archaeology ahead of the development of the Fengate industrial estate in Peterborough in the 1970s, Maisie and I discovered more and more about the long and rich history of the Fens and how they were formed, and we began to realise that we wanted our own Fenland garden. At first, neither of us mentioned the idea, but eventually one of us said something. To be honest, I can't remember precisely how or when this happened, because it coincided with my mother's unexpected and sudden death in 1980. But by then, we both knew what we had to do next.

2

# The Wisbech Fens, 1981:
# Our First Fenland Garden

*Limetree Farm: early days • Waving Willows •*
*Greenhouses and Munch Mowers • The Central Border •*
*Pattern and Purpose*

T he house we eventually settled on, as our first home
together, lay in the Fens west of Wisbech in countryside
that traditionally grew apple orchards, many of which were
still in use. Large areas of the Fens close to Wisbech and
the Wash are slightly higher than the deeper Fens further
south, around places like March, Ely and Chatteris, and
were extensively occupied in the Middle Ages, whereas the
lower-lying areas were often not drained until the seventeenth
century. Our house, which I will call Limetree Farm, was
located in open fen near a substantial village with excellent
views, over land that had once been communally farmed
medieval open fields, towards a large medieval church. In the
other direction were extensive orchards, which grew Bramley
apples on ancient trees that had been pruned over the years
to resemble open mushrooms or damaged umbrellas. Modern
orchards in the area are grown on dwarfing rootstock and are
far less distinctive.

The building itself was far from spectacular. It was built in the early twentieth century and was very typical of small farmhouses in the area: square, slate-roofed, with chimney stacks at each gable end, which helped give stability in the silty soils. The builders had used darker facing bricks for the front of the house, but the other three walls were made from cheap Phorpres bricks made in nearby Peterborough. When we were prospecting for the house, we noticed that there were hundreds of almost identical two-storey houses in the area. Most seem to have been built between 1870 and 1910. They generally feature a three-bay layout, with a prominent front door at the centre. Unlike many of the others we had visited, the actual building at Limetree Farm showed no signs of cracking or subsidence, which was vitally important if we were to have any hope of raising a mortgage. The old farmyard, which the farmer still owned, lay to one side of the house and was still occasionally used by him. However, the long-abandoned strawberry field, which lay on the other side of the house, was now part of our property. The boundaries of the strawberry field followed the line of a disused medieval droveway, along which sheep and cattle would have been driven to other farms and to markets in Wisbech town. In essence, this was an elongated rectangular plot of just over an acre: an ideal size for a garden.

The soil around Limetree Farm was heavy clay-silt: very fertile indeed, but also very stiff and prone to cracking in hot summers. A little research revealed that the fields that spread before us, when we went upstairs and looked out of the back of the house towards the fine church almost a mile away to the north, had been laid out sometime before the start of the thirteenth century. These major transformations of the local landscape took place during the second phase of the area's drainage in the early Middle Ages.[1] A more recent field survey of the area we could see from our window had revealed pottery of the fourteenth century, which would fit well with this date.[2]

Before its enclosure and drainage in the Middle Ages, the landscape had been occupied during drier periods in Roman and Saxon times. The fertile soils had been laid down very much earlier, in the Neolithic, Bronze and Iron Ages, mostly as a result of flooding up tidal creeks and old river valleys. Not surprisingly, there is evidence in prehistoric and Roman times for a substantial local industry, extracting salt from seawater that had been dammed up in tidal creeks over summer.[3] Much of this salt would have been used by communities living along the edges of the Fens, further inland.

When we took possession of Limetree Farm on 12 May 1981, most of our efforts went into getting the building and garden into a state that would survive the following winter – which in the event proved to be very severe. Over that winter, I managed to do a little digging in various places across the garden and soon realised that the soil was by no means uniform: some areas were richer in clay and the ground was much damper and poorly drained. The paler silts were higher up the roddon mound that was quite clearly discernible on the surface. The original owners had placed the vegetable garden on the most silty ground, which happily lay near the back of the house. This was a very sensible decision and was probably made when the house was built. In those pre-supermarket days, self-sufficiency was very important in rural areas and people would have looked after their vegetables with enormous care. I'm sure the state of their cabbages would have been a hot topic every winter among customers at the local pub.

*

Limetree Farm was located little more than a dozen miles south-west of the point where the River Nene flows into the

Wash, Britain's largest bay. The Nene is one of three main rivers that drain into the southern shore of the Wash, the others being the Welland (to the north-west) and the Great Ouse (to the south-east). The area of tidal soils around the Wash was traditionally called 'Marshland' and is well known locally for the higher silty ridges that run sinuously across its large fields. These banks, composed of fine sands and silts, are the fertile roddons I mentioned in Chapter 1, when I described the purchase of our new field at Inley Drove. Viewed from above, roddons can be seen to form a tree-like network of larger banks that seem to be fed by smaller ones. When I first saw them on an aerial photograph, I immediately recognised them as networks of extinct watercourses with major rivers being fed by smaller streams and tributaries. They couldn't have been anything else. The sands and silts within them were either carried downstream from off the uplands, or were laid down by the action of high tides flowing up into the rivers that drained into the Wash. As the flow of the rivers or tidal surges slowed down and began to reverse, they would shed the sands and silts they were carrying in suspension. Such particles will always settle out when the water around them ceases to move. It's rather like those tea leaves that escape the strainer and end up in your cup: when you add the milk and let it cool down, they eventually fall to the bottom.

You can see similar networks of tidal creeks and streams around the Wash today and also in the tidal marshes of Essex, on the north side of the Thames Estuary. The silty soil found in roddons is well drained and unbelievably fertile, once the seawater and saltiness have been washed out by rain. It's a type of soil that is found widely across the Lincolnshire Fens. Today, it grows most of the green vegetable and salad crops sold in Britain's supermarkets. Further south, and inland from the Wash, such soils are mostly confined to roddons.

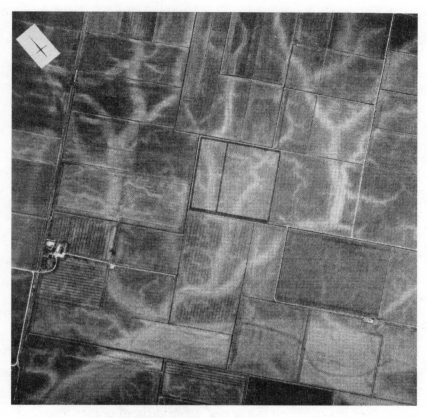

A network of old river and stream channels, known as
roddons, seen from the air. They normally show up best in autumn
and early winter when fields are freshly ploughed. A few meandering
dark lines mark the paths of the final watercourses. These roddons
were photographed in March 1982 near the village of Ramsey
Mereside, Cambridgeshire.

As soon as we moved into Limetree Farm, I was keen to get
out into the small, overgrown strawberry patch that came with
it and take a closer look, as I had high hopes that it might have
silty soil. I stabbed the ground with the archaeological trowel
I used to carry with me everywhere and, to my huge delight, I
immediately saw that it *was* silty. I was overjoyed. I sincerely

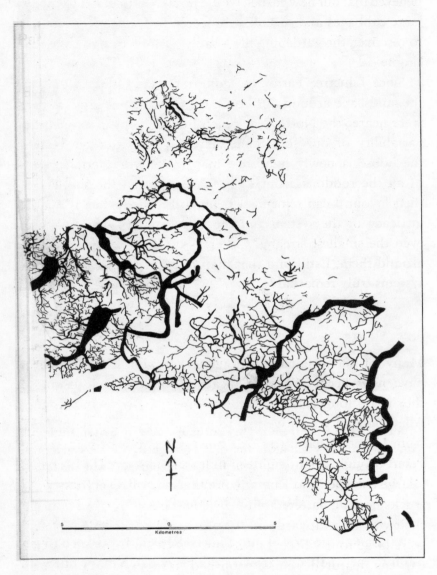

A plan of roddons as revealed on air photographs taken around
the Wash. This plan was first published in 1996.

believed that our new garden would now grow huge cauliflowers, large cabbages and succulent broccoli. But as we were shortly to discover, the gardening life – sadly – is not always quite that simple.

Since Limetree Farm was quite far inland, the roddons in the landscape around our house weren't quite as large as they were nearer the North Sea, which I think helps to explain the variability of our soil. Some sixteen years after we bought the house, a newly published map made from aerial photos of all the roddons around the Wash revealed the subtlety of their layout. I can remember being astonished when I saw the intricacy of the system and the extraordinary way in which even the smallest streams and creeks seemed to respect those around them. I still find that map of extinct pre-Roman river systems truly remarkable.

*

Many of the original road names around Limetree Farm have now been given the local authority PC clean-up, so they're no longer as colourful as Tinker's Drove and Rogues Alley, both of which we had to pass along on our daily drive from Limetree Farm towards our excavations at Flag Fen in Peterborough, about eighteen miles to the west. The area had a large traveller and Romany population and, every day, light trucks bearing battered old cars would pass our front door on their way to scrapyards on the other side of the village. There were large four-wheeled caravans everywhere and many back gardens featured semi-demolished trucks, cars and vans, rather than potatoes or broccoli – let alone roses. I knew from personal experience that rural landscapes are rarely scenes of chocolate-box Cotswoldian gentility, but this was certainly going to be a challenging environment in which to create a new garden. In the event, it took us more than ten years to achieve, but it was well worth the effort. Of course, it's sad, if not altogether surprising, that our once cherished garden no longer exists. Its destruction still hurts a bit and even today we both find it very difficult to drive past its few surviving plants: one or two trees and possibly a rose or shrub poking out through the enveloping rubbish. Recently, Maisie checked it out using Google Earth and you could still detect the outline of the main border and possibly also the pond. As I looked at the images on the screen, I found I was thinking about them and interpreting them in much the same way as I would have done when closely examining an aerial photograph of a long-vanished Bronze Age barrow cemetery – but it was my own garden. It felt a bit odd.

*

I can't remember a great deal about our early days in the new house and garden, but I do recall a wonderful feeling of optimism. My mother had died just before Christmas the previous winter (we buried her on Christmas Eve, 1980), and the warmer days of May, when we moved in, seemed to offer hope for the future after such a sad time. Perhaps it was just as well that we both felt so cheerful, because the garden we inherited was to prove something of a horticultural nightmare: if there was a persistent perennial weed, then it was there – and thriving.

The last farmer, who still owned land nearby (and whom we got to know very well), had sold the house and garden about five years earlier. Unfortunately, the people who bought it off him had been urban folk, who seemed to have known nothing whatsoever about gardening. Consequently, the once fertile vegetable garden was ridden with couch grass and bindweed.

Even worse than these notorious pests, we discovered when we attempted to grow our first crop of winter greens that all the cabbages, sprouts and other brassicas failed to thrive. I pulled up a seedling and took it round to a neighbour, who immediately recognised the problem as brassica club root. It took us about five years of strict hygiene to defeat this notorious pest (a root fungus). Club root results from growing brassicas repeatedly on the same plot of land. If you leave ground fallow, or carefully circulate the brassicas around your vegetable garden, you won't get infected.

The acre field alongside the house (and part of the property) had been used, like many others adjacent to farms in the area, as a small field for growing strawberries. The Wisbech area was then well known for its strawberries (the variety grown was 'Cambridge Favourite'). Trays of these were taken to London by local merchants in June every year. I can remember seeing stacks of trays (punnets) of strawberries accumulate at central collection points in all the local villages, where they were rushed to the crowds at Wimbledon. Today, strawberries are grown by larger farmers and distribution is handled by anonymous 'supply chains'. Sadly, piles of punnets are nowhere to be seen. Beside our new house, the once abundant strawberry field had long ago reverted to rough grass, but it still offered a wonderful view across open fen, towards the fine medieval church about half a mile away. This set us thinking.

Lovely or dramatic views have always been an important part of English country house gardening. In the eighteenth century they would often be 'improved' by the addition of battlements to distant buildings, or the creation of fake towers, spires or whatever. Capability Brown was a great one for adding lakes – or indeed long avenues of stately trees. Such 'borrowed' landscapes are very evident at places like Stowe in Buckinghamshire, one of the most important of the great

English landscape gardens, which we had recently discovered for ourselves when we were starting work on the garden at Limetree Farm. But we were also very aware that gorgeous views can cause big problems. For Fenland gardeners, by far and away the biggest enemy is the wind, which at certain times of the year will scythe through the flat landscape rather like a laser or a lethal cheese-wire. Unfortunately for us, the beautiful church we could see from the Limetree garden lay due north-east of us – and we both knew, from many winters excavating in exposed quarries and building sites, that the bitterly cold north-easterly gales of winter and early spring are the most deadly of all. To use a much-quoted old Fen saying, the north-easterly is a 'lazy old wind': it would rather cut through you than go round you.

A view across the old strawberry field at Limetree Farm in 1982, at the end of our first year. The greenhouse has just been erected and in the background are the supporting posts for the protective screen of willows along the north-east boundary.

A view along the screen of willows six years later (1988).
The longer grass around the trees was planted with daffodils.

The old strawberry field at Limetree was rectangular, roughly twice as long as it was wide, and aligned north-east–south-west. This alignment made it very susceptible to those 'lazy' winds, which would make establishing a garden very difficult unless we did something to cut them. So we decided to plant a belt of native British trees along the north-easterly boundary, parallel with a deep dyke that was regularly maintained by the local drainage authority. Fortunately, the drainage engineers didn't require access to our land for this work, so we could plant our trees quite close to the dyke. The outer two rows were entirely of tough, fast-growing white willows. Along the inner side, we planted two less formally arranged rows of alder and ash, together with the occasional decorative shrub. The ground beneath the trees was resown with native grasses, other than the very invasive couch grass, known as twitch (*Elymus repens*). The old strawberry-growing ground had been entirely taken over by this vigorous pest, whose tough rhizome roots are a gardener's nightmare.

We wanted to plant bulbs under the trees, but the couch grass roots made it impossible. I looked up ways to control twitch and none were fast or particularly effective, especially if the infestation was large and well established. The one exception was a general application of glyphosate (Roundup®) in the autumn, followed by spot applications the following spring, as and when needed. By applying it in the late autumn, the twitch plants would take the chemical in as they started the process of closing down to survive winter. I still find that a rather horrible vision: like poisoning a hedgehog's food as it gets ready to hibernate. We neither of us like using chemicals, but when it came to rampant twitch, we decided we had no choice. A farming friend kindly applied the autumn spray and I followed up with my hand-sprayer the next year. And it worked. Permanently.

The use of chemicals in the modern garden requires careful thought, especially given the largely man-made climate crisis we have been living through for the past century or so. Maisie and I have a golden rule: we will only use chemicals in small quantities and then only if we can be reasonably certain that their use will enhance biological diversity. I know this sounds a bit pompous and worthy, but I have cared quite deeply about the environment for the past four or five decades and I'm becoming increasingly aware that views such as mine are not welcomed by vegans and rewilders, whose perception of the way forward is far simpler and much more rigid. I have been fascinated by evolution ever since I was an A-level student and it's something that still fascinates me. Darwin clearly showed that nature was about the survival of the fittest, but evolution has also revealed that the environment can be very tolerant: all sorts of unusual species can survive in certain unexpected niches. I see our gardens past and present as places where diverse plants and wildlife can thrive. It's not something that we try to make explicit – we don't plan to plant a Tolerance Border or dig a Kindness Pond – but we try not to exclude nature from our grass, beds or borders. I'm afraid this means that our current lawns at Inley Drove Farm are far from neat; they are full of clover and creeping buttercup, but dozens of hares, hedgehogs and deer love to graze and feed on them. It's great to see visiting youngsters' eyes grow wide as a hare's tall dark ears are slowly raised from the edges of a border. Modern lawns can become too controlled. I don't like stripes.

I make no apology for that necessary diversion, but now I must return to our first garden, at Limetree Farm. It was that cold north-easterly wind that made us both decide that, much as we loved it, we couldn't make the view of the distant church the focus of the entire garden. And besides, I'm not sure that having a single, commanding view is always a good idea; sometimes country house gardens can overdo the grand approach, which can make one feel rather uncomfortable. Such creations are often more about the proclamation of personal power or family wealth and influence than anything else. I find that views can often make more memorable impressions if one comes across them unexpectedly or sees them in passing. So we arranged an extra, informal line of willows along the north-east side of the garden in such a way that paths through them allowed one to catch glimpses of the open fen, and with it, the church view, from time to time. Such glimpses can be so tantalising.

We knew that the willow screen along the north-east side would be crucial if our new garden was to thrive. So it would have to be quite dense, but not too thick, as it would occupy about a quarter of the garden's area and it would be nice if we could combine the trees with other plants, such as bulbs and a few shrubs. We briefly thought about buying the trees from a nursery or garden centre, but soon abandoned the idea when we realised what they would cost. It also didn't help that many of the plants were rather 'gardeny' varieties: with pretty bark or variegated leaves. We just wanted robust, wind-baffling willows. So during our first winter in the house, we went out and about gathering cuttings from roadside trees and hedgerows. I can remember spotting piles of offcut branches lying by the side of the causeway across the Nene Washes between Whittlesey and Thorney, near the wonderful pub at Dog-in-a-Doublet sluice. At the time, I was returning home from our excavations near Peterborough. It was the weekend and the council workers, who only worked on weekdays, were nowhere to be seen. Nobody was actually cutting back the many ancient pollarded willows that line this rather lonely route across a very wet tract of fen. So I stopped and loaded several branches into the back of the Land Rover. In the past, the two rows of willows would have guided travellers to stay on the causeway, while their roots would have helped to stabilise the road itself. Today, the trees are very gnarled and old, but it's great to see they are still maintained by regular pollarding.

I was planning to root the cuttings in water and then pot them up, but Maisie suggested that we simply push them into the wet ground and then wait for them to strike roots in the spring. In April, every single one started to bud up, then a few leaves appeared and, before we knew it, small side branches had started to grow. By the end of that first growing season, many of the new trees were waist- or even shoulder-high. Those people who built the Whittlesey causeway certainly knew their willows and which ones would thrive in damp Fenland soils. In just a couple of years, our screen of emerging trees was starting to have a noticeable effect on winter gales at ground level, if not at six feet up. After three to four years, the effect was dramatic: the new garden felt far less barren and hostile; tender younger plants became much easier to establish.

*

As well as the willow cuttings we had collected from the roadside out in the open fen near Whittlesey that were growing so well along the windy northern side of our new garden, other plants were starting to get going too. In a couple of years, we had established clumps of daffodils, which thrived in the longer grass around the willow trunks – and of course they looked superb in springtime. The enormously successful French novelist Alexandre Dumas was absolutely right: nothing succeeds like success, and this is particularly true in gardening. Plants that you think won't thrive in your soil and conditions sometimes turn out to be spectacularly successful. I can remember we tentatively bought a few pots of the very beautiful *Verbena bonariensis* (purpletop vervain) when we visited Christopher Lloyd's garden at Great Dixter in East Sussex.[4] When we got home, we looked it up in a gardening textbook, only to learn that it preferred the ubiquitous but strangely elusive 'well-drained soil'.

Regardless of the textbook, Maisie planted it in the Limetree Farm garden. That winter, it poured with rain; many of the borders were permanently flooded, some of them for weeks. Then, in April, to our astonishment those wet parts of the garden were covered with dozens of tiny seedlings, which we didn't recognise at first. After a few days, Maisie identified them as *Verbena bonariensis*. This wonderful plant subsequently became a mainstay of both our Fenland gardens. It continues to thrive in the damp soil at Inley Drove, every year giving us tall, elegant plants with purple flowers from spring to November. It was particularly long-lasting and prolific in 2021.

Those Whittlesey willows set us on a path that we are still following – or perhaps exploring is a better word. (I never thought I'd live to see willows with black catkins, such as the charming *Salix gracilistyla* 'Melanostachys', but two of these plants are now flourishing by our pond at Inley Drove.) We started contemplating other varieties of willow for the Limetree Farm garden. In those days, we were still thinking big: about trees and large shrubs that would form a sheltered environment for the establishing of further beds and borders.

One of the things I like about gardening is the fact that gardeners are quite open about pinching or borrowing other people's ideas. In any other profession – in art, or in literature – it would be regarded as blatant plagiarism. But not in gardening, where such things are often explained as 'being influenced by' or 'fondly recalling'. So we all visit each other's gardens, as frequently as our own one will allow. In our early horticultural days, Maisie and I spent a lot of time in the Cambridge University Botanic Garden off the Hills Road, a brisk ten-minute walk from the station. I first discovered the Botanic Garden when I was a student studying archaeology. I could remember my uncle Dr Mark Pryor, a distinguished biologist at the university, holding forth about the highly unusual plants that grew there. At that time, I found such talk a bit awe-inspiring and not a little daunting, so I didn't get round to visiting the garden until quite late in my last year as a student. And when I did, of course, I was immediately completely hooked. It was the most extraordinary garden I had ever visited. But just two years after graduating from Cambridge I moved to Canada, and trips to English gardens became impossible. It wasn't until I returned from Toronto in 1978 that I found my thoughts turning to such horticultural matters. I can't be at all precise about the date, but shortly after Maisie and I bought our new house at Limetree Farm, in May 1981, we decided to visit the Cambridge Bot Garden (as we have called it ever since) for ideas and inspiration. On a later visit, which took place in the late autumn of 1982, I made a most remarkable find there, using a tried-and-tested archaeological survey technique.

One of the best ways of finding new archaeological sites is simply to walk through the landscape with one eye on the ground. You might think that this would lead to crossed eyes and a very stiff neck, but you soon develop a technique and after a few years it becomes second nature. 'Fieldwalking', as this methodical ground inspection is known among archaeologists, has long been a habit: if ever there's a trench open in a local town, I will mentally fieldwalk the loose earth piled alongside it, looking out for fragments of pottery and pieces of flint. When I'm visiting a National Trust garden, I'll automatically check the surface of freshly dug or weeded rose beds on the off-chance they might reveal something of interest. I suppose that sounds a bit obsessive – and I suppose it is – but it's how things are. And I've learnt to live with it. But on this occasion, it paid off handsomely.

Trees and shrubs with brightly coloured stems look their best in autumn and winter and the Bot Garden featured a particularly striking red-barked willow, which positively glowed in the low sunlight of that time of year. If you want garden plants with colourful bark, such as willows (*Salix*) and the even more spectacular dogwoods (*Cornus*), you will have to cut them back regularly – in some cases every year. Incidentally, I've always been interested in plant names and I can remember being told that dogwoods acquired theirs because of the nasty smell they gave off when burnt on a bonfire. However, when I burnt some to find out if this was really the case, rather disappointingly they turned out not to smell horrible at all.

Subsequently, Wikipedia has told me it's because of an old opinion that their fruit are 'edible, but not fit for a dog'. Still, the name stuck.

It so happened that the willows with the spectacular red bark, which the excellent plant labels of the Bot garden informed me were *Salix alba*, var. Kermesina, had just been given their winter pruning.[5] Fast-growing trees, such as white willows (*Salix alba*), use a lot of sap and freshly cut branches can bleed freely if pruned in spring or summer, when the sap is still rising – and this bleeding can be very difficult to stop. So winter pruning is essential. But the Cambridge Bot gardeners were not like the chaps who had cut back those pollarded willows on the causeway outside Whittlesey. They hadn't left piles of brushwood to spoil the harmonious vistas of the various beds and paths around them. Almost everything had been tidied away, but then I spotted there were a few more freshly cut scars on the willow trunks, together with chainsaw chips and other clear signs of recent pruning. I could also detect the telltale shallow scratches left by wire rakes in the grass of the path. Those gardeners had been true professionals and had cleared up thoroughly. But I was a professional too. I was determined not to be defeated by their horticultural cleanliness.

Maisie always carries a small notebook with her when we visit gardens, especially ones like the Cambridge Bot. On this occasion, I asked her if I might borrow it. She looked at me oddly. But I knew what I was doing: I had a plan. One of the things we like about the Bot Garden is the gardeners, who are always pleasant and well informed. They are also everywhere. Mindful of this, I stopped to examine a border close by a pruned willow, pencil and notebook in hand, as if I were deeply curious about a scattering of small ground-cover plants that had just been planted. Of course, I wasn't even slightly interested in them. Instead, I was doing a detailed field survey of the ground around them. And it didn't take long: after less than ten minutes I had found three small, freshly cut red twigs, complete with several buds, of that gorgeous and recently pruned red-barked white willow, 'Kermesina'. I slipped them into my pocket. Maisie saw what I'd done and knew what she had to do next. In one of his books, the greatest gardening writer of all time, the late, great Christopher Lloyd, had recommended that aspiring gardeners should always carry a few empty paper bags in case they should be given – or happen upon – seeds, when visiting other people's gardens. Such sound advice.

As I stood up from bending over the flower bed, I felt the rustle of an archaeologist's plastic bag against my right hand. Without looking down, I inserted the three twigs in it and pressed the mini-grip seam closed. Maisie was well aware that plastic was better than paper as it would keep the twigs damp. I have to confess it felt slightly odd not then adding the site code and grid reference on the bag's white panel. But this wasn't an archaeological survey and people might be watching us and I didn't fancy having to make a long explanation. Later, when we were safely aboard the train, I said nothing as Maisie took the bag from me and wrote 'CU Bot Gdn 82'. Phew! It was now properly labelled. That made us both feel much better.

When we got home, I placed the cuttings in a jar of water and they all rooted. They grew into splendid trees in our Limetree Farm garden and today their grandchildren are thriving at Inley Drove, where their glowing bark can light up the dullest of Fenland evenings. Thank you so much, Cambridge Bot Garden: and of course you're always welcome to take an infinite number of free willow cuttings from us, at any time.

*

One of the first things we did after we moved into Limetree Farm was to buy a small greenhouse, which we placed on the edge of the existing, and much neglected, vegetable garden. As greenhouses go, and certainly by current standards, it was small and cheap, but it served its purpose more than adequately. It grew us excellent crops of cucumbers and tomatoes, which tasted superb. It's also worth recalling that commercially grown tomatoes in the 1980s were never sold on the vine; they were always large, under-ripe and absolutely devoid of any flavour whatsoever. We also used the greenhouse for propagation and for germinating seeds, and we soon discovered that its frost-free conditions could easily be extended with a low-cost paraffin heater. A year or two later, once the trees sheltering the garden had started to become established, we erected a small octagonal greenhouse further out in the flower garden. We used this entirely for non-food, house and garden plants, and as an attractive way to display some more exotic flowers in summer. As you will probably have guessed, I was generally to be found in the tomato house, while Maisie preferred the octagon.

For the first couple of years progress seemed very slow, after what had seemed like an impossibly rapid start. The farmer who had owned the house and land before selling it to the previous occupants from London very kindly agreed to till the old strawberry field and plant it with grass seed. At this stage, in February and March 1982, it looked extremely bare and bleak, but once the seed began to germinate everything was suddenly transformed. It was something we were to experience for a second time in our Lincolnshire garden, and even then, when we both knew what we were going to experience, the actual sight of the new grass massively raised our spirits. I hate to think what lowland Britain would look like if the grass died away every summer because of global warming.

I soon realised that the new expanse of grass at Limetree Farm would require more than the unpowered push mower we then possessed. And there were other unforeseen expenses, such as a powered hedge trimmer to cut back the old hawthorn hedge that ran alongside the road, on the garden's southern boundary. We certainly needed that hedge, because the road sat on top of a low medieval flood-defence bank (there were many of these in the area). Although the traffic wasn't very heavy, we did want a little privacy. On the other side of the road was the long-established and attractively pruned Bramley apple orchard, which we could admire from our bedroom window at the front of the house.

We learnt all sorts of useful lessons as the garden at Limetree Farm started to take shape. The first large ride-on mower we bought was fitted with a side-discharge blade, which seemed destined to pepper all delicate border plants with fine mowings that turned slightly acid as they started to rot down and were very destructive to newly planted-out young flowers. After a few years I discovered mulch mowers, which an elderly gentleman in the village used to call my 'munch mowers' – a *much* better description, I'm sure you'll agree.

Munch mowers are brilliant. Obviously, those horrible heaps of mowings cease to be a problem, but they also ensure that the turf remains richly organic and drought resistant. In dry seasons, our lawns remain green when those in surrounding villages are starting to looking pale and arid. I also try to avoid cutting the grass too short, as that discourages insect life. But there is one drawback to my approach to lawns: bouncy turf and finely mulched grass cuttings do not encourage the neat, rolled, stripy effect that some (deluded?) folk regard as somehow archetypically English; sooner or later they will always ask me whether I don't regret the absence of stripes. I give them a quick justification for using a munch mower and finish with the thought that lawns shouldn't look like an overblown zebra crossing. Inevitably, when they depart, their looks of quiet pity leave me in no doubt: I haven't convinced them. Gardening opinions, like the plants themselves, can become *so* deeply rooted.

*

Both Maisie and I love mixed borders. When I say 'mixed', I mean beds where perennials, annuals, shrubs, small trees and roses can be grown together – and notice I also say 'can' be grown together and not 'must' be grown together. Sometimes shrubs and roses are appropriate, but not always. If we do have a general rule, it is that smaller plants should be planted nearer the front, with taller shrubs and perennials towards the back. Gardening in such a windy environment, we quite frequently like to plant a tall hedge as a backdrop to the border. In the damp and often rather heavy soils of the Fens, we find that hornbeam (*Carpinus betulus*) grows better than beech and doesn't seem at all worried about standing in water for long periods in winter and early spring. Like young beech trees, youthful hornbeams retain their leaves over winter – at which time our hedges are invariably mistaken for beech by all our visitors. When regularly trimmed in a hedge, both beech and hornbeam will keep their youthful characteristics – leaf retention is a young tree's way of insulating itself from the coldest frosts of winter.

Once the grass had started to grow, the centre of the old strawberry field at Limetree Farm was crying out for a garden feature of some kind. We briefly toyed with the idea of a large round bed with something at its centre: maybe a statue or a large container, deftly planted with something exotic and showy. But we weren't convinced, and it didn't help that garden statues (whether blushing Venuses or balletic Cupids) were invariably not to our taste and large containers were eye-wateringly expensive – at a time when we were completely broke. So, as something of a compromise, we decided to drop the idea of a central feature and instead place a mixed border through the centre of the rectangular expanse of grass. This soon proved to be a very sensible decision. The new border ran parallel with the screen of willows along the north-east side of the garden and benefited from their protection within a couple of years. It also had both sunny and more shady sides, which gave us scope for different planting schemes. Shortly after laying out the border, we decided to put a narrow paved path across it, at the centre. A few years later, we erected a rounded metal frame above the path to support roses and clematis. In a year or two, this was to become something of a central feature.

*

It was while we were laying out and planting the central border that we found ourselves discussing a very basic issue – one we really should have considered before we even started the project. It was a question that the likes of Repton, Jekyll and Brown – or indeed *any* competent professional – would have asked their clients at the outset: how will the garden be *used*? I had always had a vision of Maisie and me, exhausted after a long day's excavation in the baking Fenland sun, stumbling upstairs for a quick bath (the house lacked a shower) and then heading out into the garden for a relaxing stroll, complete with a long, cool gin and tonic. But even on those rare occasions when this actually happened, we didn't wander aimlessly. Maybe something was smelling gorgeous or Maisie wanted to see how a new rose was faring in the heat of summer. Often, I'd want to check if something might be ready for supper in the veg garden. So walks were never pointless: they always had purpose.

The trick, we both began to realise, was to make the routes leading to the vegetable garden or the freshly planted roses as attractive as possible. When the garden was better established, we would be delighted when visiting friends were drawn away from something they had come to see by a particularly fragrant rose or a succulent-looking raspberry. I love gardens that divert and surprise, but they can only succeed in this if they have a well-thought-out underlying structure.

We British have made some major breakthroughs in literature, science and technology, but we are perhaps less well known for our contributions to the visual arts. There are, however, two notable exceptions. The first, which dates as far back as the Iron Age, is the achievement of British craftsmen and artists in the style broadly known as Celtic Art. Shields, helmets, brooches, swords and mirrors were made across Europe in the second half of the first millennium BC, but reached their peak of design perfection in Britain in the final three centuries BC. It's a style of art I love, with swirling curvilinear designs that still seem to retain their energy and life force, despite being more than two thousand years old. The second almost exploded into life in rural areas of England in the eighteenth century. Before the designed landscapes of places like Stowe, and the landscape gardeners behind them – people like Capability Brown – gardens were generally confined within walls and their layouts often reflected this: small borders and parterres of tightly clipped box hedges. I can see many conceptual links between ancient, pre-Roman Celtic art and the designed landscapes of the eighteenth century, especially movement and freedom, but all the patterns and shapes are held together – are given coherence – by a fundamental structural discipline. I can remember a great textbook on pre-Roman Celtic art with a title that is so appropriate here: *Pattern and Purpose*.[6] As we were to discover when we came to lay out our second Fenland garden, purpose would be just as important as the more visible, and perhaps obvious, pattern.

While we were working on the central border, quite late in the life of the Limetree Farm garden, we had to consider how it would be viewed. Initially, we saw it as a long bed with two sides and we tried to entice visitors to walk along it. We did this by adding what we hoped would be an intriguing curve at the far end. I don't think it was a huge success, but at least we tried. We weren't aware of it at the time, but we were starting to visualise one of the design principles that has been of fundamental importance to the development of our current garden at Inley Drove. As time passed, we realised that beds and borders were more than destinations in their own right. They were also features that we could use gently to guide visitors towards parts of the garden they might not otherwise visit. You don't need spectacular vistas to tempt people. We were learning so much – and so fast.

# 3

# The Move to Lincolnshire

*Our First Pond • Pleached Lime Trees • Propagation and Potting*
*• The Sound of Chainsaws • Harry Salmon • Harry's Patch*

The summer of 1988 was notoriously wet, but most of the weather systems were coming in from off the Atlantic. Often these systems then veer north, towards the Lake District and western Scotland, or south, towards Wales and the south of England. When this happens, the east Midlands, the Wash and much of northern Norfolk remain dry. I think this is the best explanation for the summer of 1988, because I firmly recall it was a good year for gardening: not too wet or too dry, especially in the warmer months. Although we had started to improve it after about six years of adding manure and rotten compost, the soil at Limetree Farm was still far from perfect. In dry years, the heavy clay-rich soil used to bake like concrete and seemed to take forever to soften: one or two heavy showers would make very little impression on it, and then – before you knew what had happened – you were standing in a sticky, muddy mess.

The previous summer, we had carefully laid a paved path across the centre of the main border, effectively dividing it in two, but we now realised that this path had to have a point: it needed to lead somewhere. It wasn't enough simply to get to the other side of the border; we both agreed it was an anticlimax: you crossed the border to be met by an area of lawn with a tall hedge behind it. My immediate reaction was: So What? Something had to be done about it.

The previous year, when we laid the path across the main border, we had to do the work at weekends. This was because we were spending every summer weekday of 1987 at Flag Fen, constructing the Mere. The Mere was an attempt to stop the three-thousand-year-old timbers that lay deeply buried in the peats from drying out — a result of long-term fen drainage, recent flood-control measures and, of course, climate change. We knew that if the ancient timbers dried, they would first crack, then shrink and eventually turn to dust. So we constructed an artificial lake to keep them wet.[1] At the time, I wasn't too sure that the Mere would prove sufficiently watertight, but it has — and to my delight I can say that it's still there, thirty-five years later, continuing to do its job.

Constructing the Mere was very difficult and, looking back on it, quite dangerous work too. The trench that held the lining was deep and very narrow, and although none of us ever entered it, we were always worried about the soft peats collapsing as we lowered in the continuous sheets of water-proof lining. I suppose that as the Mere was constantly in our thoughts day and night (and yes, I did have scary nightmares about it), it was hardly surprising that we should come up with the idea of a pond as the focus of the new path across the border in the Limetree garden. I don't know whether it was the fact that the Flag Fen Mere's success was due to a plastic lining, or because most garden centres have prominent displays of pond liners, but for whatever reason we both agreed that our new pond would have to be lined. I had never made such a pond before and I have to confess the price of the lining made me gasp. It was *vastly* more expensive than the cheap damp-proof plastic we had used at Flag Fen. We knew in advance that there'd be a big price difference, because at Flag Fen we were able to use cheap plastic damp-proof sheeting because it would be buried below the reach of sunlight (which quite quickly makes plastic turn brittle). Still, we didn't need to eat prime steak when Maisie could make a fabulous spaghetti bolognese with our own minced lamb, so we ate frugally and bought the pond liner.

Maisie in the new pond. Note the step around the edge for pots of reeds, rushes etc., as recommended in all garden textbooks.

Digging out the pond felt rather strange for us as archaeologists, because we weren't carefully checking the loose soil for finds as it was shovelled into the wheelbarrow. I think we may have spotted one or two broken clay pipe stems and the occasional fragment of glass jam jar or small sherd of blue willow-pattern plate. But if we did, we didn't keep them. That felt professionally naughty, but strangely nice: it made us feel that we were now gardeners, not archaeologists.

When the digging was finished, we carefully levelled in the top – what in Fen-dyke-speak one refers to as 'the brink' – and then laid the lining, which we secured in place with paving slabs. Next, I connected the hose and filling began. Today, I would be far more ecologically aware and would use rainwater run-off, not tap water. But in those days, things were a bit simpler.

Starting to fill the lined pond with water.

Soon the pond was filled, and we laid the few remaining paving slabs around the edge. After waiting for a couple of days to allow any added chlorine to evaporate, we started putting in a few plastic baskets, filled with pots of reeds and a couple of waterlilies for the deeper parts. I honestly cannot remember what we placed where, but I can still recall the wide smile of the nice man who ran the aquatics shop in a nearby village.

His smile got even wider when finally I bought half a dozen semi-mature golden orfe, a large, goldfish-like ornamental fish, which I remembered from my childhood, in a large lake near where we lived; I knew they could survive cold winters. I have to say, I found the shopkeeper's warm smile very slightly unsettling. I'm certain he knew they were bound to be gobbled up by the dozens of herons that feed in the many local dykes. Of course, he was right. We took various measures to keep the herons away, but they only delayed the inevitable. We replaced the orfe with much cheaper goldfish.

*

It took us a week or two to clear the green algae from the pond, but by then the waterside plants, the reeds and the waterlilies were growing luxuriantly, and many were flowering. It wasn't long before the pond was starting to look a bit like something in a garden magazine. But then we had the horror of pulling out a pair of drowned voles; I imagine they were leaning off a paving slab to take a drink and fell in. I immediately made an escape ramp of pebbles and gravel, which actually looked quite attractive. The following winter, Maisie planted the lovely pale-pink-flowered climbing shrub rose 'Kathleen Harrop', which looked wonderful on the wire archway covering the border path. In July 1989 I took a photo of the arch and the pond, with the house in the background. Mercifully, the gable end of the house is concealed by a dark-leaved flowering plum tree, so you cannot view the great expanse of cheap-and-cheerful London bricks. You rarely saw such bricks around north Norfolk's lovely Holkham Hall, where we bought so many of our plants. It was run by a garden enthusiast and plantsman known as 'The Major'. I think he knew we were trying to establish a garden from scratch, because we never seemed to pay anything approaching the full price. He was such a nice man. I shall have more to say about him later.

In 1989 we still used a conventional side-discharge mower, which was one of the reasons I never cut the lawn grass very short. The other reason was that we both liked the flowers of creeping buttercup (*Ranunculus repens*), which grew wild in the area. It took us a year or two to discover that they may have been beautiful but were also very invasive and, once established in a border, were extremely difficult to control or weed out. I now much prefer the meadow buttercup (*Ranunculus acris*), which is far less invasive and normally won't flower in lawns, but grows well in longer grass.

Earlier, I mentioned the importance of pattern and purpose in garden design and I want to close my memories of our Limetree Farm garden by mentioning what can happen when pattern dominates and purpose is almost absent. Today, there is a tendency for gardens to illustrate what is fashionable on *Gardeners' World* and other TV gardening programmes, or what is being promoted by the big garden centre chains. But you can still spot regional distinctiveness, even in those parts of southern Britain where towns are expanding and new housing estates are popping up everywhere. For example, I have always liked the pleached lime trees of Cambridgeshire and old Huntingdonshire, which used to be a common feature in many small towns and villages but are now becoming much harder to find.[2] I liked them so much that I was absolutely determined to have some at Limetree Farm, come what may. So I decided that two rows, each of some six trees, would look great running down the south side of the garden, close by and parallel to the tall hawthorn hedge that used to hide the farmer's strawberry patch from the road running along the top of the medieval bank, just beyond.

Lime trees like damper soils, which may help explain why they were so popular around the Fens, in places like

Godmanchester, Huntingdon and Cambridge. I could still remember the professional gardeners of various Cambridge colleges pruning their pleached trees in the depths of winter, usually in January. As I was to discover for myself, pleaching takes a lot of work and requires not a little skill to do properly. On the upside, however, it is varied work that requires lifting ladders and pushing wheelbarrows, not forgetting eventual late afternoon warming bonfires and cheering mugs of tea. It also makes a great change from my other main midwinter job: spreading muck on the vegetable garden and digging it in. For what it's worth, we both try to find winter jobs that can be done in either wet or dry conditions because the weather can be so variable. We also find it's often a good idea to have more than one task under way at the same time. Possibly my favourite winter duty is sitting beside the Aga at the end of a cold, damp afternoon, with a mug of tea and a slice of Maisie's lemon drizzle cake. I'm aware that she really appreciates it when I offer her sincere and hopefully constructive opinions as I munch away. It's something I feel I have to do: a duty.

We spent much time agonising about what variety of lime tree to choose for pleaching. We eventually went for *Tilia cordata*, the native British small-leaved lime. It wasn't a very difficult decision at the time, because we were both strong advocates of everything native. Back in the 1980s, if you said the word 'hedge', people automatically assumed you were referring to that scourge of the British landscape, the ultra-fast-growing evergreen Leylandii, some examples of which in the rich soils of the silt fens are now growing far taller than the houses and bungalows they were originally intended to screen. So pleaching native lime trees had to be a sound idea. After about five years' growth, I have to confess I found the small leaves slightly disappointing. It was then that I discovered that most of the pleached lime trees in older gardens were of the larger-leaved variety, *Tilia platyphyllos*, which is what we would later plant in the short length of pleached hedge in our garden at Inley Drove. We didn't know it then, but the small-leaved lime produces very sticky small drips that form an invisible shower beneath them in later summer. For some reason, visitors' car parks in many stately homes are often positioned in the shade of tall lime trees, many of which were planted in the eighteenth century, when the far fewer visitors' coaches would have been parked in proper paved areas away from the trees, closer to the house. At the possible risk of appearing a bit obsessive, I would suggest that when you next visit a shaded car park in July or August, you check the trees are not *Tilia cordata* before you park beneath them. If, that is, you want to be able to see through your windscreen for the drive home. In my experience, lime-tree stickiness seems very resistant to most windscreen-cleaning sprays.

The pleached lime trees in the Limetree Farm garden. This photo was taken about five years after they were planted. Note the tall, dark hawthorn hedge that runs behind the limes, from the left.

The limes were delivered to us in wintertime, as bare-rooted two-year-old cuttings. We bought them from a nursery that specialises in top-quality hedging plants, all of which are grown on the premises from their own sources.[3] I feel strongly that, as gardeners, we have a duty to try and do what we can to slow down the spread of plant diseases, especially those that harm native trees such as elms and ash, many of which travel via the international trade in potted plants. These were vigorous plants and they grew quite rapidly. Following instructions in a number of books and journals, I trained the branches into three parallel pleached rows and it worked very well. Within about five years, what I had planted as individual trees were beginning to resemble what I wanted: a single pleached feature. But then that fundamental problem of 'purpose' made itself evident: the pleached avenue – for that is what it had become – seemed to lead nowhere, from nowhere. It ran parallel to the road and to a pre-existing hedge, but that was all. I can't say that I was very downhearted at the time, because I wasn't. I enjoyed tying in branches and snipping off side shoots; it was very satisfying work. The realisation that the pleached limes had pattern but lacked purpose only really came to me after a local development that was to affect us profoundly – and over which we had no control whatsoever. And like so many disturbing moments in the 1970s and 80s, when hedges and trees were being felled right across Britain, it involved the sound of chainsaws.

\*

Waking up in a busy farmed landscape isn't always a peaceful or a relaxed process. Most often the new day is greeted by the song of robins or the sound of cattle lowing as they make their way to their first session in the milking parlour. But increasingly today these natural sounds are being replaced by the reversing beeps of large articulated trucks, or the roar of massive diesel-engined tractors. Contractors flail-cutting verges or those few surviving roadside hedges can be particularly noisy too. But nothing, absolutely nothing, can be as sharp and harsh as the sudden scream of high-revving chainsaws. And that was the sound that shattered the peace in our bedroom at Limetree Farm one early morning, at the start of spring 1989.

To be honest, I can't be absolutely sure about times and dates as I was too caught up in what was happening to keep a diary, but I can remember parting the bedroom curtains that morning to see a gang of workmen cutting down the lovely old Bramley apple trees in the orchard directly across the road, opposite the house. We had had no intimation that something like this might happen, which was unusual in a village where most of the people who ran small farms or other rural businesses knew one another – and of course there were always the pubs, which seemed to help news travel even faster than it does in today's digital world. We made appropriate enquiries, most likely in the pub, and soon learnt that the orchard owner had sold the business to a non-farming investor – we were told they managed the capital assets of a prominent trade union. Apparently, there were grants to be had for felling old orchards and ploughing the land – all of which duly happened.

We hated to see the old trees destroyed. Had they been cut down to be replaced by young trees on modern growth-restricting rootstock, that would have been a shame, but an understandable one: successful enterprises have to evolve. But it was the thoughtless felling, and with it the cutting down of the tall informal hedge around one side of the orchard, that annoyed us so much. That informal hedge had been planted with wild plums and other flowering trees and shrubs to attract insects to pollinate the Bramley apple blossom. Every year, too, we would get to collect windfalls (with the orchard owner's permission, I hasten to add) and we would watch the pickers at work among the trees and in the packing barn. We also witnessed the careful and very expert over-winter pruning, which gave those old trees their graceful arching profiles. But then those nasty chainsaws put an end to everything. We didn't know it then, but things were about to get even worse.

Local rumour had it that the speculators who had felled the orchard had then sold the land to a local developer. The person in question did not have a good reputation. Of course, we had not seen his planning application, but when we heard about it, we checked it out and immediately lodged a strong objection. A few days later, our Limetree Farm house was broken into by thieves, who smashed the kitchen window at the back of the building and climbed in. They stole our television set and the amplifier for the hi-fi system, two token thefts that wouldn't have had much resale value. In those days, police were better resourced than they are today and were able to visit the scene shortly after the crime had been committed. Chatting to the officers, I could see they thought that the break-in hadn't been about robbery, as such. I suppose you could say it had been a threat – and quite an unpleasant one that completely removed any sense of security we might once have had. Fear, especially long-term persistent fear, is profoundly disturbing. It was clear to us that the police thought those who had carried out the break-in had had other motives.

The next day, I happened to be standing in the garden at the front of the house when I heard the sound of a vehicle approaching. It was slowing down. I turned round to see if it was the postman dropping a delivery off with us, but the small van wasn't red – and it wasn't stopping. Instead, the driver leant towards the open passenger's side window and wagged his finger at me reproachfully with an expression on his face that said: 'Naughty boy, you're going to behave better in the future, aren't you?' And with that he drove off.

Talking to people in the village, most had a very clear idea who was behind the break-in, and in retrospect I suspect the police had a pretty shrewd idea too, although, of course, we never heard any more from them. It seemed to be common knowledge that the people behind the crime had very influential and powerful local contacts, and, to be honest, we neither of us had any stomach for an extended, emotion-sapping row. By then, Flag Fen had received much media coverage and I was fast becoming a local celebrity, of sorts. I'm sure I could have given the criminals behind the break-in a good fight – and the media would probably have loved it. But we had just been through a major political battle to stop funds suddenly being withdrawn from the new Flag Fen visitor centre and we neither of us fancied yet another prolonged public dispute. More importantly, we didn't want to be diverted from our archaeological work, nor from gardening – which was now very important to both of us. So we decided to move elsewhere: to cross the county boundary into a new administrative area, where we hoped people and standards would be very different. It was such a wise decision: sleepless nights can really make one feel low.

*

We initially thought we'd be able to find a suitable run-down property, which we could renovate. But in the early 1990s, house prices were still rising and older houses in need of renovation seemed to be rare. We had in mind a disused farmhouse with a few outbuildings, which we could convert into useful working spaces, both for Maisie's research into ancient woodworking and to serve the garden that we hoped to lay out in the surrounding fields and paddocks – much as we had done at Limetree Farm. But when it came to the reality of the property market, any older farmhouses were being sold at vast prices for conversion into luxury homes, while outbuildings were carefully set aside as potential smaller residences, or flats. Any land attached to these places that might be suitable for a garden was instead sold as ideal for 'equestrian' use – at grossly inflated rates. These were the years when small horsey enterprises were springing up everywhere – and they were very popular too, to judge by the many shiny cars and Range Rovers parked outside them.

Then in the mid-1990s the property market slowed down quite rapidly, and we still hadn't sold Limetree Farm. So rather against our estate agent's advice, we cut the price we were asking by about 20 per cent and, before we knew it, we had buyers knocking at the door. One reason we decided to drop the house price was that we had been told about farmers' sales run by a Wisbech-based firm of auctioneers and valuers. Many of these sales did indeed involve auctions, but most were for smaller lots of land, such as single fields or disused yards. I phoned them and explained that we were looking to buy a field across the county boundary, in Lincolnshire. I slightly expected them to say that they only sold land in Cambridgeshire, but no: they often had sales in South Holland, the district of Lincolnshire that we were interested in. And that was how we found the field that would later become our Lincolnshire garden at Inley Drove Farm.

The destruction of that lovely, peaceful Bramley apple orchard continued to affect us both profoundly. The laughable attempt to turn the ground that once lay beneath the trees into an arable field seemed to have slowed down – doubtless because of the roots and stumps – but it was soon followed by the erection of a steel silo directly opposite our house.

We raised objections and it was removed, but we knew this would be just the first of many similar incidents. We had to do something to bolster our morale. By now it was the late summer of 1992 and we were in the final stages of purchasing the new land in south Lincolnshire. Of course, we didn't know for sure whether or not we would gain planning permission for a new house and garden, but we did know that we wanted to keep sheep, which would mean we would have enough land to ensure that the rich collection of garden plants we had accumulated at Limetree Farm could be transferred somewhere else. We urgently needed a temporary local growing-ground for them.

You can't keep dogs without taking them for walks. Limetree Farm had an old yard next door, which was great for letting the dogs off their leads for a rapid dash, frantically following the odorous trails of rats, hares, foxes and other interesting scents. But when it came to that all-important sustained daily exercise, nothing could match a good long walk down a cart track or country lane. As large areas of the peat Fens of Cambridgeshire were quite recently drained, they lack the diverse range of old footpaths and rights of way that you find in older British rural landscapes. The silt Fens further north, closer to the Wash, were occupied much earlier; indeed, many villages can trace their roots back to Saxon times, several centuries before the Norman Conquest of 1066. An easy way of dating these villages is to look at their parish churches: if the church is medieval, then the parish around it is going to be medieval too.

The neighbouring village to Limetree Farm had the fine medieval church we could see from our garden and it didn't come as a huge surprise to me to discover that the parish also offered some interesting footpaths, several of which made excellent dog-walking routes. One of these led past a rather run-down bungalow, which came complete with the almost obligatory long-abandoned strawberry patch. One day, when we were returning from a long walk with our lovely black Labrador Major, a very elderly man came down the path through the bungalow's front garden. I suppose if this scene had taken place in an urban setting, we would have smiled kindly and he might have smiled back or, more probably, ignored us with haughty disdain. But that's not how things are in the Fens.

He greeted us with a wave and a call of 'Afternoon' ('Good' often gets dropped). I was immediately struck by his voice, which reminded me of the way people used to speak in the East End of London when I worked at Truman's Brewery in the late 1960s. I introduced him to Maisie and Major and he told us his name was Harry, although he pronounced it, firmly, as 'Arry. It turned out that he had sold fish in Billingsgate Market, where he specialised in salmon and was known to other traders and the many porters as 'Arry Salmon. I couldn't resist mentioning my days at Truman's, which seemed to go down very well indeed. I can't think why. Harry was plainly quite a shy man, but I could see he enjoyed our meeting – especially with Major, who tried to lick the skin off his hand – and we weren't surprised when he appeared, smiling broadly, at his door the next time we walked past.

It was during one of these informal dog-walking chats that I asked him about the old strawberry patch. He said he owned it, but he now had arthritis, so he couldn't do anything with it. I mentioned that we were thinking of moving and needed a small growing-ground to transfer garden plants. I also suggested that we could put some pleasant flowering shrubs into the hedge that would scent the air and lift his spirits during winter. I was thinking of what is possibly my favourite garden plant, *Viburnum* x *bodnantense,* and its heavenly scented pink flowers that appear continuously from autumn to spring. I guessed

Harry would love it. His face lit up with a huge grin – and I knew we had a deal.

\*

For the next three years, that little patch of ground alongside Harry's bungalow would be a regular part of our daily lives. We would never make a trip from Limetree Farm to our new field at Inley Drove (just six and a half miles to the north) without calling in at our growing-ground at Harry's. By this point, we knew we wanted to plant a large garden, but we hadn't really confronted what that would entail in plant purchases. We all get so used to seeing borders being designed and planted out on television and in gardening magazines, but we tend to forget that many of these are done by growers or nurserymen in order to promote their products – which of course they are very good at. Maisie and I know from our own experience that plants that are currently popular at Chelsea will sell like hot cakes if we're lucky enough to stock a few when we open the charity plant stall on our garden open days. Having recently installed a heated greenhouse, we've started to sell non-hardy plants, including a distinctive variety of houseleek, which has adorned many of our windowsills and the more sheltered parts of the garden in summer. Unfortunately, it has an impossibly complex name: *Aeonium arboreum* var. *atropurpureum* 'Zwartkop'. Our labels just say: 'Aeonium purp.' I know because I wrote lots of them when I propagated several in the winter of 2020–21. Thanks to Covid, Chelsea 2021 was delayed until the autumn and was fresh in people's memories when we opened our garden for the weekend, late in September. I didn't know it, because for some reason we hadn't followed the Chelsea coverage that year, but a dark *Aeonium* had been a huge success. So to our delight, we sold every single one on the stall. We should have doubled the price.

If you don't propagate your own plants, and simply buy in replacements and plants for new beds, it can prove very expensive indeed – which is one of the reasons I would never employ a garden designer. You can always tell bought-in plants: they are so closely similar to each other that they almost appear artificial. They also lack the low or misshapen side branches that inevitably remain when one digs up rooted suckers. Plants should look natural, not neat and perfect. Of course, I could be saying this because I'm an archaeologist, not a banker, and I know for a fact that I'd never be able to afford such a garden. By the time we had bought our new field, we had been gardeners for long enough to know that propagation would be the only way we'd be able to afford plants for it. Harry's little growing-ground was going to earn its keep.

Ever since they had felled the orchard and we had made the decision to move away, we had made assiduous efforts to propagate every single plant in the Limetree Farm garden. I can remember the intensity with which we set about it. It was as if any plant we failed to replicate or move to the new garden was a victory for the chainsaw people. Every successful propagation was our quiet way of showing those unpleasant people two fingers. So we started our campaign a couple of years before we obtained Harry's Patch and we set about it carefully – calling it a 'military campaign' (Operation Propagate) would perhaps be over-egging things somewhat, but we were certainly closely focused on and very methodical about what we were doing. Maisie kept exhaustive lists, itemising every pot and plant.

The area we chose for Operation Propagate at Limetree Farm was quite close to the vegetable patch and had ready access to the greenhouse and to water. We were also careful about choosing a part of the garden where the soil was very silty. It was on the edge of a large drainage dyke that was regularly cleaned out by the North Level Internal Drainage Board (NLIDB), which meant that it was always kept clear and was never blocked. Our new garden was across the county border in land controlled by the South Holland Internal Drainage Board (SHIDB), and dykes that formed our southern and eastern boundaries would be regularly maintained by them. Having good IDB-maintained dykes is very reassuring during these decades of climate change, when rainfall is heavy and the likelihood of flooding increases; but we soon discovered that these benefits also came with legal restrictions on ploughing and fencing, which affected what we could do close to the dykeside.

Summertime in the Fens can be very hot.* The east coast tends to miss many of the Atlantic storms and heavy showers, which are much reduced by the time they reach us, so we usually have to get longer periods of warm sunshine. Our rain and snow generally falls in winter and early spring when high pressure dominates, and the air that circulates in a clockwise direction around anticyclones is cold and damp, and often carries snow from off the North Sea. Fen gardens rarely dry out over winter, but desiccation in summer can be a big problem – and it can strike fast: pots of plants that looked bright and fresh in the morning can be stone dead by teatime. Fen gardens need lots of shade and part of the skill of arranging interesting shrubberies and flower beds is providing them with suitable shade, which can, of course, vary hugely – depending on what you plan to grow. It's not just a matter of shade or sun, nor of deep versus dappled shade. It's vastly more complex than that: do you

---

* In July 2019, the Cambridge Botanic Garden recorded what was, at the time, the highest temperature ever recorded in Britain: 38.7 °C (101.7 °F). But this record would be broken just three years later, on 28 July 2022, when the temperature at Coningsby in Lincolnshire (about 25 miles north of Inley Drove) reached 40.3 °C (104.5 °F).

want the dappled shade to be interspersed with sunshine in the morning, or would it be better to restrict afternoon shade to those damp areas that are likely to favour the growth of wet-loving primulae? We were faced with a similar, if somewhat simpler, problem when it came to the storing of plants to be moved to the new garden.

How were we to keep them wet? We tried regular sprinkling with a hose and putting them in large shallow trays filled with water. But such conditions don't suit all plants. Some of them – including the peonies, which prefer stable conditions – didn't like the regular switching from very dry to sodden; it was clearly stressful for them. In addition, too many changes can induce disease, such as clematis wilt. I'm not certain how we came upon the eventual solution, but we found that pots that were partially buried in soil were able to go much longer without being watered. I think they also benefited from having cooler roots and by being more stable when the wind got up, as it always did in the Fens in October. Several pots of plants that were stored in this way had to be repotted at least once, sometimes even twice, before we were able to move them to the new garden.

# PART II

*Inley Drove Farm:*
*Planning and Planting the*
*Basic Structure*

# 4

# Creating the Wood

*Playing with Maps • Framing the Picture • Trees Come First •*
*The Farm Woodland Scheme • A Living Skeleton •*
*Walking the Dogs • Lifting the Gloom*

While Operation Propagate was in full swing at Limetree Farm, there were pressing matters to address at Inley Drove. By now it was spring 1993 and we still hadn't sold Limetree Farm, but we had managed to borrow enough money to make a start on setting up the new farm. When you apply for planning permission from a local authority, you have to put things on a map. At Inley Drove, we now had a field that had absolutely nothing on it and we needed to show the authorities where we intended to place our proposed new house and barn. As both Maisie and I had studied Fenland archaeology for almost two decades, we were well aware of the possibility of future flooding. So we decided to position the house at the highest point in the field, which we had spotted immediately when we stood at the field gate the previous autumn. The low mound was the remains of a rodden (a silt-filled creek or channel) that had been formed in the Iron Age, just over two thousand years ago. At that time, our field would have been part of a marshy backswamp, behind the tidal sandbanks that ran along the Wash coastline.

This patch of slightly higher ground also fitted in well with the way we thought we could best arrange the house, farm and garden. So we drew up a sketch map showing where we wanted to position the house, the barn and the access road. I assumed this would be approved by the planning authorities as it seemed to me to be based on common sense and entirely non-controversial. So I was a bit surprised to receive a note from the planning officer dealing with our case to the effect that he thought the house ought to be positioned nearer the tiny single-track droveway that ran along the field's western edge. He put a mark on the sketch map and I altered it, moving the barn to what was, in fact, slightly higher ground than the position we had originally chosen. We agreed to it because we were both more than a little nervous that the planning authorities might suddenly turn round and refuse us permission to do anything at all – and at least we now knew where the house and barn were to be built. It was progress, of a sort. Mercifully, he left us alone to cope with a building inspector who insisted that we must fit air vents to the lower brickwork. I pointed out that these would let water in if the area flooded – and he looked at me uncomprehendingly. It had plainly never crossed his mind that the Fens are liable to flooding. Since then, I've managed to block up most of those stupid vents.

Early in 1994, we heard from the estate agents that they had been approached by clients who seemed quite serious about buying Limetree Farm at its reduced price. I gathered they weren't locals and I sort of assumed they were Londoners who had long wanted to move to the country. I was almost right: they were Londoners who wanted to find somewhere cheaper to live. They knew nothing about gardening and I didn't think they would have understood if we asked them for permission to take a few cuttings after they'd moved in. So we spent the next few weeks frantically moving plants up to Harry's growing-ground.

As soon as we had sold Limetree Farm, we invested some of the proceeds in constructing the timber barn at Inley Drove Farm. We needed the barn not just for sheep, but to house materials when we started to build the house. Permission to build the proposed house was (and still is) legally linked to the farming enterprise that went with it. To this day, I can report that sheep still peacefully graze in the paddocks of permanent pasture that surround the orchard, the woodland, the central meadow and the borders. The many large bales of hay cut every June in the central meadow are fed to our sheep over winter. The farm and the garden are still part of the same entity. So we have kept our undertaking to the planning authorities and I think that's important: a successful planning system is essential to the maintenance of open countryside and controlled urban growth. Increasingly today it seems that planning is something simply to be 'avoided': the vast, palace-like houses with three or more garages that are springing up around smaller country towns and villages are wrecking their character and appearance. Long gone are the days when beautiful medieval parish churches dominated the scene: today they must compete with vast, glitzy modern eyesores.

When the new owners of Limetree Farm moved in at the end of 1994, Maisie and I decided our cheapest option was to get hold of an old caravan and park it next to our smart new timber barn. Over the summer we had had the barn, and then the caravan, connected first to mains water and electricity, then to the phone. Life in our temporary home would prove remarkably pleasant.

*

Everything must be contained. This applies as much to religions, pandemics or national ambitions as to the humbler aspects of our own lives. Weekends frame and contain the working week. Boundaries mark the limits of counties, farms, fields and gardens. The trouble is, I don't like walls, fences or tall clipped hedges when they are used to keep people out or to tell the world that an imposing residence lies within. Those seemingly endless stone or brick walls that bound the parks of so many lovely country houses are the one feature that puts me off. I suppose they give meaning and purpose to statuesque gatehouses, but I still don't like what they stand for, or what they represent. I greatly prefer landscapes where fields, woods, roads, rivers and hedges blend together into a seamless, peaceful whole.

These were some of the reasons we decided to edge the Inley Drove garden with a varied planting of trees that would be thin and quite hedge-like in some places, while other parts would be more like a conventional wood, with oak, ash and other native British species. That at least was what we were thinking, but the reality that faced us was altogether different. The field was bare except for an overgrown hawthorn hedge along its northern and western sides, and of course there was that slight rise caused by the ancient roddon. It was the hedge along the northern edge of the field that set us thinking. We both knew how bitterly exposed these open fen fields could be in winter and this hedge would provide limited protection against the worst of the north-easterly gales. I say 'limited' because it was an old hedge that had been cut down repeatedly over the years, so its hawthorn bushes were just that: multi-stemmed bushes. They would never grow into anything very much taller.

Our initial plan was to put parts of the formal garden on the sheltered side of the existing field boundary hedge. We made the decision early in the spring of 1993 and planted two rows of daffodils on either side of what was to be a main border. Then

A general view of the Limetree Farm garden showing the central border, taken in early summer 1987. The large hedge to the right runs parallel with the road and a medieval flood protection bank. Behind the hedge you can see the tops of trees in the Bramley apple orchard.

Snowdrops growing in the wood at Inley Drove Farm.

A view down the drive, with the apple and pear trees of the orchard visible immediately beyond the grazing sheep. Note the rose hedge along the left-hand side of the drive.

The nut walk in mid-February. By this stage of the year the snowdrops, *Galanthus nivalis*, are in full flower, but the hazel catkins have largely finished.

A view of the segment of the vegetable garden given over to onions, shallots and garlic, taken in mid-July 2015. Note the covered brassica plants to the right.

General view of the vegetable garden in late May, with the greenhouse in the background. Three of the four rotational segments can clearly be seen, with onions in the foreground.

Here I am on my brand-new tripod ladder mid-way through the early January pruning of the pleached lime windbreak, between the back of the house and the barn.

A view of the Hot Garden from the yard, taken in July 2016. The pampas grass, *Cortaderia richardii*, is about two years old. In the foreground are self-seeded plants of dark mullein, *Verbascum nigrum*.

The Hot Garden in September 2015. The orange-red flowers are of *Kniphofia* 'Prince Igor'. Note also the silver leaves and brown seedheads of the giant sea holly, *Eryngium giganteum*.

The roof of the Poop Deck in May, with flowers of *Wisteria sinensis* visible between the joists.

The Front Garden in early summer. This view is taken from the front door of the house, along the path through the wirework dome, out to the driveway, with sheep grazing in the meadow beyond.

A closer view of the wirework dome in late summer. The hardy *Fuchsia magellanica var. gracilis* thrives in our clay-silt soil and looks at its best in late summer and early autumn.

The front of the house, with the *Wisteria sinensis* in full flower.

we changed our minds. We realised that such a layout would place the formal garden too far away from the house and I couldn't see us keeping it properly maintained. On reflection, we decided to use the shelter provided by the hedge as a way of getting a belt of trees rapidly established – much as we had done at Limetree Farm. But we have never got round to digging up those two rows of daffodils, which now appear every spring in an area of lawn to one side of the main meadow, where they look hopelessly out of place. Still, they remind me that plans can change. And besides, I rather like the way they puzzle the more earnest of our visitors.

I was tempted to plant protective rows of willows, but the new garden seemed even more exposed than our first one; after just ten years of growth, many of the Limetree Farm trees had started to shed branches in stormy weather. What we needed were stronger, more durable woodland trees, such as oak and ash. Slowly, we were thinking our way into doing something that I had wanted to do all my life: to plant a wood. The more we thought about it, the more it made sense. I was just starting to contemplate the cost of such a project, and feeling more than a little daunted (we had no money whatsoever at this stage), when we heard about the government-funded Farm Woodland Scheme, which had been set up a few years previously, in 1988.[1]

Establishing a small farm 'out of the blue', as it were, is quite a complex process. You need registered holding numbers and all sorts of other stuff, which we couldn't possibly have dealt with without the assistance of the local agent who helped us find the field. He's a lovely man, who has guided us as we slowly expanded the farm over the past three decades. I'm delighted to report that we are still good friends.

During the 1980s and 90s, woods and hedges were vanishing from the English countryside at an alarming rate as farmers took advantage of the many financial incentives to extend and intensify their arable acreage. Tractors, combines and farm equipment were getting bigger too, and although they hadn't achieved the ludicrous sizes that are normal today, they already seemed far too large for the fields and lanes of rural England. Following its preventable introduction from Canada in the late 1960s, Dutch elm disease had brought about the destruction of Britain's most distinctive hedgerow tree. I still miss those huge, elegant elms. And now of course our ash trees are threatened by a deadly fungal infection, ash dieback. The vanishing trees, the disappearing hedges and the open arable 'grain plains' were destroying the character of eastern England's rural landscape. It made me feel both angry and frustrated. Landscape isn't a mere productive commodity that can repay suitable investment. Those trees and hedges, together with the villages, lanes, cottages and gardens where they once grew, represented the lives and achievements of generations of rural people. Their destruction has been a historical and spiritual – not to mention an environmental – catastrophe.

We were aware when we planted our wood that we would not be providing a replacement for the rich diversity of the ancient woods and hedges cut down in recent decades. You can't replicate the subtleties of local adaptation and cross-fertilisation over hundreds of years with a vanload of saplings from a commercial tree farm. But we hoped we might be able to offer a habitat for surviving wildlife whose existence had been made more precarious by the welter of recent destruction. We were also becoming increasingly irritated by the growing number of people who just *talked* about environmental degradation and climate change. We wanted to *do* something about it. So one day, in the temporary office we were using at Flag Fen, I put my portable site drawing board on my desk and sketched in the outline of the new field at Inley Drove. Then I can remember staring at it. One question filled my head: what now? I was having an experience I would come to recognise when I started writing books: it was that blank sheet of paper or empty screen moment.

*

The weather outside the Portakabin office at Flag Fen was getting colder. Winter was approaching. Having thought about the garden for several weeks, we had both become increasingly convinced that we must first augment the hedge along the north-east side of the field to provide more lasting protection against the chilling and destructive winds, so I started to sketch the outline of a narrow belt of trees. But then I remembered about the Farm Woodland Scheme. I checked through some of the papers they had sent me earlier and read that the minimum size for new grant-aided woods was about eight acres. That was almost half the area of our new field. I measured in an eight-acre belt of trees parallel with the north-easterly side of the new field. It looked horrible: a great rectangular block – no, a brick. I was about to erase it completely when I stopped and reread the scheme's regulations. The rules and regulations had plainly been written by civil servants, rather than farmers, and I had assumed they would have included detailed guidelines about the shape and layout of new woods, which would probably have to be straight-sided and square or rectangular, like so many other features of the rapidly changing agrarian landscape. But no, I could find nothing – just stuff about planting distances and suchlike. That lifted my spirits considerably as I picked up my pencil and rubber. It was time to get started.

The first thing I did was to erase the southern side of the rectangular wood. Then I extended the easterly side right the way along the big drainage dyke. I left the edge straight along the dyke, but the other side, facing the house and garden, I allowed to waver in what I hoped was a natural-looking way. So far so good, but how was I to treat the southern, or inner, side of the original rectangular block of woodland? Nothing was coming to me. When I can't remember a name, or am having trouble writing about something, I tend to set it aside and think about something else. So that's what I did.

In the mid-1990s, I was thinking about the development of the Fens in the Middle Ages and I was doing a lot of basic background reading. The book at the top of the pile beside my desk was by the great landscape historian W. G. Hoskins. *The Making of the English Landscape* had been published some forty years earlier, in 1955. Having studied pre-Roman archaeology at university, I had never read it closely before. But now I found his well-written and lucid account of landscape development over the past two thousand years absolutely riveting. I had finished it a few days earlier. So I picked it up and idly started to thumb through, trying to put my immediate problem to one side. Then I spotted that I'd left an empty book of postage stamps in it, as a marker. It was in chapter 3, on The Colonisation of Medieval England. Why, I wondered, had I done that? Glancing down the page, my eye came across a word in italics: *essarter*. Then it all came back. It was a word in Old French meaning 'to grub up trees'[2] and it became the origin of the medieval term 'assart', which referred to an area of old woodland that had been cleared of trees to make fields. A few medieval assarts still survive in the modern landscape and they often have a very distinctive curved, almost semicircular, shape. The more I thought about them, the more I realised that a curved assart-style edge would fit nicely on the south side of the wood. It would also provide a graceful, natural-looking backdrop for the hay meadow that I had wanted to plant for many years. I looked down at that sketchy plan, but it had changed; somehow it now felt reassuring – no, comforting. At last, our garden was starting to take shape.

*

The woodland area to the north and east of the field was one of the few parts of the garden that we designed in some detail on paper. That was quite simply because it depended on the Farm Woodland Scheme, who needed to know, quite reasonably, what they would be spending public money on. The plan we adopted was quite simple. First, we would plant only native British hardwoods. The main belt of trees that ran along the cold, windy north-east boundary was in two halves: ash and oak to the west; oak and alder to the east. The big 'assart' – the bay-like meadow to the south – was bordering both areas. Then, further south, along the south-eastern boundary, the oak and alder planting gave way to a mixture of hazel interspersed with groups of oak trees. This was an area where we would start to coppice in about five to ten years' time. Around the outside of the entire woodland, including the hazel coppice, the oak, ash and alder gave way to more hedgerow-like trees, including field maple, hazel, blackthorn, hawthorn, wild cherry and wild pear; I ensured that a few oak, ash and alder also found their way there during the planting. The trees would be supplied as young seedlings or rooted cuttings, about two to three feet high.

Our scheme obtained official approval and we were free to get quotes for the supply of plants and for contractors to do the actual work of planting. Our professional advisors told us that we would be expected to accept not the most expensive, nor the cheapest, but the *second cheapest* bid – which we duly did. One of the reasons Britain has so many fine hedges, whose plants reflect regional variations in flower colour, leaf size or vigour of growth, is that the people of the Middle Ages and later who planted those hedges along fields, country roads and tracks did so using species that grew locally. This is particularly true of the enclosure hedges that were planted in the eighteenth and nineteenth centuries, many of whose component plants were from cuttings taken in the locality.[3]

Being hopelessly naive, I assumed that we would be able to continue this tradition of regional distinctiveness. But it turned out that the second-cheapest bidder obtained their plants from abroad. Continental hawthorns belong to the same species as their British cousins (*Crataegus monogyna*) but show some subtle variations, including a habit of flowering a few weeks earlier, in late winter. So the lovely hawthorns of Inley Drove Farm are out long before those in older hedges in the area. Similarly, our cherry trees are not the rather sour-tasting native British wild cherry (*Prunus avium*), but derive from seedlings germinated from cherry stones collected from a central European jam factory. In very hot summers, the many cherry trees on the edge of the wood have produced a rich crop of very dark, succulent fruit that do indeed make the most delicious jam (and a yummy sweet sauce to go with ice cream). But disaster has struck our ash trees, all of which are from continental European stock, which is highly susceptible to ash dieback. Sadly, I don't think the subtleties of regional variation in hawthorns, cherries and ash trees are ever likely to interest the politicians or civil servants who plan these funding schemes – with the best of intentions.

I'm still quite pleased with my fake 'assart', which we supplemented with a few more ornamental trees planted thinly around the edge. Trees scattered around the fringes of woodland can be a characteristic of real assarts and they certainly look very pleasing wherever I have seen them: all too often, modern rural landscapes have sharp boundaries that can never be softened or made to look more natural. We made sure that the trees we planted next to our curving 'assart' were well spaced and featured some spectacular specimens that stand out when they are seen across the meadow, especially in autumn. They include a yellow ash, an American red oak, a pair of birches with very white bark and, best of all, a spectacular native British oak with a remarkably upright (fastigiate) habit. The trees at the edge of the meadow were planted shortly after the contractors had finished the wood and everything with the Woodland Scheme seemed to be running smoothly. Each year we received a grant for several hundred pounds, which we used to pay contractors to trim around the young trees and cut down the largest weeds, invasive elder and blackberry bushes, etc.

In the early 2000s, about ten years after we had planted our trees with the help of the Farm Woodland Scheme, we were contacted by a civil servant who said he had evidence that we had started to cut down trees and that this flagrantly violated the conditions of the scheme. So he was stopping our payments, forthwith. In a panic, Maisie phoned him and asked why he thought we were doing something quite so crazy. He explained that the 'assart' curve looked exactly as if we had been cutting away at the woodland edge, a fact that was proven by the few trees left standing in the meadow. Happily, she was able to explain everything and sent him photos to prove her point. In fairness to the official, he apologised profusely and explained that he was working from satellite imagery alone. She then showed him pictures of the maps and plans we'd submitted during our original application to the scheme and he agreed that, yes, our recreated 'assart' did indeed look like deliberate tree-felling. When Maisie had finished explaining, he had the grace to laugh about it. Indeed, it was quite funny. But it had been a very anxious moment: our clever plan had so nearly been *too* clever.

*

We all use our gardens for a range of different activities, which tend to vary depending on the time of year, the climate or when our personal circumstances change. A successful garden must be able to cope with these differing types of use, some of which are likely to occur simultaneously – especially when the garden's owners have large families. At one and the same time there may be young children playing on the lawn, teenagers enjoying themselves in the summerhouse, while father weeds the vegetable garden and mother repots her pelargoniums.

By contrast, some of the ways we use our gardens remain more or less the same throughout the year. A good example of this in our case is dog walking. One of the main reasons I enjoy taking our two dogs, Baldwin (a Jack Russell dog) and Pen (a black Labrador bitch with some Border collie genes), for three walks a day is that I get to see the garden at different times and from a variety of perspectives, including from the outside. I always think that people who deliberately set out to 'screen' their houses and gardens from the world around them are actually being rather selfish: why try to hide them away so completely? You don't have to reveal everything; it's only natural to want to keep certain parts of your garden private – such as the places you might retreat to with friends to drink Pimm's in summer. The trick is to hide them without making the concealment obvious. This was something that came naturally to the Georgians, but was lost on the Victorians, with their penchant for tall walls and thick laurel hedges. There are times I fear we might be slipping back to the nineteenth century.

I have always held footpaths and walks in high esteem. They are great places to exercise dogs, but there is far more to them than that. Despite always having loved walking through parks and gardens, it wasn't really until I began to write books, in the mid-1990s, that I found I was taking several walks a day, with or without the dogs. I didn't take those walks as part of the process of writing – as a way of coming up with new ideas or as a means of dealing with problems. No, I took them because quite simply I found them relaxing: I believed that on a walk, my brain could switch out of writing and into gardening mode. What brought about a change in my approach to walks was a visit to Charles Darwin's home at Down House near Bromley, in Kent. I remember a wonderful feeling of quiet contentment when I came across the Sandwalk, a footpath that Darwin had carefully laid out along the edge of his garden and which not only looked out across the peaceful Kentish countryside but also wove its way through deep woodland.[4]

I was immediately struck by the Sandwalk's calming tranquillity. There was nothing dramatic about it whatsoever: no commanding views nor striking revelations. It could never have been designed by Capability Brown.

As time has passed, I have found that my own variants of Darwin's Sandwalk have been extraordinarily beneficial to me. I used to see them as the skeleton of the garden, the physical framework that held its disparate components together. Now, I take a far more rounded view: yes, they do indeed provide structure, but like the skeletons of living organisms they do far more than that. Bones contain marrow that produces white blood cells that help fight infection; they also give protection to blood vessels and nerves. So I see the network of stepping-stone paths, the carefully arranged mown grass walks and the informal woodland paths as far more than a mere framework. What one might think of as the 'destination' features, the flower

89

beds and borders, change with the seasons: rose beds are less exciting in early spring than they are in late spring and early summer; while herbaceous borders, after a quiet April and May, can reach spectacular climaxes in mid-June or September.

The paths, lawns and walks at Inley Drove define and link the garden's set-piece features, but they also develop a character of their own, which often cannot be created by design. Their appeal can be softer and more subtle than that of a colourful herbaceous border: the gentle curve of a tall, well-clipped hedge, for example, or a distant glimpse of a pond or sundial. Walks and paths are also a way of easing people into an area that may at first sight seem less restful than other, more obviously welcoming, parts of the garden. Open meadows can seem hostile in December or January, but even so, I firmly believe you should never ignore them. You may well be surprised by what they have to offer. Nothing inspires as much hope as the first glimpses of snowdrop and aconite flowers through snow-covered or frosty grass in early January. It's a dark time of the year that I have always found rather depressing, but sometimes during those short days I can feel very close to my garden. Lawn walks and woodland paths come into their own in the depths of winter: like old friends and close relatives, they can provide both comfort and emotional warmth.

*

Like everyone else living in rural Britain, I like to compare the progress of the seasons year on year, and fixed points in the calendar, such as Christmas, make the task much simpler. In late December 2021, I was taking the dogs on their second Boxing Day walk when I noticed that the branches of the hazel we were walking beneath had sprouted one or two pendulous greeny-yellow catkins. That was *very* early: we don't normally have hazel catkins until mid-January – at the earliest. As I stood staring in astonishment, I was almost pulled off my feet by our black Labrador, Pen, who had detected a delicious aroma – probably a lovely patch of fishy heron poo, which she adores rolling in at this time of year. Plainly, she had no interest in catkins; neither did our Jack Russell, Baldwin, who had just come across a superb piece of long-dead blackbird. In short, neither of them chose to look above their heads, so I couldn't have asked them what they might have thought, but I was absolutely convinced that the catkins had not been there on Christmas Day. But then, of course, I started to have doubts: had I looked quite so high above my head yesterday? I remembered it had been raining, which meant I wouldn't have been staring into the sky. I resumed my walk, my head full of doubts.

I had taken about ten paces and the dogs were just starting to find new sets of even more delicious scents, when I almost whooped with delight. There, just on the edge of the path, was the first clump of fresh, clean, green and pointed snowdrop leaves! That really made my spirits rise – and on Boxing Day, too! Normally, the snowdrops keep us waiting until at least the end of the first week of the New Year. So both the hazel catkins and the snowdrops were early. Maybe the aconites wouldn't be too far behind. I was feeling much more cheerful. All I needed was for the sun to emerge, but this was a typical late December day, with misty drizzle and a continuous ceiling of pale grey cloud. Sometimes a crow would call and at one point we disturbed a buzzard perched in an oak tree high above our heads. All the action was with the birds, hares and muntjac deer. The murk was closing in. Time for a hot mince pie.

*

Nothing lifts the gloom of midwinter better than the flowers of the first snowdrops and aconites. As I write, we're near the end of the second week in January and those early snowdrops, which I spotted just after Christmas, appear to have stopped growing. Mark you, I don't blame them: it has been a very cold, damp winter, dominated by high pressure interspersed with vigorous rain and snow showers from off the Atlantic. Slowly, however, the days are starting to get a bit longer. I always rather enjoy the way mornings in early January remain late and dark, while afternoons quite quickly start to get lighter. I used to think there was a problem with my perception of time and light, but in fact, if you check the precise times of sunrise and sunset for this time of year, you'll see that my perception reflects reality: following the winter solstice (21 December, the shortest day), sunrise doesn't start to get any earlier for almost three weeks, whereas by the same time in mid-January, afternoons are twenty minutes longer. I gather that the lack of day-length symmetry is a result of the Earth's wobbling in space as it orbits around the sun.

We're very fortunate with our weather here in Britain. I lived in Toronto for nine years and I can remember those Canadian winters very well indeed. Before I went there, I used to think of places like Toronto as being close to the Arctic Circle, many, many miles north of London. But in actual fact Toronto is about five hundred miles *south* of London, on roughly the same latitude as Marseilles. This only becomes really apparent in summertime, when the heat can be almost unbearably humid thanks to nearby Lake Ontario. Inland areas of Canada, such as the region around the Great Lakes, have continental climates, with a short spring and autumn (fall) and a sometimes protracted summer and winter. It's the speed with which fall happens that helps to give those maple woods of Ontario, Quebec and New England their astonishing colours: they have to be seen to be believed.

I can remember my first Canadian spring. In late March or early April, the ubiquitous snow suddenly melted and for a couple of days there was deep slush everywhere before it all drained away. I recall walking through Queen's Park, near the Royal Ontario Museum where I worked, and being amazed to see bulb leaves shooting out of the ground, rather like asparagus on amphetamines. Snowdrops were up, flowering and dead within a couple of weeks; daffodils were the same: they looked fabulous for a few days and then died off. Almost before I was aware of it, spring was over – and we entered the long, hot days of summer, which continued for almost six months, until sometime in late October.

I still haven't quite got over the extraordinary difference between the continental climate of inland Canada and the maritime weather of Britain, where the seasons are much longer and more evenly divided. Temperatures are less extreme and the start and finish of each season can be very unpredictable; there is also far more by way of precipitation, whether in the form of rain, showers, snow, sleet or drizzle, but snow rarely stays cold for long enough to accumulate on the ground. When people struggle to describe the way that climate change is altering the British weather, I think of my years in Canada. I would suggest that Britain's climate is becoming more extreme, more continental and of course far more unpredictable.

I always think of snowdrops and aconites as the first flowers of spring, but they bloom throughout January and February (both winter months), and in very warm seasons they're finished by early March.* In fact, the first flowering plants in most

---

* In this book, I use the meteorological definition of each season: winter (December, January, February); spring (March, April, May); summer (June, July, August); and autumn (September, October, November). See also: www.metoffice.gov.uk/weather/learn-about/weather/seasons/spring/when-does-spring-start

modern gardens are the fragrant winter-flowering viburnums and honeysuckles.* We always have a few plants near the back door. Their scent used to make the night-time trudge to the lambing pens a positive pleasure.

*

We decided not to plant bulbs in the wood until the trees had become quite well established and were providing sufficient shade. My parents' house in Hertfordshire was rich in snowdrops, but like many old plantings the many varieties had interbred and would often produce unexpected seedlings: perhaps of extra-large size, or with double flowers. We wanted the snowdrops in our new wood to look and be 'natural'. Most garden reference books describe *Galanthus nivalis*, the common snowdrop, as being 'native' (i.e. indigenous) to Britain. However, at the time we were planning the new wood, back in 1993, both Maisie and I were quite familiar with pollen records that extended back to the Ice Age – and snowdrop pollen was never mentioned. But even if they were not a 'true' native species, those simple plain common snowdrops are still absolute perfection. Vast amounts of time, labour and effort have been expended so as to produce superior – or just different – hybrids, but although some are both striking and unusual, none have the quiet grace of the original, *Galanthus nivalis*, which is now thought to have been introduced to Britain roughly five hundred years ago – sometime in the 1500s.[5]

People who collect and understand the complexities of snowdrop breeding are known as Galanthophiles, and while I can't claim to share their delight in the intricacies of snowdrop identification, I can understand how it might appeal. Roses

---

* Such as *Viburnum* x *bodnantense* and *Lonicera fragrantissima*.

are probably even more diverse, and their breeding and distribution are important components of the horticultural industry. I suspect, too, that many more people collect roses than snowdrops – and yet their interest hasn't been dignified with a name. For most gardeners, roses are special, but they are seen nonetheless as part of something larger. Very few private, non-botanic gardens have areas where roses are grown entirely on their own. Most are planted in beds, along with other plants that can enhance their appeal. At Inley Drove, we like our roses to be seen in mixed borders. Even our Rose Garden, which was initially intended to be just that, has developed into a series of smaller mixed beds, where roses play a very important part – but they don't sit in glorious isolation.

So why are snowdrops treated so differently? The answer is quite simple: snowdrops are seen on their own because that's how they grow. With the exception of a few aconites and perhaps an early crocus or two, snowdrops dominate the garden in late winter and early spring. They have no competition, which is something we both like: there is something so appealing about starting the gardening season with such simple, straightforward displays of pointed green shoots emerging through the frost to reveal their graceful white flowers, which open their petals at the first hint of sunshine. We wanted the snowdrops in the wood to be *Galanthus nivalis* alone, with no hybrids. It's reliably early; flowers for a long time; is scented and graceful. Superb. We had wanted it for our Limetree Farm garden too, and contemplated buying it from seed merchants and garden centres, but we weren't entirely confident that hybrids would not appear in the mix (we had had bad experiences with other plants we'd bought in packets). They were also very expensive. Then, in the winter of 1984/5, Maisie spotted a piece in a gardening journal reporting that Walsingham Abbey, in Norfolk, was selling bare-rooted bulbs of *Galanthus nivalis* at a very reasonable price.[6]

On a summer visit to Walsingham a few years previously, we had learnt that the abbey had a good display of snowdrops in the grounds. A winter trip to Walsingham, avoiding the hordes of Chelsea tractors that clog up the narrow roads of north Norfolk in summer, seemed like a good idea. And so it was! Neither of us had ever seen a more spectacular snowdrop display, which covered an area of about twenty acres, mostly in woodland. We could also see why they were selling off bulbs, as many of the clumps were very congested. We bought several large bagfuls.

I have long known that snowdrops are best transplanted 'in the green' with leaves and roots still intact. Their bulbs are not happy about being dried and quite often won't re-germinate. They're also best planted in small groups of two or three, rather than as single plants. Isolated single plants make easy targets for squirrels and other pests and they also take much longer to form into good-sized clumps. Snowdrops look much, much better in clumps than as single flowers, although I gather that pots of rare hybrids, each with a single, treasured bulb, can change hands for large sums in the specialised sales of the Galanthophile fraternity.

By the time we made the move from Limetree to Inley Drove Farm, our clumps of *Galanthus nivalis* snowdrops were huge. We must have taken many thousands of bulbs with us, safely protected and kept damp in large blocks of silty clay. Most of the small clumps I planted in the new wood were in the area that is now dominated by ash trees, many of which are suffering from ash dieback disease. Once we realised that the wood was infected, I began a campaign of transplanting and managed to move many bucketfuls of snowdrop bulbs to the areas of woodland dominated by oak. That was almost ten years ago. Today, they are looking very spectacular. Let us pray that the healthy oaks don't fall prey to yet another horrible disease.

No English wood would be complete without bluebells,

which must be planted in different areas from snowdrops, because their leaves obscure each other's flowers. As most readers will probably be aware, the native strain of British bluebells (*Hyacinthoides non-scripta*) is in danger of being swamped by the larger and more vigorous Spanish bluebell (*H. hispanica*), which is still widely sold in garden centres. We greatly prefer the British bluebell, not for jingoistic reasons, but because their colour – a darker, more intense blue – is very much better. The Spanish bluebell also holds its flower stems more stiffly: they don't nod and sway like their more elegant British cousins. Near my parents' old house in Hertfordshire is a well-known bluebell wood, Graveley Howe, from which my grandfather would regularly transplant bluebells into the garden; he favoured especially the pink seedlings, which sometimes pop up in old bluebell woods (I think they are natural one-off variants). My grandfather had to take a break from gardening when he went off to spend four years in the trenches of the Somme in the Great War; but in his absence the bluebells flourished and became well established.

We didn't really start serious planting at Limetree Farm until the late spring and early summer of 1981, the year we moved in. This was also the year that the government passed the Wildlife and Countryside Act, which made it illegal to uproot wild plants without the landowner's permission.[7] So I didn't go up the hill to Graveley Howe wood, but instead removed a couple of buckets of my grandfather's bulbs from my parents' garden. I can't remember if I asked my father's permission. But I can assure you, they're British native bluebells without so much as a hint of Spanish blood (or should that be sap?). Unwanted cross-hybridisation can cause problems for modern gardeners. The trick is to stay alert!

\*

Today, a large part of the garden at Inley Drove Farm is enclosed by the protective woodland we planted. The transition from highly structured formal garden to this outer, seemingly unstructured zone of trees, hazel bushes, brambles and stinging nettles happens in a tranquil, pleasant fashion as you follow the straight path, framed by the two pampas grasses, across the open Hay Meadow. Just before you enter the wood, you come upon a far less spectacular mown path that follows the edge of the trees, where climbing roses and scented shrubs offer you an alternative, perhaps more relaxed, stroll, if you don't feel in the mood to enter the shady, cooler realm of the trees. I quite often follow this wood-edge path when I'm walking the dogs, which I keep on those extendable leads when near the wood to protect the dozens of hares who live in and around the many piles of shrub and woody herbaceous prunings we have carefully heaped around the inner edge of the wood, as winter protection, mostly for young hares and hibernating hedgehogs. The dogs love this path between the wood and the meadow: I think of it as a canine tapas bar, offering them occasional mouthfuls of delicious hare poo and a vast array of smells – and all for free!

# 5

# The Hay Meadow

*Sowing the Seed • Hay and Meadows • Cows' Lips •*
*Snake's Heads • No Turning Back • Genetic 'Purity'*

In the late summer and autumn of 1992, we used to visit the new field at Inley Drove almost daily. We did have small jobs to do there, but in reality I think we were just getting used to going there. These visits may sound rather dull and routine, but they weren't at all. In some ways, we found them almost exciting: it was all about anticipation, about living in the future. Every time we headed across the county boundary, the Inley Drove project seemed to get larger and more challenging. We also couldn't help noticing that the small number of weeds that had remained after the land was harvested the previous year were now multiplying and growing very rapidly. Self-seeded oilseed rape plants were the most vigorous of these and one or two were even showing the early signs of flower buds. If they reseeded, it would be a disaster. I made a mental note that we must do something about it. If the weeds had grown this fast earlier in the year, I honestly don't know what we'd have done – we might even have been reduced to spraying them off, which would not have been a good way to start an environmentally friendly garden. But Maisie and I had work to do. We both agreed on the size and broad outline of the wood, so I could now start doing something about the growing carpet of weeds.

The next day I drove into the village and went to see Fred, the farmer we'd bought the land from, who I knew would have the right equipment for the job. I explained to Fred that first I wanted to harrow the weeds (which would require his help), and then to sow grass seed, which I would buy. Nineteen ninety-two hadn't been a bad year for drilling (sowing) next year's wheat and barley, so Fred was well ahead and reckoned he'd easily have the time to do our little job.

While Fred got on with the harrowing, Maisie and I spent a couple of very pleasant days marking out the edges of the wood, which we did with bamboo canes and lengths of plastic hazard tape. I bought the grass seed from a local seed merchant, who tried to sell me various commercial mixes, all of which featured large quantities of North American ryegrass, which livestock adore, but sadly isn't native to Britain. Many of the off-the-peg grazing mixes contained red clover, which is also very nutritious, but can give sheep bloat when they partake of it too freely. I wanted small-flowered white clover (*Trifolium repens*) and native British grasses only. It took them a day or two to assemble the mix. I don't recall exactly what it cost, but I do remember it wasn't cheap.

The seed merchant delivered the bags of seed to Fred's farm and within a few days the job was finished. Grass seed sprouts quite quickly in a warm, damp late autumn, and just over a week after seeding you could clearly discern the outline of the wooded area, which had been harrowed but not seeded. It was wonderful to watch as the garden and meadows slowly took shape in the grass and clover that would feed successive generations of sheep and lambs. Maybe it was my excitement at observing the transformation of the previously bare field, but I couldn't help thinking that young grasses have a particularly delicate shade of green. I still find it a colour of hope.

As the grass grew, we fenced the paddocks and the following year we had sheep grazing on them in the spring. They plainly loved the white clover, which, like the native grasses, responded well to light grazing. By the end of the summer, the paddocks all boasted a good rich sward that looked as if it had been there for decades, not months. I knew at the time that it was, strictly speaking, a mistake to include clover in the grass we sowed in the garden, but it wasn't practical to sow the two areas in separate operations – and besides, all the seed bags contained clover. I do love to see the chirpy white clover flowers in the lawn and they certainly attract many bees, but clover is a creeping, invasive plant and if it escapes from the lawn and gets into the flower beds, it can be very hard to get rid of. But do I regret planting it? No, I don't. It looks particularly good in one large area of grass that is used neither for grazing nor for lawn: the Hay Meadow.

*

English gardens have long been known for their lovely, natural-looking meadows. You wouldn't have thought it possible for them to get any more popular, but in recent years they certainly have. Much of this is down to the Dutch garden designer Piet Oudolf, whose book *Planting the Natural Garden* (2003) remains highly influential. I can't say I'm wildly enthusiastic about the low-growing grassy 'carpet bedding' that is such a feature of his borders, but then that's just me: I prefer my borders to be taller and a bit more exciting. Living in the depths of the rural Fens, I like beds and plantings that contrast with the natural landscape – or what is left of it. I also find many modern horticultural recreations of meadows to be far too rich in flowers. I sometimes wonder what would happen if they were cut for animal fodder: would all those exotic plants dry evenly and form hay, or would they rot down and make a rather slimy compost? I suspect the latter.

We knew when we started to think about the detailed planning of the new garden that we would have to include quite a substantial area – certainly more than an acre – that we could cut every year for hay. When we were living at Limetree Farm we kept three or four orphaned lambs, which we'd buy cheap from neighbouring farmers who were only too pleased to be rid of them during the frantic weeks of lambing. So after a few years, we had learnt a little about sheep-keeping. Eventually, we understood enough to know that the agricultural justification we would need to gain planning permission for the new house and garden would have to be based on a self-financing sheep-farming enterprise. Every winter, the in-lamb (pregnant) ewes must be taken off the outdoor grazing and housed before lambing begins. This allows them to put on a bit of weight before the lambs are born; it also ensures that the pastures can recover, ready for the return of the ewes and their young lambs in the springtime. Considerable quantities of top-quality hay are needed to feed the ewes when they are housed. Since the 1970s the price of hay has risen sharply, largely because so many rural smallholdings have been given over to the raising of horses. These people buy in their hay and are quite prepared to pay good money for it. We frugal sheep farmers prefer to grow our own, although on rare occasions we have been known to sell surplus large bales for horses – providing, of course, the price is right.

Every year, our meadow is cut for hay and normally yields about a dozen large round bales. We never apply any fertiliser because meadow flowers thrive much better in slightly undernourished soils. At first, I was worried in case the drop in soil fertility might damage the yield of hay too severely to make it cost effective. But I shouldn't have worried: every year our naturally rich clay-silt soils grow luxuriant crops of grass.

Baling hay in the meadow, July 2021. The 'assart' curve to the woodland edge is visible in the background.

Most of the hay grown by UK farmers today consists of grass – usually ryegrass – and maybe one or two other nourishing herbs. Before the Second World War, hay was often cut on common land or on areas of the farm that weren't suitable for ploughing because the soil was thin or poor. The land kept for hay wasn't ploughed and no artificial fertilisers were used. So in time the meadows became very rich in certain wildflowers that could flower, and set their seeds, before that time in summer when hay cutting was allowed. In many villages there were strict rules governing when common land could be cut for hay.

The old hay meadows of England were devastated by modern farmers who wanted to replace them with more productive crops of newly sown grasses. Today, old meadows are protected by law, but only a tiny proportion have managed to survive. Many seed companies offer packets of meadow flowers, which we did consider using. But we decided not to. I think we were both rather put off by the 'sameness' of seed-packet meadows. There was nothing distinctive about them. Ours was going to be a Fen meadow and we didn't want it to resemble something one might see in the Cotswolds or on the flood plains of the upper Thames. We also knew that the footings of old hedges nearby and the edges of local dykes still contained wildflowers, such as dead nettle, creeping buttercups and daisies, which would eventually find their way into our meadow. I'm glad to say that I think it has proved to be the right decision. But there were two flowers that I was absolutely determined we should have – and I was prepared to buy them if necessary.

*

The heavy, wet clay-silt soils of the south Lincolnshire Fens are ideally suited to cowslips and snake's-head fritillaries. Cowslips acquired their name because their trumpet-shaped flowers were thought to resemble cows' lips. I used to think this inexplicable until one day, when sitting on the ground in warm spring sunshine, I found myself staring at a particularly fine cowslip and yes, it suddenly seemed obvious: the petals did indeed look just like the lips of a pouting cow or milk-hungry calf. By great good fortune, we grew cowslips in the long grass beneath the willows at Limetree Farm and were able to move quite a few plants out to Harry's growing-ground, where they thrived.

Once the recently sown areas of grass in the new garden were starting to get established, I subdivided the plants at Harry's into dozens of tiny plantlets, some of which had very few roots. Maisie thinks I over-reduce plants when we're dividing them up or potting them on – and of course she's right: more often than not we'd then have a spell of dry weather and 90 per cent of them would shrivel up and die, but in this instance it paid off handsomely. Those dozens of tiny cowslips, which I had planted in widely separated groups of twos and threes right across the sweeping bay-shape of the new Hay Meadow, all took root. Within weeks they had become healthy young plants. One or two even managed to flower, which I can still remember finding strangely moving: those short-stemmed young cowslip flowers had a strength of colour that seemed more intensely yellow than was normally the case. Even though the grass around them was still quite thin, and the trees of the wood were only just starting to poke out of their plastic growing tubes, it was possible to get a feeling for how the Hay Meadow might one day look. But what surprised us both was the speed with which it happened.

The second year after planting, the young meadow grass grew rapidly and I couldn't help thinking that somehow it had overwhelmed the cowslips. I looked for them everywhere, but could only spot one or two. Then, two years later, when the first crop of hay had long been removed, I was walking through the meadow in the depths of winter when I was astonished to spot cowslip plants that were showing signs of putting on new leaves, ready for the spring. Where I had planted patches of two or three, there were now half a dozen – even more. Every day I spotted new plants. Very soon, there were too many to count. Over the next five years, those few dozen over-reduced plants I had so carefully inserted into the still quite soft meadow soil had started to form distinct drifts of springtime yellow. Today, they form a huge floral carpet that must contain hundreds of thousands of flowers.

In the season before we moved the cowslip plants out of Harry's growing-ground, they grew well, flowered freely and eventually produced seeds, which we collected regularly and put in an envelope for safekeeping. Once the trees had been planted in the new wood, we came face to face with the reality of what it meant to leave a thirty-foot-wide strip along the drainage dykes that run along the field's south and east boundaries. This strip was required to allow access for the large diggers that the Internal Drainage Board deploy in the autumn to clean out the dyke, in readiness for any winter flooding. We could graze sheep in this strip, but we would have to be prepared to move them whenever the IDB needed access. With this in mind, we fenced the strip and sowed it; but even when we had done that, it didn't resemble anything other than what it was: a rather brutal-looking access strip. By this point we had moved all the cowslip plants out of Harry's, but then I remembered that envelope I'd filled with seeds – they were certainly still fresh and should germinate. Having said that, I didn't hold out huge hopes: those strips looked *so* bleak and hostile.

I waited for a still, calm day because the seeds were tiny and would be scattered at random in a wind. I originally intended to spread the seeds evenly, but I soon abandoned this in favour of a few areas of less thinly spread plants. The two strips ('brinks' is the local term for the land along dykesides) were far longer than I had initially imagined when we collected the seeds, but when I came to do it there was only enough to spread some uneven patches along the eastern dyke. This, however, turned out quite well: germination was remarkably good and soon the patches of tiny seedlings grew into small plants. Within a couple of years, the patches looked entirely natural – as if they had spread there from out of the young wood (where the primulae would actually have been the more shade-loving primrose, *Primula vulgaris*, rather than the sun-loving cowslip *Primula veris*). Slowly, as the trees in the wood grew taller, the once rather severe-looking brinks acquired a rustic charm all

The brink behind the main area of woodland, with wild cherries in flower. Baldwin (Jack Russell) is in the foreground and Pen (Labrador x Border collie) beneath the cherry blossom.

of their own. They look particularly fine when the cherry trees are in flower. I love taking the dogs on their winter walks there: the morning sun, even in early January, feels wonderfully warm and relaxing as it shines on the trees. As we walk past, we often spot hares, muntjac and roe deer sunning themselves, safely sheltered from the cold winds blowing in from the north.

Cowslips were fairly straightforward to find, but snake's-head fritillaries were to prove more problematic. For a start, they were very expensive and at the time we were very broke. Sadly, archaeology isn't a financially rewarding profession and we had other, more urgent, expenses to attend to. But then something happened that I could never have imagined in a thousand years.

In the late 1990s, most of the people living in the area either worked on the land or had jobs in local towns, like Wisbech, Holbeach or Spalding. Some people commuted to Peterborough – some twenty miles away – but cities like Cambridge and London were just too difficult to reach daily by train. Maisie and I worked on archaeological sites around Peterborough and in the nearby Fens. There were only a few people who worked in London, and those who did usually spent three or four days there, staying overnight during the week rather than travelling to and fro every day. I suppose you could say that it was all rather parochial – or perhaps old-fashioned would be a kinder way of putting it. But then a genuinely exotic couple bought the only large house in the neighbourhood.

You could easily spot their house from upstairs in our house, before the woodland started to grow. As the crow flies, it's about a mile and a half away to the south-east. It's an architecturally outstanding building, built in the late seventeenth and early eighteenth centuries. I think it owes its distinctiveness to the fact that it hasn't been given elaborate doorways and windows – there is no flamboyant stonework. In fact, it is built from brick, in a plain, straightforward fashion. I find this lack of ornamentation not just modest, but comforting. The house sits very well in its restrained Fenland setting, on a low, natural rise in the silt fen. It had been neglected for many years; local people remembered the days when there was an oak tree growing out of it, its branches projecting through the roof. Then it was bought by a couple who restored it sensitively. With fireplaces in every room, it was a characterful and welcoming place, especially on cool winter evenings.

I can't remember precisely how we got to meet our new neighbours, but very soon we became firm friends. I mention this because one of them was the now very well-known and distinguished garden designer Arne Maynard.[1] We were at pains not to pester him with questions, but, having said that, we always had lots to talk about whenever we met, which was quite frequently. Arne redesigned large areas of their garden, often quite elaborately. We soon realised that potential clients would be shown round the garden so they could see what Arne would be capable of doing for them.

Arne and his partner, the photographer William Collinson, spent most weekdays working in London. While they were gone, we would nip round and have a cup of tea with their resident gardener. Perhaps because he was working alone in a large and isolated property, he was always happy to chat. We picked his brains at every opportunity, and he was very generous in the information and knowledge he imparted. By way of returning the favour, we invited him to visit our wood and help himself to as many hazel rods and poles as he needed from our by now rapidly growing area of coppice. It felt good to be contributing to what was becoming an increasingly well-known local garden.

I mention our new neighbours not just to drop a huge horticultural name, but also to explain how I suddenly acquired bulbs of snake's-head fritillaries. One day I mentioned to Arne that I would dearly like to get hold of some for the meadow. I wasn't hinting at anything and forgot that I'd even mentioned it, so it came as a huge surprise when, at the correct planting time in the autumn, he gave me several bags full of fritillary bulbs, which he said had been 'left over' from a contract. I planted them in small clumps and over the years they have seeded and spread. They clearly love our wet, heavy, silty soil – and of course they look fabulous in the spring, when the cowslips are also in flower. The spring meadow is now one of the most successful and popular features of our garden.

Arne's collaboration with the distinguished Dutch garden designer Piet Oudolf produced a garden that not only won them a Gold Medal at the 2000 Chelsea Flower Show, but also the most prestigious award of all: Best in Show. Maisie and I were fortunate enough to be visiting the Flower Show on the day of their triumph and had the pleasure of witnessing their excitement and delight. Half a dozen years later, Arne and William sold their Fen house and moved across the country, to South Wales. We still miss them.

One of the things I love about gardens is their wonderful habit of springing surprises. Maybe that's one of the reasons why, despite my admiration for Arne, I'm generally not very keen on gardens that are overtly designed; I dislike imposition and prefer a light touch approach that allows for the possibility of nature taking its course. In our meadow, for example, we were able to control the arrival of cowslips and snake's-head fritillaries, and they certainly look very attractive indeed; but they are also natural to the setting. I was surprised by the speed with which they became established and started to spread – all of which was very pleasing – but their presence wasn't a surprise. Then, about a couple of years after we had taken possession of the new field, something unexpected *did* happen. I remember being annoyed by the arrival in the meadow of creeping buttercup (*Ranunculus repens*), which seemed to be everywhere. I soon established that they were thriving on the dykesides and I assumed they were probably present in the soil when we sowed the grass. I was fairly sure they would cease to be a big problem when we started regularly mowing the lawn and cutting the hay, and in general that has been the case.

Then one day in late May, probably in 1995, I was walking along the edge of the meadow when I thought I spotted a few plants of creeping buttercup growing in the grass that we were about to cut for hay. I was slightly irritated by this, as I wasn't very fond of them, but then I took a closer look. There was something not quite right about them. The buttercups in the long grass were a bit different from *Ranunculus repens*: for a start, their flowers were on tall, elegant stems, quite unlike the short stalks of the creeping buttercups; their shade of yellow was also subtly paler and I thought I could detect a very slight scent. Suddenly, I realised these were meadow buttercups (*Ranunculus acris*), and not the pesky creeping weed that I disliked so much. I was well aware, from walking the dogs, that meadow buttercups grew along the dykesides, but for some inexplicable reason I had never thought they might spread into the meadow. I made a mental note of where they were growing and then I got on with other jobs. Three weeks later, we cut the hay.

The following year I should have been looking out for them, but at that stage in the garden's development I had other, more pressing, things to think about. I can remember walking along the meadow's edge, some distance from where I had spotted the flowers the previous spring, when my eye was caught by several long-stemmed yellow flowers growing further away from the edge. Immediately, I went back to the spot where I now remembered I had seen meadow buttercups the previous year and to my surprise, and delight, the little patch appeared to have doubled in size.

I disapprove of the notion that a flower meadow is only meant to be viewed from the outside. I like to get up close and personal with a meadow: I love looking at the bees and other insects that inhabit it. I also enjoy the scents and subtle changes of texture that develop as the season progresses. A walk through our meadow is also the best way to judge when the hay is starting to mature. So we have two mown paths through it. The first is straight and runs from the small, hedged

Rose Garden, out into the meadow, where it passes between two large pampas grasses before joining the wood at its main entrance, at the apex of the 'assart's curve. The second path is longer but slightly narrower, and runs in a gentle semicircle from the east (or pergola) end of the long border, all the way to the Tea Shed. It crosses the straight main path close by the clumps of pampas grass.*

I walked along all the paths and spotted little patches of meadow buttercups everywhere. At this stage I reckoned I could possibly have delayed their development with spot applications of lawn weedkiller, but I didn't want to. In my heart of hearts, I knew I'd grown more than a little attached to them. I liked the rather cheeky way that they were insinuating themselves into our garden, uninvited. But most of all, I was starting to like their colour en masse. Today, I am addicted to it. When they're in flower, I walk along those meadow paths several times a day. So I try to cut the hay slightly later than I would normally, when the buttercups have set their seeds. Within less than five years, the few scattered patches of flowers had become drifts and by 2010 they formed a stunning carpet, which in some respects even outshines the earlier displays of cowslips and snake's-head fritillaries. That carpet of meadow buttercups returns every year and it always seems to get better. We both found it particularly cheering in June 2020 when everyone was having to live through the unpleasant months of the first Covid-19 lockdown. Wildflowers can be so comforting.

*

Capability Brown and Humphry Repton understood very well that large garden, park or landscape features will appear

---

* I discuss this straight path in the final section of this chapter.

even grander if they are framed, constrained or broken up in some way. There's nothing like a small island or two to make a medium-sized lake appear far more imposing – and of course a great country house looks positively palatial when seen at the end of a huge avenue, usually of limes. Ultimately, I think features such as avenues of limes are about providing us normal folk with steps that we can use in our minds to enter these larger worlds, many of which are otherwise completely out of reach.

When the new wood had been planted, the area we had marked out for the Hay Meadow seemed far too big. We thought about the matter for some time, and decided that the easiest way to reduce its size would be to extend by about half an acre the parts of the garden that would be occupied by lawn. I was slightly daunted by the thought of having to mow such a huge additional area, but that's what we decided and, at first, it didn't seem to be too much extra work. Looking back on those times, I now realise that, since the borders and some of the more formal gardens hadn't yet been fully planted or indeed even planned, there was generally less routine maintenance to be carried out, which made the additional mowing doable.

When we first laid out the wood, we made no provision whatsoever for paths or access. It was just a block of trees. But when it came to the business of planting it, the contractors needed a route for our rather aged Suzuki four-wheel drive to tow trailers full of young saplings, stakes and protective plastic tubes to where they'd be needed. This access route formed a large curving path that swept rather majestically, I now realise, through the centre of the wood. It's still in use today and in one or two places you can still see shallow grooves where the four-wheel drive and trailer got stuck in the mud.

I'm well aware that those plastic tubes played a vital role in protecting the young saplings, but we knew they were going to be a pain to get rid of. We had been told by officials and contractors alike that the green plastic tubes would never need to be removed because they would rot away within five years. We were assured that they were made from a special short-lived plastic that was specifically designed to break down rapidly when exposed to direct sunlight. But after about seven years they were still in perfect condition and hadn't even gone slightly brittle. So in the end we had to remove them all, by hand (I remember, because it was very hard on my back!). The few tubes that we retained for use elsewhere in the garden are still in mint condition and very flexible. I suspect the lab that tested the plastic for its resistance to sunlight was probably located in Death Valley, California, the hottest place on Earth. But on the positive side, the few tubes we retained still have the strength to deter hares, deer and any other predators of young trees.

I was rather fearfully planning to burn the tubes we'd removed in a bonfire, which I knew would stink and I felt bad about causing such nasty pollution, but dumping them in a local landfill site would be just as bad – if not worse – and could prove quite expensive. Anyhow, I had to do something. So I piled the tubes into a rough heap next to the place where we have bonfires, while waiting for a south-easterly wind, which we knew would not blow the acrid smoke across our neighbours' properties. By the time we'd finished, the heap had become very large and could clearly be seen from Inley Drove. One day, a passing Land Rover towing a horse trailer pulled into the drive and a smiling lady got out. She was about to plant a wood on land that she had just bought and couldn't believe her eyes when she spotted our heap of tubes. It turned out that they fitted comfortably into her horsebox and she drove off delighted. She also offered to pay, but even I couldn't allow that.

The large, curved access path through the wood ran from a side branch of the drive all the way round to Chicken Lane, which had not yet been thought of as a potential feature in its own right.* At this stage, it was simply a means of linking the wood with the barn and farmyard. As the trees slowly began to poke their heads above the sea of green plastic tubes, it became apparent that the long 'assart' curve to the edge of the meadow was quite attractive, but somehow it lacked impact – or purpose. It was crying out for a prominent feature. I suspect Capability Brown would have suggested a small Ionic temple[2] or a granite obelisk. Sadly, we lacked the cash.

At the time we were thinking about the problem, Maisie was rereading, for the umpteenth time, Christopher Lloyd's superb *The Well-Tempered Garden*. It was a book that she often returned to during the darker months of winter, as it gave hope and inspiration for the following summer. It was early December 1994 and we were contemplating moving out of the barn and into our new house at Inley Drove. Evenings were getting cold and there were mice everywhere. She had got to the pages where Lloyd was discussing pampas grasses and how they can be used to form wonderfully prominent garden features. He was particularly keen on one of the biggest, which from midsummer onwards also has the palest, largest and most prominent plumes: *Cortaderia selloana* var. 'Sunningdale Silver'. Lloyd's description made it sound extremely spectacular and time has shown that, as usual, he was dead right. By great good fortune, we then came across two plants in a local nursery. But where precisely should we plant them?

My initial reaction was to put them on the woodland edge, to break up the long, rather samey 'assart' curve of shrubs and

---

* Chicken Lane is discussed in Chapter 14, pages 286–89.

tree trunks. I know that sounds fairly straightforward, but I wasn't altogether happy about it. Something was missing; it felt rather like we were papering over cracks. It was time to step back and take a broader view.

I found myself thinking about my concern that a curve in a woodland bordering a meadow might possibly be slightly monotonous. Why should that matter so much? It then occurred to me that I was thinking about the garden simply as a piece of design. Instinctively, I knew this was wrong: gardens are about much more than this. A garden isn't something merely to be looked at; it is not a picture hanging on a wall. Gardens are there to be experienced; they are places where you can smell scents, see insects flying by and sometimes even experience the shock of a sting. They are also places where many people come face to face with profound emotions: with love, with loss, and sometimes with loneliness too. Many gardens open to the public can be imperfect, with monotonous, repetitive planting schemes and large areas that have apparently been abandoned – but they can have an unexpected appeal. When I'm visiting one of these properties and find myself walking through a neglected early nineteenth-century walled garden, my imagination peoples it with beautiful girls in Jane Austen dresses and young men in long, pointed tailcoats. You can hear their laughter as you look at the broken panes of a near-derelict summerhouse. Sadly, we were both well aware that history was a dimension our new garden would lack and we would have to provide something very memorable in its stead. But what?

In the first five years or so, while we were still actively planning and laying out the new garden, we would make frequent trips to other gardens for inspiration. We weren't after specific features, or ideas; I suppose we were seeking some form of theoretical or philosophical guidance. Anyway, I think it was sometime in the summer of 1995 that we visited an elaborate and expensively arranged garden that must have employed at least half a dozen gardeners. It was a garden full of spectacular views and fabulous fountains and we should have found it a memorable experience. But we didn't. In fact, it was a huge disappointment. The next day we were walking along the main double border of our own garden, trying to decide if it should have a spectacular focal point at one end. We knew we couldn't afford to build anything on an appropriate scale, but maybe we could plant something like a brightly coloured fastigiate tree or shrub – which could only get better as the years passed. But then our eyes met: no, that wasn't what we wanted at all. But what *did* we want? I knew that neither of us had a clue. Sadly, I'm not very good at managing frustration so I decided to change the subject:

'Can you remember the end of the rose border yesterday?'

Our eyes met again. We both knew it had been a terrible disappointment. What should have been a, if not the, high point of the visit had just ended with a tall, finely clipped yew hedge and a large, mega-expensive Lutyens-style garden seat. But that was it. We had turned round and retraced our steps along the other side of the border. Fairly soon we were in the car, on our way home. As we drove back, we discussed why the grand garden had been so disappointing and Maisie made the good point that features like the main border were simply there in their own right. In other words, you saw them, walked through them and then looked at your map to decide where to go next. It was like being a child and eating your way through a bag of liquorice allsorts: a series of nice bites, but nothing to link them together into a more rewarding experience. There was never anything to lead you onwards, to tempt you to explore beyond the rather limited delights on offer. It was a severe case of take it or leave it: rather like reading a collection of formulaic short stories. Don't get me wrong, I love good short stories, but they rarely pack the emotional punch of a great novel. And that's what that big garden had lacked: it had no real punch, no narrative force. We determined then and there, while driving along the road to Peterborough, that none of our garden features should have dead ends. Our visitors must never find themselves turning back. When they arrived somewhere, they should be tempted off in a different direction or, better still, in several competing directions.* Henceforward, we would adopt the design principle of 'No Turning Back'. It's a shame the phrase has so much political meaning, as it's actually very useful.

*

As we worked together at Inley Drove, we realised that we were shaping the garden, rather than designing it remotely on paper, or screen. We had to work with the real garden and, in the Fens, this inevitably meant dealing with issues relating to soil drainage – or the lack of it. But not always. Sometimes our actions were influenced by much simpler things, such as the two pots of pampas grass that we had acquired just before Christmas 1994 and which were now (in early spring 1995) starting to show the first signs of growth. They needed planting – and soon. But we were growing increasingly aware that this wouldn't be just any old planting: those large, dramatic grasses could well become one of the most dominating features of the entire garden. We had to get their positioning right. It was an important decision and one that I would normally assume would best be considered on paper, where one could see the garden's overall structure and layout. But that wasn't what

---

* This was something we tried to achieve when laying out the long border (see Chapter 13).

happened. We were unexpectedly helped by the wheel ruts I had left in the ground the previous autumn, when I had taken the garden tractor (which was also the lawn mower) into the wood to spray off the large weeds that were threatening to overwhelm some of the young trees. We only needed to spray Roundup in this way for two or three seasons, but I'm glad we did, as it certainly saved many of the oaks, which were slower to get going than the more vigorous ash and alder.

I had taken the garden tractor around the edge of the wood-to-be, along the 'assart' curve. I entered at the apex of the curve and drove for a few yards into the rows of one-year-old trees. There was a particularly large patch of vigorous weeds at the spot where the contractors had temporarily dumped a pile of tubes and posts in the late winter of 1993, at the start of the main planting campaign. The heap of tubes meant that there was a slightly wider gap between the rows of trees at this point. Incidentally, the rows of trees in the wood were laid out diagonally, which created a more natural, less grid-like impression when you walked through them. Just over a year later, in the early spring of 1994, when we were faced by the pampas grass planting dilemma, the wheel ruts leading up to the temporary tube dump formed quite a prominent feature at the apex of the 'assart' curve. My immediate reaction was to get a spade and remove them, but then I thought of those two pampas grasses. Maybe we could use the route to the tube dump as another way into the wood? It was beautifully positioned at the apex of the curve and could readily be joined to the main path running through the centre. It would look even better, and more dramatic, if the two pampas grasses could frame it.

Given our new 'No Turning Back' way of thinking, it struck us both that the new path into the wood must be positioned in a way that might entice people to use it. Another thing we had observed when visiting established gardens was that large pampas grasses are often positioned in a way that allowed them to be appreciated from many directions. Smaller grasses are fine in beds and borders, but not pampas. After a few years of moving from garden design to garden shaping, we soon learnt that problems involving layout, positioning and arrangement are best approached from several directions. We spent much time walking to different spots and then standing and discussing – and not always with gin and tonics at hand.

By mid-spring 1994 we still hadn't planted the pampas grasses, whose roots were now starting to poke through the bottoms of the pots. A decision was needed urgently. I remember discussing the problem from the edge of what was to be the more formal garden at the place we had chosen as the site of a clipped archway through the tall hornbeam hedge with which we planned to enclose it. We wanted visitors to be presented with a sweeping view of the meadow that might tempt them out to explore it. But the more we thought about it, the less appealing a great expanse of maturing hay sounded. And how could you 'explore' it? No, we had to have mown paths around it and, most importantly of all, a prominent path through it – a path that people would use when the daffodils, cowslips and snake's-head fritillaries were out in spring and the buttercups in early summer. In effect, this path would be the central axis of the more informal meadow garden. Immediately, we knew that the two pampas grasses should mark the spot where the new path started. At the same time, they would frame the new entrance into the wood, which we could emphasise and slightly enlarge by judicious trimming of the trees and shrubs that framed it. Today it forms a dark and slightly mysterious cave-like feature, which visitors' children find especially intriguing – another reason to go exploring.

A view of the Hay Meadow showing the two clumps of pampas grass *Cortaderia selloana* var. 'Sunningdale Silver'.

After about ten years of mowing the enlarged lawn, I came to my senses and realised a) that I was wasting time and petrol cutting such a huge expanse of grass and b) that it was completely unnecessary. So we kept a curved inner mown path that followed the edge of the old enlarged lawn and extended the straight central path to slightly more than double its original length. And it really worked: by now, the well-established pampas grass plants could hold their own and looked fabulous when seen from afar, with tassels gently swaying in the wind. Meanwhile, we had to transplant several patches of cowslips and other flowers in the hope that they would expand and make the extended meadow as floriferous as the original one – a process that was surprisingly speedy. After about five years you couldn't tell the two areas apart.

I want to end this chapter with a quick cautionary tale. As I think I've made quite clear, I love meadow gardens dearly, but I feel quite strongly that they are all the better for not being too obviously 'planted'. If you look at photos of Christopher Lloyd's fabulous meadow garden at Great Dixter, you can see the cowslips are often brightly coloured, whereas they should all be shades of pale creamy yellow. I noticed the same thing when I visited Miriam Lane's beautiful natural garden at Ashton Wold, near Oundle, in Northamptonshire, when I had the great privilege of being one of her tenants. Miriam was a most extraordinary person.[3] Her father, Charles Rothschild, had bought Wicken Fen and had established it as the country's first nature reserve. He was also a leading entomologist and natural historian. Miriam too was a highly distinguished scholar and the world's leading expert on fleas, particularly the ones that like humans. She was also an enthusiastic gardener and her meadow garden was stunning. But I had one problem with it: like the cowslips in the picture of the meadow at Great Dixter, most of those at Ashton Wold were brightly coloured. One day I asked her about it, and she told me that cowslips and primroses very readily cross-pollinate with the brightly coloured primulae that were so loved by Victorian and Edwardian gardeners and have remained popular at garden centres ever since. This was the reason Maisie and I decided never to buy any bright cultivated primulae for our new garden, and (touch wood) we have managed to keep our primroses and cowslips clear of bright colours. So has it been worth the sacrifice? I think so. Every time I look into those delicate cowslip flowers, they seem to be thanking us for leaving them alone – for letting them just be.

# 6

# The Orchard and the Nut Walk

*Whetting the Appetite • Of Biffins and Pippins • Pruning for
Form or Fruit • A Dark Journey • Cobnuts or Coppice*

Gardeners love visiting other people's gardens. When the
weather's wet and you're fed up with potting plants in
your shed or working in the greenhouse, nothing lifts your
spirits more than looking round another garden – even if it's
a bit wet and windy. We always look forward to the moment
when you turn off the main road and head for the house or the
car park. Unless it's raining very hard, I wind the car window
down. My nose is seeking scents and smells, my eyes are alert
and my ears are pricked up – anything that might start to reveal
the delights that, I hope, we are about to experience.

Of course, no two gardens are ever the same and the clues you
detect when you first arrive often prove wrong or misleading:
the large walled garden you glimpsed from the road has been
long abandoned and the double avenue of limes you'd read
about in an old edition of Pevsner had been cut very short
when they built an airfield runway across it in the 1980s. I also
think it's rather a shame that many historical country houses
are now approached, as it were, via the tradesman's entrance.
Car parks, souvenir shops and cafés tend to be around the

back, often within the old stable block or coach house. So visitors are frequently deprived of that carefully set-up view, beloved by landscape architects and owners alike, along the great drive, which frames and reveals the palatial mansion in its full splendour. It always makes me a little sad that this set-piece approach, which the original owner wanted all his guests to enjoy and be impressed by, is now only rarely experienced. Today, us ordinary folk must start our visits from the rear.

I fully realise that a modern Fenland farmhouse is in no way comparable to a large country house, but our house is surrounded by quite a substantial park-like garden and we neither of us wanted our visitors to see everything the moment they arrived. As time has passed, we have grown increasingly aware that the garden will be much more enjoyable for visitors if they can discover things for themselves, which is why we have tried to provide paths and plenty of opportunities for people to change direction or to try a different area of the garden. We could offer them temptations and inducements, but it was always the individual visitor to the garden who made the actual decisions.

In recent years, certain disused warehouses and factories have been turned into antiques centres, which are occupied by different individual traders. Each antique dealer occupies one or two rooms, which are linked together by a network of corridors, and it's up to the various traders to attract potential customers out of the corridors and into their displays. That's sort of how our garden is arranged, except that the 'rooms' vary in size enormously and some of the corridors can broaden out into lawns, meadow, orchard and shrubberies. I probably shouldn't admit it, but sometimes, when we open the garden for the National Garden Scheme, I will be approached by a visitor who had been told not to miss a particular feature, but hadn't been able to find it. I have to say this rather pleases me: I like gardens that can retain their secrets.

So what were visitors to see when they turned off Inley Drove, the narrow single-track lane that runs in a fairly straight line from Old Fen Dyke to New Fen Dyke? We were both in no doubt whatsoever: it wouldn't be flowers or shrubs. We wanted something less obviously inviting. It's not that we didn't trust the people driving past our entrance, but it somehow didn't make sense, especially in the early years when things were far more open and exposed, to appear to be waving a flag that loudly proclaimed: 'Look folks, we're here!' We knew we'd be travelling up and down our drive, to and from work or on shopping trips, every day. We also knew from experience that certain parts of a garden need regular inspection and the most important of these is the orchard. Apples and pears can ripen very unpredictably and when they start to fall you can lose an entire tree's fruit in a very short time – especially if it's the windy season, as is so often the case in the South Holland fens in the autumn. From several points of view – practical, aesthetic and others – it made sense to plant an orchard at the start of our drive.

The Fens around Wisbech and up into Lincolnshire have long been famous for their large apple orchards, many of which are still thriving. The traditional variety grown locally has long been the Bramley cooking apple, a naturally large tree that was kept under control by regular pruning. Tall central trunks were discouraged in favour of spreading side branches, and well-pruned orchards could look very elegant, even graceful, especially in spring when the pink and white blossom covered them. Another distinctive feature of these orchards was the tall screens of column-like Lombardy poplar windbreaks – so necessary when the fruit were ripening in the late summer and early autumn. I had found the recent felling of so many traditional Bramley orchards very disturbing, which is why the sudden disappearance of the trees opposite Limetree Farm had upset me so much.

The same view as the image on page 6, but taken twenty-four years later, in August 2016. The drive curves gently to the right, passing through the orchard, with the much taller trees of the wood in the background.

Many orchards weren't completely destroyed. The old trees were removed, but the poplar screens remained and new Bramleys were planted on modern growth-reducing rootstock, which made picking both quicker and safer, as ladders weren't needed. I prefer the look of the old orchards (and a few do survive), but fruit growers must move with the times and the new-style orchards are developing a look of their own, which can be very attractive. Incidentally, although it's not widely known, the area was also home to cider orchards; the Norfolk cider company Gaymer had a large one near the Lincolnshire border, not far from Wisbech. Sadly, it has been felled, but there's still a sign advertising the cider, which is now produced in Somerset and is much more bland – perhaps 'corporate' would be a better word – than the sharp, tangy original, which I loved and I'm sure must have included many local Bramleys.

Maisie and I love home-grown nuts and apples, so the area around the driveway was planted very early with various apples and pears, including a Bramley and a very vigorous Ribston Pippin. The plants for the Nut Walk were bought from The Major in the walled garden at Holkham Hall, probably in autumn 1992. He had a wonderful selection and we lined them out at Harry's growing-ground before moving them into the Inley Drove field early in the winter in 1994/5, as soon as Limetree Farm had been sold. Work on the main apple and pear orchard started in 1993 and gathered pace in 1994. We've been adding trees on and off ever since. I wish I could say that it has been an ordered, logical process, determined by the form and shape of the orchard, but I'm afraid it hasn't been like that. We were led by our love of the taste of apples and pears. We would never make it in the modern orchard trade...

\*

Both Maisie and I could remember how apples tasted in the days before New Zealand imports became widely available, and greengrocers still sold many different varieties of English apples. It was these old types of apple that we wanted to plant and Maisie had several books that listed what was available, together with their strong points and weaknesses. Over the years, we've sadly lost quite a few trees (usually after very wet winters), but those that have survived are generally growing strongly. A stroll through our orchard, notepad and pen in hand, reveals the following: Rosemary Russet, Ashmead's Kernel, Sturmer Pippin, Ribston Pippin, Jonagold, Jupiter, American Mother, Bramley, Beauty of Bath, Sunset, Orleans

Reinette, John Downie (a crab apple), Norfolk Beefing, Worcester Pearmain and New Rock Pippin.

Today, the Royal Horticultural Society and the guardians of the national fruit collection, the Brogdale Horticultural Trust, at their farm in Brogdale, Kent, offer much apple information online, and Brogdale even provide an apple identification service. But in my old-fashioned way, I think there's no substitute for a good book. The one we use is *The Book of Apples*, by Joan Morgan and Alison Richards, which contains beautiful pictures of apples and their blossom, painted by Elizabeth Dowle.[1] The first half of the book is devoted to chapters on the history of apples and how they were used. The second half is a detailed directory of apple varieties, which describes their taste, when to pick them and how long you may expect them to store. We bought our copy in the mid-1990s, when we were just starting work on the Lincolnshire garden, and it is very well thumbed, but in surprisingly good condition. It's a sturdy and well-bound book – but even so, it's a bit too classy to be kept in the potting shed.

Most modern commercial apple orchards grow just one or two varieties, so their flowering season is usually quite short, but in a small orchard like ours, which has a range of different apple types, the first blossom can appear in mid-April and there will still be flowers on other trees in late May. Apple blossom has a very delicate scent, which can hang on the air in the stillness of a late spring evening. I always look out for bees feeding on the nectar of the flowers while unconsciously pollinating the fruit for us humans. Sadly, however, it's very noticeable how bee numbers have declined in recent years.[2]

I always love it when the fruit-picking season starts, usually in late August, because at that point we haven't eaten any apples for the best part of three months. We grow two early varieties, one of which is a huge success, the other a miserable failure. The success is Worcester Pearmain, which keeps surprisingly well for several weeks and has a texture and taste that simply cannot be beaten. It's probably my favourite apple. The different varieties of apples have their own growth patterns, which are hard to predict or to control. This is why trees in orchards have usually been grafted on to apple rootstock that will determine the size and vigour of the tree.* Our Worcester Pearmain tree hasn't grown as big as I would have wished, and I suspect the plant we ordered from a grower in a neighbouring county hadn't been grafted on to the right rootstock. This particular grower, who subsequently went out of business, muddled up our grafting requirements on several occasions, so some of the trees in our orchard are on vigorous rootstock and inevitably the largest are the ones we like the least. By the same token, the smallest have proved to be those we use most often. Our small Bramley gives us a good crop of cooking apples every year, which are very popular with keen cooks in the area. You can't make proper English apple pie without the delicious, slightly fluffy cooked texture of Bramleys. Some of the heavy crop of windfalls from our trees grafted on to giant rootstock ended up with Val, a nice lady up the road who keeps horses. She takes several bucketfuls of them every autumn for her hungry animals. Horses, like our lovely, eat-anything Labrador bitch, Pen, love apples.

The early apple that has proved so disappointing has a very inviting name: Beauty of Bath. In the purely visual sense, it entirely lives up to its name. It is a well-proportioned tree and has delightful blossom. It looks gorgeous growing by the drive, especially when its branches are weighed down with inviting

---

* The rootstock is the root system of a tree with a part of the stem, to which the fruiting part of another tree can be grafted. The size of the rootstock (from dwarfing to vigorous) determines the size of the tree that is grafted on to it.

bright red and orange fruit. Every year, this fine tree loyally delivers us a good crop. Several times I've spotted visiting white-van drivers with long arms helping themselves – and good luck to them: the apples are sweetish, but otherwise tasteless and with a slightly soggy texture. Every August I try one or two in case it is an exceptional year, but they never merit more than one tentative bite before I chuck them in the dyke. Most of them end up down the road in Val's stables.

As its name suggests, Beauty of Bath is an apple that comes from the West Country, where it was first bred in the 1860s. It has won numerous awards and has an excellent reputation as a sweet and very early dessert apple. And yet ours are barely edible. The only possible explanation must be that local conditions don't suit it. Maybe the climate around the Wash is too dry and our clay-silt soils are wrong in some way? Having said that, the tree has grown lustily and always looks in the peak of good health. We've had trouble growing other old varieties, including Irish Peach, although here the name should have warned us what to expect: Ireland is mild and wet, Lincolnshire is cooler and drier? My advice, when planting traditional varieties of apples and pears, is to use your common sense. It seems that older fruit trees – rather like elderly people – can be a bit fussy.

Norfolk Biffins (also known as Norfolk Beefings) were first recorded on the Mannington estate of the future prime minister Robert Walpole in 1698.[3] Norfolk Biffins were roasted in bakers' ovens in Norwich in Victorian times and were then sold on the streets of London, where they became very popular. Charles Dickens mentions them in *A Christmas Carol*: 'Norfolk Biffins, squab and swarthy, setting off the yellow of the oranges and lemons, and in the great compactness of their juicy persons, urgently entreating and beseeching to be carried home in paper bags and eaten after dinner.' We planted a Beefing tree about ten years ago and it has never really thrived, although each year it manages to yield a small crop of up to a dozen dark-skinned, rounded apples, which Maisie dries in the oven of the Aga on a bedding of hay, beneath a heavy weight. They are quite nice to eat; but having said that, I sometimes wonder why they had such a big reputation. The tree also frustrates me: why won't it thrive? I thought about the disappointing fruit from our Beauty of Bath and wondered whether the soil and climate may not be suitable. It might just be the *soil* that's at fault, because the Fenland climate is very like Norfolk's. But then it dawned on me what the problem must be: they are *Norfolk* Beefings and we're in Lincolnshire. Even today, Fen folk in Lincolnshire raise their eyebrows when asked to cross the county boundary into King's Lynn, and Norfolk. As the people around here so often say: 'They're different in Norfolk'. It's no wonder those ancient Biffins refuse so stubbornly to travel.

At the other end of the Orchard, slightly set back from the drive, is one of the largest apple trees, which I used to try to control by pruning – a practice I have long since given up. It's a Ribston Pippin[4] and its apples are beyond praise: perhaps not quite as sweet as Worcester Pearmain, but with a more complex flavour, and one that develops as the apples mature. The tree is quite close to the semi-wild hedge that runs along Inley Drove and birds love to perch in its branches, especially the green woodpeckers that nest in the nearby pollarded willows. You might think they'd love to peck at slightly unripe fruit, but I've never spotted so much as a single woodpecker's peck mark in an apple. I think the tree provides them with a good vantage point to look at the anthills in the meadow alongside the Orchard, where they really do like to feed. This meadow is visited by many birds of prey, including sparrowhawks, buzzards and kestrels, and we've noticed that other birds like to perch safely in the nearby fruit trees. I would imagine that if I ran the orchard commercially, I would have shrouded that large tree in netting because its Ribston Pippin apples look so tempting. I have seen grey squirrels eat them, but they only seem to go for windfalls.

One of the main reasons we decided to grow many of the more unusual apple varieties was their ability to be stored and kept. Every year we continue eating our own apples right through spring and sometimes even into June. But we find that each season is different: the apples mature at varying rates and their flavours are never quite the same from one year to the next. Very occasionally we have lost stored apples to a sudden severe frost. Connoisseurs keep their apples in old, defunct freezers, which we will probably do when our chest freezer decides to die. In the meantime we use cardboard boxes, which live in the barn. Each box is labelled with the apple variety and its eat-by/storage dates. Within the box we put the apples into old plastic bags – about six in each bag – this helps prevent the spread of mould, if one or two go rotten. The bags must also be punctured to allow air in – Maisie does it with a pencil. When frosty nights are forecast, I cover the boxes with newspaper, old sacks and carpets – anything thick and insulating.

Ribston Pippin store very well, but like many keeping varieties they are best picked before they are ready for eating. Ribston Pippin are best picked in September and can be stored and eaten throughout October to January – although this will vary considerably from season to season. A range of picking and storage dates for each variety is given in the directory of apple varieties in *The Book of Apples*. We have had a lot of success with Sturmer Pippin, a late-keeping variety that should be picked and packed in October, but can be stored from January/February to April or even into June in exceptional years. If you choose the right varieties and the weather gods are feeling friendly towards you, there's no reason why you shouldn't be eating your own apples for anything up to ten months a year. That's quite a saving at the supermarket, but it's also worth remembering that if you grow your own apples you can remove, or massively reduce, the use of sprays and other chemicals. Most important of all is the taste, which is constantly changing as you move from one variety to another, but is never predictable. Every year, late stored apples are a source of delight. Indeed, it's now well into March and I'm still savouring the last few bites of an early season Ribston Pippin. Delicious!

Any gardener will tell you that home-grown fruit and vegetables taste very much better than the ones you can buy in a supermarket. Very often, the lack of flavour in bought produce is a reflection of modern intensive commercial horticulture, which often involves the use of artificial fertilisers. But I don't intend to lambast all commercial growers, many of whom have greenhouses and fields near where I live. I think they do an incredible job, given the constraints, both practical and financial, that they have to face. The problem lies not with them, but with the widespread, largely urban belief, much encouraged by Westminster politicians, that food should be cheap. Today we spend a tiny part of our domestic budgets in supermarkets, compared with previous generations. British households in 2020 spent just 8 per cent of their budgets on food, whereas in India the figure was 30 per cent. Admittedly, that figure also reflects the average earnings in the two countries, but it is worth noting that British food spending dropped by half between 1957 and 2017.[5] Given such constraints, it is hardly surprising that our growers have to increase the yields from their fields through the widespread use of chemical sprays and fertilisers – which also have a major impact on the environment. But the taste and variety of food can decline for other reasons.

Plant breeding is making extraordinary advances in its ability to create new varieties that can resist drought and disease. The flavour of fruit is a close reflection of what people in supermarkets want to buy. In Britain, the public taste is massively in favour of sweetness, especially when it comes to apples. People also like skins that aren't too tough and fruit that is crisp when you bite it. I can remember my father and grandfather peeling the skins off their breakfast apples in late winter and spring, as they ate fruit that had been stored in a shed outdoors, for weeks. Nobody would do that today, but what would they be losing? Were my grandfather's tough old apples tasteless too? No, they weren't. On the contrary, their flavours were subtle, even sublime. When my grandfather died, my father inherited his house and garden and with it a few of the apple trees (sadly, many had blown over and died in the late 1950s). However, the surviving trees continued to provide us with fruit that made a lasting impression on me, particularly when I was a student at Cambridge, when every year I would return to my rooms with boxes of apples, which I soon polished off with help from my friends – but there was a downside to the non-use of pesticides in those days. At least once, a girlfriend sitting on the edge of the bed in her mid-1960s mini-skirt got scared quite badly by an emerging creepy-crawly hairy caterpillar, seemingly intent on attacking her knees. I soon learnt to check that all the old apple bags were removed from under the bed as soon as they were emptied. The smell of home-grown fruit used to linger in the room for weeks.

*

All gardeners have strengths and weaknesses, and when it comes to pruning I have taken an inordinately long time acquiring any skill. Maisie, on the other hand, is a natural pruner. We grow a huge variety of roses, including many 'old-fashioned' groups, such as *Gallica* shrub roses, hybrid musks, rugosas, spinosissimas, climbers and ramblers – and all have to be pruned differently. Maisie knows instinctively how to do them all, and rarely makes mistakes. But it's quite an ordeal: depending on the warmth of the season, she starts in midwinter and continues, more or less non-stop, until the end of March (although in very wet years she has been known to finish in June). My job is to collect prunings for the bonfire, and every so often I'm instructed to take a mechanical hedge cutter to a rugosa and cut it off a few inches above ground. Every year I marvel to see it grow back vigorously and then produce flowers in abundance. Quite often I forget to feed it, but this rarely seems to make a difference: our silty soils are so astonishingly fertile.

Our border collie sheepdog Twink poses in front of the screen of espaliered apple trees that edge the vegetable garden. This picture was taken in November 2012 when the espaliers were barely ten years old. The vegetable garden had just been raided by muntjac deer; hence the presence of Twink and the electric livestock netting immediately behind.

So while roses are well beyond my pay grade as a pruner, I have found two areas where I can wield my secateurs quite usefully. The first is in the vegetable garden in late summer, when I cut back the fruiting branches of the espaliered apples and pears that line the main path. The second also involves tight cutting back and happens in midwinter, when I pleach the lime trees that run part of the way between the house and the barn. Those four trees provide much-needed shade and wind protection in high summer. So I do know something about pruning, but for some reason that I don't understand, I have never been much good at pruning non-espaliered apples and pears. I can look up what to do in one of my spiral-bound, much-loved and often consulted Royal Horticultural Society's *Encyclopaedia of Practical Gardening*.[6] The volume in question, simply titled *Pruning*, is by Christopher Brickell. It is clearly written and with abundant illustrations – a superb book. My copy got slightly singed when I left it on the ground while I was burning apple prunings. We had had an attack of woolly aphids and I was keen that all the prunings should be destroyed. Then there was a sudden breeze, the book flew open and a red-hot twig landed on the title page. I snatched it off the ground, but it had left its mark.

*

I think there is always a danger when you're focused on a large project to become too obsessed with it. Quite minor problems can keep one awake at night and original, imaginative solutions get bypassed or missed because one becomes too involved with issues that in retrospect appear unimportant. Sometimes the day job can provide an alternative focus that helps to set the project at home in some sort of perspective. In 1987, Maisie and I set up Flag Fen as a public excavation and prehistoric park. Then, in 1989, the site acquired its new, permanent visitor centre. By the early to mid-1990s, we were still battling with the problems of staffing and financing an on-site museum, shop and visitor centre. We both had some practical experience of working in shops and bars, when we were students, but this hardly qualified us to deal with security, accountancy and HR problems. We were both on a near-vertical learning curve, which was not at all relaxing. So were we crazy to start a large new garden project in 1992? Looking back on it, I think we must have been mad. But that was not how we saw it. At the time, we both believed that the project would provide relief from the stresses of the day job. As time passed, I'm glad to say, we were proved right: the new garden was where we found both peace and relaxation. But it was still hard work.

Despite being busy on so many different fronts, we continued to pay visits to country houses and their gardens, and to castles and other historic places – especially if they had a good shop and/or cafeteria. These visits helped us to relax, but they also gave us opportunities to talk to the people behind the counter and discover what they sold, why they sold it, and for how much. (Maisie has always been good at concealing her tiny notepad, where the prices were duly recorded.) Phone cameras had yet to appear, but I owned a very small 35mm camera, with an expensive Leica lens, that took the most amazing photos on high-ish speed film, and without a telltale flash. So we were enjoying ourselves, but were also doing useful research for the shop at Flag Fen.

On several of these garden visits we came across so-called Nut Walks of tall hazel bushes, just wide enough for two people to pass through side by side. They were wonderfully dark, shady and not a little mysterious. Then it suddenly came to me that a Nut Walk was just what we needed to conduct people into the wood, away from the warm sunlight of the lawn at the edge of the formal garden, near the pond.

I decided to take a risk and make our Nut Walk much wider than the mostly Victorian examples we had seen on our various visits, because I wanted more people to use it than just two. I also felt that the hazel bushes were often a bit overcompressed – a bit too squashed together: I thought they would look more elegant if they were allowed the space to arch over. I remember thinking that the narrow Nut Walks reminded me of the tunnels in a London Underground station, whereas my mind wanted something larger and more inviting: the great arched roof at St Pancras station would perhaps be a slight exaggeration, but it better captures what I was after. At the far end of the Nut Walk, the path would have to narrow quite suddenly as it entered the wood. In springtime this path is lined with snowdrops, aconites and primroses, which are later replaced by bluebells. Sadly, this area has been badly affected by ash dieback disease.

Like most sensible gardeners, I try to stay away from risky or very 'innovative' decisions, which nearly always have negative consequences. It's no surprise that gardening is actually quite conservative; after all, most of us are trying to achieve harmony with nature, not conflict. But in the case of the Nut Walk, I thought we'd try to stretch the width of a hazel arch as far as it would naturally grow, without the need for props or supports. This was particularly important because supporting poles can look terribly clumsy – especially after being replaced a few times. Sadly, we both knew we would never be able to afford the sort of elegant overhead iron arches that are such a delight in the Regency Swiss Garden, in Bedfordshire.[7] We have long agreed that it's one of the finest historical gardens in Britain. I would guess the two rows of hazels in the Victorian Nut Walk at Hindringham Hall, in Norfolk – another garden that is well worth visiting – are about two to three yards apart.[8] I can remember having my doubts at the time, but we decided to plant the bushes of Kentish and Nottingham cobnuts about five to six yards* apart, with a second, less formally arranged, row of shrubs – mostly hazels, *Viburnum opulus* and *Viburnum* x *bodnantense* – to provide additional shade and protection. The *Viburnum* x *bodnantense* flowers from late autumn to spring. Its flowers have a heavenly scent that somehow has the ability to linger on the air – especially in the still atmosphere within the Nut Walk. But most importantly of all, the hazel branches didn't collapse and met in the middle, so there wasn't a gap down the centre of the Walk. It worked perfectly and for many years we were able to reach up into the bushes and harvest huge crops of delicious cobnuts. Then, very much later, disaster was to strike. I'll describe what happened in Chapter 14, but before that I want to think about nuts and food in a more general way.

*

If you're fortunate enough to earn your living doing something you love, it's often very difficult to decide when work stops and leisure begins. This is particularly true when it comes to archaeology and gardening, both of which involve considerable knowledge of plants and a lot of digging. One of the big research questions in prehistory has always centred on the introduction of farming and food production, which happened at different times around the world. In Britain and western Europe, the arrival of farming is marked by the use of cereal crops, mainly wheat and barley, together with domesticated

---

* When I lay out informal or semi-formal planting schemes, I always do it by eye rather than with a tape measure. Plants have to look right, whatever their actual position in the ground.

animals, especially cattle, sheep and pigs. These momentous events happened in Britain in the centuries just before 4000 BC, some six thousand years ago, and marked the transition from the Mesolithic (or Middle Stone Age) to the Neolithic (New Stone Age). It was always assumed that before farmers and farming arrived from the continent, the indigenous Mesolithic people simply gathered their food from their surroundings. It was believed to be a simple process that didn't change much through time: hunting with bows and arrows, digging up roots with digging sticks and collecting wild nuts and berries.

The change from the Mesolithic to the Neolithic was a period that interested me profoundly, as my team excavating on the edge of the Fens, at Fengate in Peterborough, had discovered the foundations of one of the earliest Neolithic houses then known in England. The first farmers also brought with them the knowledge of how to control heat and fire, which enabled them to produce the first pottery from local clays – and of course fired pottery can survive in the soil more or less forever. We were fortunate enough to reveal quite a few bits of pot in the house's foundations, and I can remember the feeling of awe as I held one in my hand. I had just scraped it from the ground with my trowel. It still had a sharp break and I don't think it had been left lying on the floor for long before it was pushed into the narrow trench that was still partially open, at the base of the house wall. This was probably done by the person who had broken it. I remember wondering what he or she was thinking. They must have been annoyed, but had they also been scalded by hot liquid and now had more urgent things to do? Maybe a young child or a pet dog was also involved? For a few moments it felt like I was intruding into a private life, albeit one six thousand years ago. To make things worse, I was now kneeling in the remains of their home – and without their permission. Sometimes, small things can be very affecting.

There has been a huge amount written about the arrival of farming and farmers in Britain and it's hard not to emphasise the great contrast between the new, very settled way of life, with its farms, fields, stockyards, animal shelters, grain storage facilities and so forth, with what had gone before, when people were assumed to have been more mobile, even nomadic, with lightweight houses and shifting settlements. That at least was the more traditional view. Today we are discovering much more about the earlier, hunter-gatherer way of life and there is increasing evidence that not everyone spent their lives moving about. Some people lived in settled village-like communities in houses that were permanent and clearly intended to be occupied for long periods.[9] The fact that you gathered and hunted your food did not mean that your life was somehow disordered and chaotic. People have always planned the ways they chose to live their lives and our Mesolithic ancestors were no exception. I have to confess that I used to belong to the school of thought that tended to rather look down on pre-farming communities. I didn't do it consciously, but in retrospect I patronised them: I assumed they weren't very sophisticated and led a rather simple if not 'primitive' lifestyle. But planting and then managing our own hazel bushes at Inley Drove Farm taught us a great deal about gathering food – and we discovered it wasn't a simple, unsophisticated process at all.

Many archaeological sites of both the pre- and post-farming eras have revealed small holes dug in the ground for the storage of hazelnuts. Each of these mini-pits held the equivalent of about an hour's picking – if, that is, you were picking nuts in a modern cobnut orchard.* If, on the other hand, you were picking nuts around the edges of a wood, I'd guess they represent about half a day's work. Either way, these are collections that were picked

---

* Cobnuts are commercially bred hazelnuts.

in a serious, not haphazard, fashion. If you wandered out into a wood with a basket hoping on the off-chance to collect a few hazelnuts, you wouldn't fill half – maybe even a quarter – of one of those pits.

I was thinking these thoughts while I was working in the two or three acres of the wood we had reserved for hazel bushes. We had planted hazels not so much for nuts as for straight rods and poles that we could use for making hurdles or temporary frames for climbing plants. Hazel wood lasts much longer than willow, which grows faster, but is very much softer. By and large, willow rods will survive one winter before turning brittle, whereas hazel will last two, or even three, if they are thick enough. I was cutting stands of hazel that had been planted about fifteen years earlier, and although they were still quite young, they had been coppiced (in other words, cut back to the ground) at least once and were now growing into straight and vigorous rods. This tendency to grow upwards, reaching for sunlight, was encouraged by the planting of well-separated oak trees, known as 'standards' in a coppiced woodland. The hazel bushes around the oak standards deep in the shade of the coppice woodland were very different from the ones we had planted to produce nuts, which were far more bushy and low-growing. The long, straight hazel rods in the coppice did produce a few nuts high above my head, but they were nothing like as prolific as the bushes around the fringes of the wood or in the Nut Walk, which, as its name suggests, had been planted – in the early years of the garden – specifically to produce nuts. It's quite simple really: if you want long, straight hazel rods you need shade, and if you're after nuts you must look for bushes in sunlight.

The bushes we had planted in the Nut Walk, when we were initially laying out the garden, were all intended to produce nuts. The two main varieties were Kentish (*Corylus maxima* 'Kentish

Cob')[10] and Nottingham cobnuts (*Corylus avellana* 'Pearson's Prolific')[11], together with a couple of plants of unimproved native hazels (*Corylus avellana*), which we hoped would help to pollinate the cobnuts. We planted the Nut Walk away from the shade of the wood because we didn't want the hazel bushes to become etiolated, or leggy, as so often happens when they have to reach upwards into the wood's canopy to catch any sunlight. We also wanted the fruiting bushes to remain quite low and compact, which would make them easier to pick. We coppiced, or cut back, the rod/pole hazels regularly at ground level; many of these went to our neighbours Arne and William, whose skilful gardener wove them into decorative supports for roses and clematis. Every year they took several hundred rods, which meant that the hazel was regularly coppiced and none of the wood was wasted. Judging by the large quantities of nuts found on archaeological sites, it seems to me that prehistoric people were well aware that hazel bushes needed to be treated very differently, depending on whether they were to produce nuts or rods.

I suspect they knew perfectly well how to plant them, too. Anyone who has watched a squirrel bury a nut in the autumn and then witnessed the nut burst into life the following spring will share my view that prehistoric people would have been perfectly capable of planting groves of fruiting hazel bushes on the sunnier land outside an ancient wood. Put another way, the cultivation of hazel could be seen as a variant of farming that was fully understood many millennia before the first 'official' farmers arrived in Britain around 4000 BC. I won't say that my insight into the growing and cultivation of hazel was particularly profound – it certainly wasn't on the same intellectual level as that falling apple in Sir Isaac Newton's Lincolnshire garden – but it was a direct result of tending and working with actual plants in real life. Today there is a prevailing view that nearly all knowledge comes from books, scholarship or laboratories, but we shouldn't forget that ordinary daily life can still teach us important lessons.

But now it's time to pick up a spade and enter the vegetable garden.

# 7

# The Vegetable Garden

*Food Comes First • Saviour Sleepers • Following the Rules •*
*Ambrosial Asparagus • Fruit of the Gods •*
*Muck and Manure • My Spade*

The principle that 'food comes first' has been fundamental to the way I think about and arrange any garden I might be planning. If all I had was a window box, I'd plant it with lettuces or radishes rather than flowers. I can remember being very frustrated when I lived in Toronto for nine years, from 1969 to 1978. The Canadian winters were so cold that you couldn't reliably grow *any* salad plants, brassicas or green vegetables. Even plants like roses, which we in England take for granted, couldn't be pruned before April and were frequently killed by sharp frosts. Some of those winter frosts were severe enough to cause frostbite, even on downtown streets, if you weren't careful. So I used to look forward keenly to returning to England for the summer season of excavation. I lived in various rented flats and cottages and I would always plant vegetables shortly after I arrived, even if it meant digging up part of the lawn (which I did several times). Each summer season would last from about April to October, so it was possible to get good crops of salads, some brassicas, but *lots* of spinach, peas, broad beans, French beans and runner beans. New potatoes, planted as soon as I landed back in Britain, would be ready for digging by late summer. I can remember wishing I could take some of my home-produced vegetables back with me to Toronto, but there were strict regulations preventing the import of anything green and fresh. Even I, with my extreme dislike of supermarket food, knew it wasn't worth taking the risk. Sensibly, I obeyed the rules.

I returned to Britain full time in late 1978 and a couple of years later, as we saw in Chapter 2, Maisie and I established our new garden at Limetree Farm. Maisie was also a keen vegetable grower and had learnt a great deal from her father and grandfather, who had very productive allotments. When I first met Maisie, her house had a large vegetable garden and we very rarely had to buy fresh food from local supermarkets. However, we experienced some initial problems with the Limetree Farm vegetable garden, including the dreaded brassica club root. After several seasons, we also realised that the plot we had given over to vegetables was too small. By then, however, we had decided on the move to Lincolnshire. We also had a clear concept of how large the vegetable garden should be and a firm understanding that it *had* to be positioned on the best, most freely draining and silty soil. Many seasons of bitter experience had taught us that slugs make it nearly impossible to grow vegetables on heavy, clay-rich soil.

So the position of the Vegetable Garden at Inley Drove was largely determined by the soil. Sadly, the highest silt bank – an old, probably Iron Age, tidal stream channel, or roddon – was where the planning authorities in their wisdom had decided we should site the barn. In retrospect, this was possibly a sensible decision – even if they weren't aware of it at the time. Quite a large part of the silty bank beneath the barn extended to the east, and this was where we decided to locate the Vegetable

Garden. That decision dictated the orientation of the main borders and ultimately the entire garden – which some might consider to be entirely right and proper: vegetables should always come before mere flowers. (Maisie will probably ask me, in the nicest way possible, to delete this.)

I remember the feeling of excitement when we started to mark out the boundaries of the Vegetable Garden. The soil was a bit heavy, but you could feel the slightly grainy texture of the silt and we both knew that a few applications of well-rotted sheep manure would improve it beyond recognition. Sadly, earthworms were still absent, but so was club root! – which was a cheering thought. We surveyed in the outline of the plot and decided where to locate footpaths. They were to be straight and businesslike, passing round the outside of the growing area. In the early 1990s companion-planted flower and vegetable gardens were becoming very popular, but they required a great deal of maintenance and neither of us wanted our veg garden to look pointlessly picturesque or romantic, with meandering paths or floral arches. You don't need to make a rural garden more rustic. And besides, on a cold, moonless winter's night, and after maybe a couple of glasses of sherry, I wanted to be able to find my way to the Brussels sprouts without tearing my scalp on the thorns of a rambling rose. Having said that, a flourishing active vegetable garden can look very attractive, simply by displaying so many healthy plants. I also love the appearance of freshly dug soil in good condition. The sympathetic planting of soft fruit, such as strawberries, raspberries, blackcurrants and redcurrants, can frame and enhance the otherwise rather severely rectangular main growing area. A well-organised vegetable garden certainly doesn't have to be uninviting.

We laid out the basic shape of the Vegetable Garden back in the autumn of 1993, when we were still living at Limetree Farm.

By this time, we had dug the foundations for the new house and the barn had just been erected. We decided to position the Vegetable Garden in an area where the soil was better-draining and more silty than clay, and which coincided with a roddon. As we have seen, this lined up with the main axis of the barn and gave it easy and direct access to the Vegetable Garden. The north-west–south-east alignment of the Vegetable Garden, the barn and the house determined the general arrangement of the new garden. We can't claim to have deliberately planned it this way, but it's an alignment that has proved very plant-friendly, without too many areas of cold total shade or blazing sunlight, which so often happens with strict east–west or north–south arrangements.

The smaller size of our plot at Limetree Farm had placed limitations on what we could grow; in the new Lincolnshire garden we had decided to grow some additional vegetables, such as sprouts, broccoli and cabbages (to take advantage of the club-root-free soil). At that stage the field was still devoid of shelter, since the planting of the surrounding wood had happened only very recently (in the late winter of 1992–3). We borrowed a dumpy level,* some wooden survey pegs, a few nails and a couple of rolls of string from the excavation survey kit and immediately set to work. As we hammered in the pegs and attached the lines of string between them, we became acutely aware of how very exposed the new field was. We decided that we needed to plant a hornbeam hedge around the outside for protection – and without delay. The ground was quite hard and we also had to fetch in lots of water; planting our vegetable garden at Inley Drove took time and effort. When we finished the job, the first winds of autumn were starting to blow; we realised we were going to need additional

---

* A tripod-mounted optical surveying instrument, still widely used.

protection for both the young hornbeam hedge and any growing vegetables. I bought several rolls of close-mesh green plastic netting, which I made into a five-foot-high screen with some fence posts. That seemed to do the trick. Sitting within the new mesh fence on camping stools and sipping mugs of tea in the late autumn sunshine, we felt strangely relaxed and even private – despite the fact that our screen was clearly visible to everyone for miles around.

Many of the vegetables I planted within the screened-off garden were a bit too large to have transferred from Harry's Patch, but we persisted and – with the help of a lot of water and some foliar feed* – they started to pick up. As the weather grew colder and the days became shorter, a few small Brussels sprouts appeared. I can't remember if we ever cut off (and then ate) sprout tops, to stimulate sprouts to grow on the stalk, but disaster soon struck when a winter storm ripped up much of the windproof plastic netting. It lay on the ground, along with dozens of hedge and vegetable plants it had ripped out of the ground as it thrashed around. The carnage among the Brussels sprouts and cabbages was appalling. It wasn't a very Merry Christmas in 1993 – but at least we could buy sprouts on stalks at Long Sutton market. They were almost as good as our own.

That early winter storm was the first of several more, none of which was quite as bad, but they gave us strong hints of what the next few years could be like. It was more than a little depressing. When spring came, however, and we were able to enjoy that wonderful clear, almost liquid, daylight, our mood started to improve. When the buds on the tiny hedging plants opened, I was anxious in case they dried out while we were away at work, but I needn't have worried: far from dying,

---

* Sprayed onto the leaves.

they thrived. Green leaves gave way to green shoots and as we watched, completely delighted and entranced, a row of tiny individual green bushes slowly merged together to form the first short segments of a hedge. By late summer they had doubled in size and the hedge was almost continuous. It was very heartening. As autumn approached, I was tempted not to cut the young hedge back, because I wanted its protection fast, but happily I was persuaded by a gardening friend that if I did that the hedge would never be sufficiently tight and windproof. It was important that I made the hedge bush up, and the only way of doing that was to give it a good, close clipping. Reluctantly, I followed his advice and of course he was right: the hedge is now remarkably strong and weatherproof. Today there is absolutely no danger of any of those stout hornbeams being blown out of the ground. They are there for good.

*

When you establish a new vegetable garden or take over an existing allotment, one of the first things you discover are the subtleties of local drainage and water retention. As an archaeologist, I'd learnt about such things when we studied how 'cropmarks' – these being marks that reveal the presence of natural or archaeological features beneath the surface of the soil – appear in growing wheat and barley in late April and May. From ground level you can sometimes spot them, but from the air – and nowadays of course that increasingly means from cameras carried by drones – they can look spectacular. After a bit of practice, you can identify prehistoric pits for storing grain, the shallow drainage ditches that were dug around Iron Age roundhouses or the much larger and deeper ring ditches dug to quarry material for Bronze Age burial mounds, or barrows; very often you can just make out graves within them too. Cropmarks form because cereal plants will grow faster and more thickly if roots discover the damper and more fertile fillings of ancient pits and ditches buried beneath the topsoil. If I were a wheat plant, I think I'd greatly prefer my roots to draw nourishment from prehistoric soil in Iron Age ditches than from the thin covering of earth over bare gravel that is characteristic of so many intensively farmed modern fields.

All gardeners worry about whether the plants they put in the ground will flourish. Is their soil of the right type for what they want to plant? Is it perfect, well-balanced loamy soil? Or is it chalky or sandy, clay or silt? Plant labels in commercial garden centres make it all sound so simple: they talk about certain plants preferring 'fertile, well-drained soil', or 'damp, freely draining soil', or flourishing 'in sun or shade'. Such terms are largely meaningless and are no help whatsoever in choosing a suitable location for a plant. Invariably, they fail to tell you that a particular plant will die if it is put in chalky or acidic soil. All too often, it seems that plants are sold without much thought or concern being given to their survival.

The borders and beds in long-established and properly maintained gardens will generally be quite consistent in the way they support plants. Years of digging and the addition of compost and manure allows plants to grow well and in an even manner. I noticed this in my parents' Hertfordshire garden, which was on a chalk hill with a thin covering of clay, so it couldn't be considered very fertile. The flower beds that had been maintained since my grandfather's time had deeper soil and were far more fertile than in the newer areas, such as the asparagus bed, which my father had laid out as recently as the late 1960s. However, I was slightly surprised to discover that this basic rule even applied to the rich silt fen soil of our new Lincolnshire vegetable garden. True, I was well aware that the soil was largely devoid of earthworms and other microbial life, but I thought that the 'natural richness', which one hears so often when people are writing or talking about the silt Fens, would somehow transcend everything. I shouldn't have been so naive: yes, the soil was indeed fertile, but after years of neglect and intensive farming its structure had been all but destroyed. So it still took time and frequent applications of rotted compost and manure to improve it. In retrospect, I think our impatience was understandable: we had laid out the Vegetable Garden in the weeks leading up to Christmas 1993 and I spent much of January '94 digging the heavy soil to let air in and allow frost to break it down. We were desperate to see something of our own growing in what was slowly starting to become our new garden. It just took rather longer than we'd imagined.

We decided to adopt a four-course rotation of potatoes, followed by onions, then brassicas and finally summer vegetables before the ground was dug again for potatoes. The ground was carefully strung out and then each of the four equal-sized growing plots was laid out in rows that ran from the central path down to the young hornbeam hedge around the outside of the Vegetable Garden. The silty soil formed a very low but just discernible bank that followed the course of the old stream and tidal creek that had deposited it, probably over two thousand years ago, in the pre-Roman Iron Age. The central path, which formed the axis or spine of the Vegetable Garden, ran along the top of the slight ridge. The plants growing nearer the central path were about two feet taller than those down nearer the hedge. This difference in height was also reflected in the quality of the earth, with higher plants growing on lighter, siltier soil than those below them, where the land was heavier and more clay than silt.

The very different drainage conditions meant that the seeds of plants nearer the central path were the first to germinate and they then grew briskly. By any standards, they were top-quality plants. However, everything planted down-slope near the outer hedge fared poorly, with irregular germination and rather weak growth. Many of the overwintering brassicas, especially sprouts and broccoli, were eventually killed off. It was very disheartening. I hoped that digging in manure would help, and it did, but only a little. After five years, I ran out of patience. I realised I would have to do something to raise the level of the beds nearer the hedge. There was plenty of spare silty soil near the big drainage dyke that the local Internal Drainage Board's huge mechanical digger cleared out every year, but how could we hold it in place?

Like most long-term residents in the local fen, we had visited the large second-hand junk yard run by a scrap dealer and opportunistic trader. Local legend had it that, after the war, he had once offered a redundant submarine for sale. We used to visit his bargain shop and yard regularly when we lived at Limetree Farm and we hadn't changed our ways just because we'd crossed the county boundary. I think it was in the late autumn or winter of 1999 that I found myself wandering through the junk yard on the lookout for bargains, when my gaze fell on a stack of railway sleepers. This was about the time that the railway authorities were completing the destruction of Fenland's railway network, a process that was begun by the notorious Dr Beeching in the mid-1960s. There could be no doubt that these were genuine ex-railway sleepers, because they all bore clear evidence of those iron baseplates that held the steel chocks to clamp the lines in place. Some of them even smelled of old oil – and coal.

As soon as I saw them, I knew those old railway sleepers would be just what we needed to raise the soil level in the

Vegetable Garden, although we'd require a double thickness along the path that runs beside the hedge. Today you can buy metal pegs for tying together and fixing the sleeper-like thick boards that are the rather expensive modern equivalents of those real sleepers. We fixed them in place using ex-site wooden grid-pegs, which I soaked in a bath of wood-preserver for a couple of weeks. I honestly can't remember how much I paid for those sleepers, but the scrap dealer knew I was a local and had bought stuff off him in the past. So we negotiated a price and at the last minute I asked for free delivery. He paused – we both knew I was being cheeky – then he grinned. As he turned to walk away, he nodded. Delivery was part of the deal.

It took a lot of quite heavy work, but I have never regretted raising the soil levels across half the Vegetable Garden. The results were instantaneous: every year the rows of vegetables are evenly matched and all the plants are vigorous and healthy. For what it's worth, the sleeper edging looked quite good too. It was neat and plainly very effective. I didn't do anything clever, like attempt subsoil drainage; I simply piled the additional soil scraped out of the dykes into the lower-lying areas and then added lots of manure. We didn't even lose a season of home-grown vegetables, as I was able to get the work done in the late winter, before most of next year's planting had started. I well remember many friends and garden visitors would leave the new raised Vegetable Garden looking pensive: those sleepers had put ideas in their heads. It was at about this time that I first noticed sleeper-like revetment boards being sold in garden centres and timber merchants. Presumably other people had had the same thoughts as me. Maybe the introduction of raised flower beds was the one positive outcome of those otherwise disastrous post-war railway line closures?

*

One of the great pleasures of gardening is making your own decisions. Often you make mistakes, but when you get things right it feels like time to rejoice. Bottles of cheap-and-cheerful bubbly wine are shared with visiting gardening friends on such happy occasions. But sometimes one knows instinctively that intuition and hunch are not enough. In such situations the textbooks are rigorously consulted and their recommendations followed as meticulously as possible. The club root at Limetree Farm was a case in point. Textbooks warned against transplanting anything out of the vegetable garden, and this was one of the reasons we established the growing-ground at Harry's. In cases such as club root, you must follow the horticultural hygiene rules strictly. I mention club root because it normally strikes when brassica (cabbage family) plants are grown in the same soil for several years running. The simplest way of avoiding this is to subdivide the vegetable garden into three (we prefer four) segments, all with clearly marked-out and consistent boundaries, which must never wander. Breaking the segment rule is the Sin Against the Holy Ghost of vegetable gardening.

Each segment grows different types of vegetables in successive years. At the end of the year everything moves one step to the left or right. So in segment 1 you might dig it and then plant potatoes and perhaps outdoor tomatoes, if there's enough space. The following year you dig and plant spuds in segment 2, next to it, and plant onions in segment 1, where you'd had potatoes the previous year.[1] It's a very simple system, once you've grown used to it. But one year – I think it was the year (2017?) when I had my left hip joint replaced – I shifted the rotation in the wrong direction (left instead of right). I simply can't think what made me do it. It's the sort of thing one might do when one was very drunk. But anyway, I did it – and what was even worse, I didn't notice my mistake until the following autumn. For some reason, it caused chaos for the next four years. It should have been simple to sort out, but it wasn't. Maybe I was over-concerned about my hip, but it caused me huge anxiety. I lost sleep over it. I'd never, ever forgive myself if we caught club root or, just as bad, potato cyst eelworm – another disease caused by repeat planting. This year (2021), things are back to normal: the rotation is working smoothly and, fingers crossed (!), everything still looks healthy. The tool shed and greenhouse each now display a card with the current season's rotation carefully sketched on.

That mistake with the crop rotation did make me doubt my sanity, so I blamed it on the new hip, which in actual fact was settling in very well and causing me almost no pain. Looking back on it, almost the weirdest thing was the fact that I didn't notice my mistake until the start of the following season, when I referred to the notes I'd made the previous year, which simply set out what was planted where – and if there were any particular problems. No, it was all very odd. But if you want another example of my horticultural mental failings, I've got an even better one, but this time I think the motive – simple greed – is only too apparent.

*

I'm horribly aware that I bang on endlessly about home-grown vegetables tasting better than supermarket ones. But I won't apologise for doing so here, because I think it's an important issue, for people's physical as well as their mental well-being. The growing waiting lists for allotment plots in towns and cities right across Britain suggest that the number of people who share this view is increasing – and quite rapidly. Street market vegetable stalls, especially in smaller rural towns, often have access to local growers, so their produce is almost as good as what you can grow at home, but it's never quite as fresh.

The asparagus bed in the vegetable garden in early summer, with espaliered pears and apples, left, and a hornbeam hedge, right. This bed produces enough asparagus for a large family.

A cauliflower cut from the garden ten minutes before cooking is so delicious; even one or two slugs that may have escaped my eagle eye when cutting it up for the pot seem to taste less slimy. There are, however, two ingredients of every well-stocked larder that are vastly better when grown at home. They are asparagus and strawberries. Indeed, I'd say that the out-of-season, midwinter supermarket versions of both are almost completely without taste.

Asparagus is the finest-tasting food you can eat. But it's not particularly easy to grow well. The first point to note is that it is very much a seasonal vegetable and for some reason it's that seasonality that seems to affect its flavour; every year it tastes very slightly different. However, asparagus grown out of season in greenhouses or polytunnels has much less flavour. I also think some modern fast-growing hybrids can be rather tasteless. Personally, I prefer older varieties, and the one I have grown for almost forty years, 'Connover's Colossal', is now referred to as an 'heirloom' variety and is widely available, as seeds or as young root crowns. Its origins go back to Victorian times, but its merits are entirely modern: it's a heavy cropper, it appears early in the season and its flavour is unmatched. I can't fault it, but I do get rather fed up with the seedlings that appear all over the garden. They're no real problem, provided you dig them up immediately. If they get into other plants, such as asters, they can be a right pain.

We had an asparagus bed in my parents' house in Hertfordshire and I can remember it was always something of a disappointment. My father loved asparagus, but the plants he grew were rather sad and puny. Admittedly, the soil in that part of the Vegetable Garden wasn't too good: a strange mix of glacial clay and weathered chalk. In actual fact, asparagus in the wild is a seaside plant and I can remember coming across some while filming with *Time Team* on a coastal site somewhere in Wales. I got very excited, but other members of the team looked at me rather sadly. I don't think anyone on the shoot, either in front of or behind the cameras, shared my enthusiasm. But now I must confess to my second horticultural mistake: for some reason, I failed to make the mental connection between the drained silt Fens around the Wash and that silty marine marshland in Wales. So the asparagus bed I could see in my mind's eye was based on the one in my parents' Hertfordshire garden. That bed had been very unproductive; so I made the bed at Inley Drove Farm about half as large again. The best way to start an asparagus bed is to buy three-year-old 'crowns' (dormant plants with a good mat of roots) from a reliable grower. So that's what we did. And then, the following spring, before the young freshly planted three-year-old crowns had begun to sprout, I bought some more and established a second bed outside the back door. This bed was about half the size of the main bed. It makes me blush when I think about it, but I can so vividly recall being terribly anxious in case we didn't have enough asparagus. I needn't have worried.

Even with three-year-old crowns, you're not supposed to start cutting any stems for at least a couple of years and even then you're recommended to go very steady.[2] I was astonished by how vigorously those young crowns sprouted. In the first year, I'd have said they were already as prolific as the mature plants in my parents' garden. After two years, it took several wheelbarrow journeys to take the collapsed shoots to the bonfire in the autumn. By the third year, the shoots were as thick as my fingers and even though I tried to cut sparingly, I estimate I still managed to fill a couple of buckets over the season.

I still don't know why I planted quite so much asparagus. But what was I to do about it? Once the truth had dawned, which happened fairly rapidly, my immediate reaction was negative. The simplest solution was to get rid of the second bed and reduce the size of the first one, but the actual doing of it proved too much. I can remember standing with a heavy-duty archaeologist's mattock, about to whack it down on a healthy young asparagus crown. I looked closely at my target. I could imagine picking it up, with severed roots; its tender young shoots about to emerge. As I held it in my hand, the shoots began to weep. It was too much: I couldn't be that cruel. So I laid the mattock aside and headed indoors for a much-needed cup of tea.

Like most keen vegetable gardeners, I was quite used to having surpluses, and our various friends and relations are used to being given surplus potatoes, cauliflowers, raspberries etc. But the asparagus surplus was going to be of a different order. I did consider setting up a stall at the farm gate, but then a new farm shop opened in the village and they were happy to take a regular supply. A few years ago they closed, but by then people living in our neighbourhood had begun informally exchanging their surpluses too. People would arrive at our house with boxes of half-a-dozen eggs, or apples – even strawberries. Now I admit, my weekly round of asparagus visits in April and May is slightly more regular and large-scale than other informal exchanges, but then people have responded with very welcome gifts of homemade wine, liqueurs and other treats at Christmas. These local exchanges increased during the Covid-19 pandemic of 2020–21 and they played a part in building a sense of community in our part of the Fens, where houses are widely spaced out and there are few larger villages. But now we're all getting to know each other better. So life moves on, and every year I very much look forward to the friendly chats and smiling faces I'll enjoy on my asparagus rounds. I'm so glad I decided to lay that mattock aside.

One final asparagusian thought. Connover's Colossal, like all asparagus plants, is open to attack from asparagus beetle, which eats the stems and fern-like leaves in the summer. It overwinters in the stems' interior, so it's essential that all the newly died-back stems are cut off at ground level, then immediately taken away and burnt. As it is, you'll probably still have a rumbling background level of beetle infestation, but it shouldn't cause you problems. If you don't burn the stems, however, the beetle will return for certain. It's not a job that you can ever afford to miss. In theory, you should select only male plants to put in your bed, as the females seed everywhere. That's fine in theory, but I don't know of anyone who does it. We all want our replacement plants from time to time. I also like to give them away, especially to younger gardeners, as commercially grown root crowns can be very expensive. I've never had any trouble giving away one- or two-year-old asparagus crowns – and it's great to know that when they're planted they'll give pleasure for many, many years.

*

Growing fruit and vegetables has many delights, but few can rival that moment when you pick the first strawberry or raspberry of the season. I know you can sense from their colour, their soft feel to the touch and just a hint of a sweet scent on the air that they're ripe; but that's never enough – or that's what I always tell myself. No, the only way to be absolutely certain is to pop the first two or three straight into your mouth and then to linger over the flavour, which slowly develops as you enjoy its sweetness and savour its complexity. I've long wondered what makes this moment so special. Writing this in February, I can now appreciate that what I'm enjoying is the taste of an approaching summer – which helps to explain why it's so different every year.

Today, there's a movement to integrate the growing of fruit and vegetables into the larger garden and not to confine them to a special area. The French love their vegetables and cook them sublimely; I love their word for a vegetable garden, *potager*. You can visualise everything growing in an enormous pot, rooted in delicious herby stock rather than topsoil. My own preference is very much in favour of a special vegetable garden, or potager, but I can understand why people with smaller gardens might want to integrate their flowers, fruit and veg. Some vegetables – scarlet runner beans spring to mind – have beautiful flowers, and some, such as courgettes and cucumbers, are attractive in their own right. Ripe tomatoes – red or coloured – always look so enticing. If placed in a border, there are always plenty of bees around to pollinate their flowers and you can also place protective companion plants nearby, such as French marigolds

(*Tagetes patula*), to protect vegetables from attack by whitefly. All of this makes perfect sense, but I don't see why it obviates the need for a vegetable garden. Certain plants, such as potatoes, would look extremely odd in a flower garden, especially when you start harvesting the first earlies. I also don't think onions and garlic are ideal border plants. Strawberries are possibly OK, but raspberries, with their invasive runners, would be insanity if placed in a border. I think I've laboured that point sufficiently.

We tend to move the strawberries every few years, as this seems to stay on top of diseases, which are rife in this part of the Fens, where strawberries have been grown commercially for a very long time. Fungal infections can be a big problem and for some reason they are less persistent if you keep moving the plants. It's also a good idea if you remove the straw quite quickly when they have stopped fruiting – which is something I nearly always fail to do. Wet straw must look like heaven on earth if you're a fungal spore looking for a nice place to overwinter.

Raspberries tend to stay in the same bed, which is usually bounded by mown grass or something like a brick wall, or reinforced concrete, to prevent those invasive runners from spreading. The textbooks suggest you have elaborate wooden frames for raspberries, but we find a few well-placed wires attached to those cheap and effective iron road spikes (usually sold as 'road pins') do just as well, and don't get in the way quite as much when it's time to start picking. Again, garden centres and others proclaim the effectiveness of netted fruit cages. We have never netted our raspberries and although we probably lose about a quarter to birds, especially to blackbirds, I don't begrudge them. We're not so short of land that we can't afford to overplant by about 25 per cent. Strawberries, however, are very different.

I would go so far as to say that a small planting of un-netted strawberries is a waste of time: the birds will snaffle the lot. When we first moved into the Fens, there were five- or ten-acre fields of strawberries everywhere, and none of them were netted. Our garden at Limetree Farm was surrounded by them, so we blithely assumed that local birds would be so fat and bloated that they'd leave our little patch alone. But we could not have been more mistaken. As soon as our fruit started to ripen, practised and sharp-eyed blackbirds spotted their distinctive colour and shape and made short work of them. So we netted them and the problem stopped. It's worth noting here that it's not a good idea to grow strawberries under cloches or polythene-covered wire hoops. Strawberry flowers have to be pollinated by bees and other insects, who are happy to fly through netting, but not glass or plastic sheeting.

Among the features I enjoy most about Victorian and Georgian walled vegetable gardens are the trained and espaliered apple and pear trees that line paths and so elegantly cover walls. Apart from looking fabulous, especially when in blossom, they give me particular satisfaction because no fruit is wasted. Most of the fruit on our orchard trees grows beyond our reach, and although we can pick a certain amount with an adapted pole-pruner device, the vast majority end up rotting on the ground, or, as we saw in Chapter 6, as breakfast for Val's horses. We decided to plant our espaliered apples and pears on either side of the main path through the Vegetable Garden. This position allows me excellent access for pruning in late summer and winter, and even better, all the fruit is within comfortable reach for picking. I find espaliers particularly good for growing soft dessert pears since it is essential to be able to see and feel them ripen. I also hugely enjoy the process of formative pruning, which I find both creative and relaxing. Even if you only have the space to grow a single espaliered tree, may I suggest you try a dessert pear? The variety we both adore and which fruits reliably every year is 'Onward'. *Pyrus communis* 'Onward' is bred from the classic French pear, Doyenné du Comice, and has some of its flavour, but is slightly firmer (I find Comice too juicy) and very much easier to grow.

\*

Every winter, there are two key routine jobs that I have to get completed quite early in the season: digging the Vegetable Garden and pruning the pleached lime trees. Lime trees are fully dormant in the early new year, which means there is no likelihood that the scars left after pleaching will bleed sap. Apart from looking unsightly, bleeding sap weakens the plant and can be a source of infection. Digging the Vegetable Garden is the most urgent of the early winter tasks, as I want the freshly dug-over ground to be frosted a few times. There are two types of frost: air frost and ground frost. Air frosts happen when the temperature of the air drops below freezing point (0 °C; 32 °F); ground, grass or radiation frosts are the result of heat loss from the ground and they start to happen when the air temperature is three or four degrees above freezing. Light ground frosts show up as hoar frost on lawns or well-grazed paddocks for a few hours in the early morning, but they don't have much effect on the soil itself. On the other hand, a sharp air frost causes leaves to wilt and will penetrate lumps of heavy clay; these will start to crumble when they thaw. Each time the process is repeated, the air frost penetrates a little deeper. Harder air frosts usually happen in early and mid-January; so I try to have the digging finished as early as possible in January.

Normally, I aim to start the digging before Christmas, but often the weather has its own views and persistent rainfall will cause me to start pruning the limes first. So far, the winter of 2021–22 hasn't been too wet and, as I write (it's now 30 December), I've managed to get about a fifth of the digging done. Over Christmas, the weather was pretty horrible – lots of drizzle, fog and cold easterly winds – and those people at Head of Zeus seemed to think that this book's deadline was important, so I didn't get out and dig as much as I would have liked (to be honest, it was so horribly damp I was grateful for any excuse to stay indoors). I think I speak for most experienced gardeners when I say that regular, seasonal tasks, such as digging or pleaching, make long-term changes in the weather – and possibly even the climate too – much easier to identify and define. These days, hard air frosts occur later in the winter and are less common or severe than they were even twenty years ago. I'm in absolutely no doubt whatsoever that our climate is changing.

I'm a bit of a traditionalist when it comes to our vegetable garden. I learnt my vegetable-growing from a very knowledgeable gardener called Joe Aylott when I was growing up in our house in Weston, near Hitchin in north Hertfordshire. Weston was then a quiet rural village in the rolling chalk hills that overlook Stevenage and Baldock. You could step in cow pats when you walked in the roads around three of the village's cattle farms, as cows were taken in for milking twice a day and people were less fussy about their footwear (and none of the roads yet had raised or kerbed pavements). It's difficult to judge older people's ages when you're a child, but I would guess that Joe was in his fifties when I started taking an interest in gardening, from about 1955 (I would have been ten). Joe, who was my parents' gardener, came from an old Weston family and was very much a rural Hertfordian. He spoke with the local accent (which has since largely vanished) and the skills he passed on to me were also very traditional.

I have vague memories of him explaining that you should never plant cabbages or Brussels sprouts in the same ground two years running, but I wasn't quite sure why this was so important. Joe's main influence on me was to teach me how a vegetable plot should be laid out – and his rules have entered my DNA. Rule No. 1: rows of plants must always be dead straight and this is best achieved with a roll of string (which I think he called twine). Rule No. 2: rows must be kept far enough apart to allow sunlight on the leaves and access for picking or harvesting. Thanks to Joe, my parents' vegetable garden resembled a well-disciplined military operation. A small number of flowers for cutting (mostly chrysanthemums) were allowed, but these also had to be grown in strict rows, which were clearly separated from the vegetables. It was almost as if the flowers were morally dubious and might corrupt the cabbages and onions.

Weeds were simply not tolerated, which wasn't as easy to achieve as it might sound. Joe, quite rightly, didn't approve of any weedkiller in the vegetable garden and anyway, the chemicals then available were pretty drastic in their impact. My father favoured sodium chlorate, which was only to be used on paving and paths. (Sodium chlorate abhors all forms of life; it's also explosive, when mixed with sugar.*) So ground elder, bindweed and creeping twitch grass were constant problems in the Hertfordshire garden, and had to be regularly and very thoroughly hoed off or dug out. I can remember trying to do this to Joe's satisfaction; he was too polite to say that I'd done a rubbish job. but sometime later I noticed that he'd completely reworked the ground I'd so painstakingly dug a little earlier.

---

* Its use is now banned. I discuss a naughty sodium chlorate explosion in *Scenes from Prehistoric Life* (Head of Zeus, London, 2021), page 136.

Gardening on the chalk hills of north Hertfordshire is very different from the Fens, and when I first tried, I did experience problems establishing a productive vegetable garden. In our Limetree Farm garden we had brassica club root, but ground drainage also wasn't very good and the soil was somewhat exhausted. Looking back on it, we should have persuaded a local cattle farmer to give us a trailerful of well-rotted manure. Sadly, our faltering attempts at producing garden compost were not up to standard. Things weren't very much better when we started work on the new Lincolnshire garden. Drainage at Inley Drove was a slight improvement on Limetree, but – as we have already seen – the soil was very much worse, being completely exhausted and devoid of earthworms. By the mid-1990s, however, we were successfully farming sheep. We kept some of the animals on rented grazing, but the majority were on our own land, which we were able to expand by about 30 acres (12 ha) in the late 1990s. The ewes came into the Inley Drove barn just before Christmas, had their lambs between late February and March, then returned to outdoor grazing in April. A hundred or more ewes produce a lot of manure, which I would clear out of the barn with the muck bucket of my aged (1964) International B414 tractor, very much of fond memory. That muck was to prove a lifesaver in the new garden taking shape around the house and barn.

We didn't make the mistake of using fresh muck in the garden. Fresh animal dung needs to rot down before it becomes usable manure, a process that takes a minimum of six months. We allowed almost a year and didn't start spreading it until the following spring. Joe Aylott used to tell me about the importance of manure and how to dig it in. In those days we'd get ours from my uncle's cattle farm, just outside the village. The key was to flip the fork- or spadeful of earth upside down so that the manure, which had been spread on the surface, was now beneath the freshly dug spadeful of soil. It took me quite a long time to perfect the flip, but eventually I mastered it. I know it might sound a bit odd, but I never managed to regain my soil-flip trick until I tried it using our own sheep manure. I couldn't do it with garden compost. And when I did it, I could distinctly recall what it had been like when I did it as a child, some forty years earlier. Was it that slightly sweet smell of well-rotted manure? I don't know, but it was a memorable moment.

\*

No-dig vegetable gardens have become the new normal and I fully understand – and approve of – the reasoning behind them: it's the horticultural equivalent of no-till agriculture. The idea is to help the soil enrich itself, which is best achieved by not disturbing it. In the past, I tried using mechanical Rotavators and other machines, but I didn't like the way they pulverised the ground, which sometimes actually led to further compaction, especially in a dry spell following heavy rain. But when we came to mark out and plant the beds in the new field, the ground had been lying bare for two or more years and, since the topsoil was devoid of earthworms, it had become very compacted indeed. When we started to lay out the Vegetable Garden, I needed to use an iron rod simply to insert a cane. The ground was like concrete. If we had tried to dress it with a mulch of rotted manure, or even bought compost, it would have dried out and blown away in a couple of days. It's sometimes quite hard to explain just how hostile a gardening environment it was.

We found that the best way to get manure into the soil was to wait for a damp day, but in very windy, dry weather, we'd also sprinkle the surface with a watering can. First, we lightly forked about two square yards of the surface. We then spread about a barrowful of manure and mixed it in with hoes and rakes. Being quite young manure, it was full of earthworms, and although many of these were much smaller and more wiggly than the normal earthworms you find in garden soil, I'm sure they would have adapted. They certainly made me feel much better, because I had been appalled by the deadness of the topsoil on our new field. I spread manure in this way across the entire Vegetable Garden and then left it alone for two or three months.

When I came to dig the ground for our first crop of potatoes, in mid-January, I was delighted to see that the manure was beginning to be slowly incorporated into the soil. Even though it was still very heavy and felt more dead than alive, I did spot a few worms and other insects. Then I started on the serious digging, using a spade. But this proved hopeless: I couldn't drive the blade in more than halfway and, after an hour or so of vigorous pushing and stamping, the arches of my feet were aching. So I moved to a garden fork, which proved easier to insert, but before the day was out I had bent the two outer tines. You can straighten them, but they're never quite the same again. In an attempt to speed up the digging of the veg garden, I bought a heavy-duty road repairman's fork. It weighed a ton and had massive, square-section tines – one of which I eventually managed to bend. Finally, I bought a good-quality digging spade, which I religiously cleaned and kept sharp. Slowly, as the years rolled by, the work got easier: worms became far more abundant and the soil began to develop a slightly crumbly texture – at long last, it was coming to life. But it was a very demanding time. I was in my fifties, and after just a short morning's digging in the veg garden my back ached and my hip was so sore.

I mentioned the stiffness I felt when digging to Patrick, who then ran the excellent shop selling hardware, seeds, tools and garden furniture in Holbeach. The following week he suggested I try a long-handled, handmade spade, which he could order from the makers in Holland. It would cost me slightly more than three times the price of an ordinary garden-centre spade, but – having just bought yet another of these and torn its blade while digging out some rose roots – I was prepared to experiment. The new spade is about nine inches longer than my old ones and has a handmade shaft with a T-shaped end and a slightly splayed, heavy-duty blade. It took me a few days to get used to it, but now I won't use anything else. For about five years it enabled me to dig the garden, as my left hip slowly and painfully wore itself down. Eventually, I had the hip replaced, and when I was able to walk again, I returned to the Dutch spade and was digging the veg garden in less than two years after the operation. When I finish writing this section, I'll have a quick cup of tea and then head out to the veg garden for a spell of pre-lunchtime digging. I love that spade.

# 8

# Between the House and the Barn

*Unwanted Bricks • A Born-again Ewe • Stately Pleached Limes •*
*The Huntingdonshire Pleach • The Hot Garden •*
*The Self-seeded Bit • Wisteria*

Planning a garden around a house that is still being built isn't easy. So many things can go wrong, but at the same time unexpected opportunities may arise and the trick is to be there, on the ground, when they do. Early one morning in the late summer of 1994, when I was walking from our temporary home in the caravan to the shower we had installed in the barn, I saw the house builders' supervisor standing in the yard looking very concerned. I called out 'Good morning, John' and he didn't respond. That worried me, because he was normally a very polite, cheery man, so I walked across and asked what was bothering him.

He was standing next to two pallets of bricks that hadn't been used and were still strapped and wrapped, just as they had been delivered from the brickworks at the start of the project. In his hand he held a piece of paper from the brickmakers, which stated that his company would be charged for the collection and disposal of any unused bricks. At that point, the brisk morning wind grew even stronger and as I was only wearing an old moth-eaten dressing gown over my pyjamas, we headed back towards the shelter of the barn. As we walked, he asked tentatively whether I could possibly find any use for those bricks. By this point we had used a considerable tonnage of the old broken bricks that contractors had brought us to form a solid base for our yard and drive, but they had been rolled in and dressed with road planings over a year ago. I could have used them then. But not now. Suddenly, there was another sharp gust of wind, which almost removed my dressing gown. That triggered an idea.

Our new field at Inley Drove was very open indeed and the winter winds that blew there were far stronger than in our garden at Limetree Farm. Doubtless this was partly due to the proximity of the Wash, but whatever the cause, these winds could be terrible. We knew that planting trees and shrubs would help to reduce the problem, but we were also aware that Fen winds had an almost human ability to get round, or penetrate, the most tightly clipped hedge. If we were ever to defeat them, we needed something more permanent and windproof; something that would also catch the warmth of the sun. And how else were we to grow figs, my favourite fresh fruit? I knew then that what we wanted was a brick wall. I outlined my idea to John. As I spoke, I could see his eyes brighten. I told him not to raise his hopes too much and that I'd get back to him shortly.

I bought my first Apple microcomputer back in the late 1970s and was well used to using computers by the time we came to plan and manage the Inley Drove Farm project in the mid-1990s. At the early, financial planning stage of building the house, I had set up a spreadsheet, using Lotus 1-2-3 software, and it enabled me to manage the changing costs of the building works very effectively. I checked the spreadsheet after my quick chat with John and, slightly to my surprise, it showed we had a small surplus. So we might just be able to afford to build a bit of wall. The next day, I went out with Maisie and we discussed what we thought would be ideal: two walls. One would run from the house to the driveway and would give the Front Garden some much-needed shelter from north-easterly gales. The other would run from the house out towards the barn. It would be right-angled to enclose a small lawn and flower bed at the back of the house. The south face of this wall would give protection both to tender plants and to the path from the barn to the back door of the house, which we knew would be heavily used at all hours during lambing in late February and March.

I spoke to John and he was delighted. He offered to do the work more or less at cost price, which meant that we would overshoot our construction budget by only about 5 per cent. I phoned our bank manager (you could do that sort of thing back then), who was happy to provide us with a temporary small mortgage. So we went ahead. I still think it was just about the best single decision we made in the entire project. Those two simple brick walls aren't just integral to the house and garden, they are now an essential part of our lives *in* the garden.

*

As I just described, one of our two new brick walls ran south-east from the house towards the barn. Roughly halfway between the two buildings, it turned sharply to the north-east to provide shade and shelter for the small border and lawn behind the house. We decided to plant a fig tree on the yard side of the wall, close by the right-angled corner. It was a warm and sheltered spot. The spring of 1995 was the second season of lambing at the new farm and it was fraught with problems. The weather was cold and damp, but sometimes the daytime air could be strangely warm. The in-lamb (i.e. pregnant) ewes were all in the barn, out of the worst of the weather. They had lots of good hay from the garden meadow, plus plenty of fresh straw from our neighbours. But I was worried because the warmish days and very cold nights were perfect for the spread of pneumonia – which housed sheep are very susceptible to. We had injections to give if any were ill, but that's not the way sheep pneumonia usually seems to strike. Sometimes we've been able to catch a ewe that's starting to get ill and, if we can do the injection, they then quickly recover. More usually, however, you find a sheep dead in the morning, with a very runny nose, which is what tells you it was pneumonia. Sadly, that was what we found on this occasion.

I was about to drag the dead ewe round to a secure sheltered spot at the back of the barn, where we put any dead sheep and lambs when we're lambing. During lambing, the knacker visits all sheep farms in the area once a week and he always checks our shelter. But then I had an idea. I'd read somewhere that fig trees will grow very well if they're planted close to a dead animal. I was vaguely planning to go out and find a roadside casualty – probably a hare, rabbit or muntjac deer – as there are plenty of these in early springtime. But wouldn't it be better, I wondered, if I buried one of our own sheep? The new fig tree could then be a lasting memorial to her. I still like that idea, but I've noticed that some of our more urban friends tend not to finish the lovely succulent Brown Turkey figs I pick them, if I've just told them that story. The tale of the dead ewe can also come in useful on those rare occasions when figs are a bit scarce. I should add that burying the ewe and then planting the fig proved to be very beneficial, both in the short and the long term. We now have two Brown Turkey fig trees (*Ficus carica* 'Brown Turkey') close to the end of the brick wall; both are thriving and fruit very well. As I pick the first figs of summer, I always think kindly of that poor dead sheep, still lying peacefully down there, among the roots.

*

We decided that the two brick walls would have to be about seven feet tall if they were to provide adequate shelter from the Fenland gales. They were finished by the end of autumn 1994, and when the cold winds of the next winter started to pick up, they proved themselves highly effective. But displaced air has to go somewhere, which is probably why the open gap between the barn and the wall behind the house became even more turbulent. The wind now scythed its way into the young garden, lifting some freshly planted shrubs clean out of the ground. We had to do something about it – and fast.

We decided to close the gap with a row of four pleached lime trees. Thanks to our experience with lime trees at our previous garden, I had learnt many useful techniques and was feeling

Two of the pleached limes in the early days of the pleached screen. Note the central upright in this picture is a supporting pole, not a lime tree trunk.

quite confident; but I was keen that the new screen, which would involve quite a lot of work, would be clearly visible. I didn't want it to blend into the background, like the pleaches at Limetree Farm, which were overshadowed by the giant hedge that ran beside the road. The new screen would be much shorter in length, but it also had to be taller and very robust if it was to stand up to those late autumn gales. Measuring the width of the gap to be filled, we decided to plant four trees. We could probably have done it with three, but we weren't convinced that they would be strong enough.

We bought slightly taller trees than we would normally have done, because this new screen was needed urgently, but we didn't buy them bare-rooted. They needed to have a good root ball to start growing quickly. Normally we look for small plants when setting out something like a hedge, or indeed when planting specimen trees. People who pay huge sums for large plants must find it so frustrating when they see the tiny saplings planted in their less-well-off neighbours' gardens rapidly outgrow their expensive specimen trees. As a general rule, the larger the plants, the less reliable they are when transplanted. Cheap and cheerful is always best. We were probably taking a slight risk when we bought the larger plants, but the roots looked very healthy and when we told him what we wanted to do with the trees, the gardener in the nursery assured us that these ones were originally cuttings taken from the same parent plant. This was important, because it would mean that after a few years the woven-together branches might start to grow into each other (a process known as 'inosculation') and form a much stronger, unified bough when the trees were more mature. In the case of our limes, the process started at the turn of the millennium, but it hasn't taken place very evenly. I suspect this is due to the wind. So our pleaches are not a textbook example of inosculation, but where it has worked, it has been very successful – and quite subtly spectacular.

Pruning the pleached limes is one of my two most important winter tasks, which can never be omitted. The other is, of course, the digging of the Vegetable Garden. I always note in our gardening diary (where I also record rainfall, early and late frosts etc.) when I finished pruning the limes and when I had dug the Vegetable Garden, as this gives me a very clear impression of what that winter's weather had been like. Last year (2021), for instance, I didn't finish pruning the limes until early February. It had been a very wet season indeed, but there were a few dry weeks after Christmas and early in the new year and I spent these digging the Vegetable Garden – an impossible job in very wet weather, after almost twenty years of regular manuring. Once the digging had been done, I could turn my attention to the limes. I find both jobs strangely relaxing. When I'm digging the Vegetable Garden, I can closely examine the state of the soil and the number of earthworms. I'm always delighted when a lovely robin redbreast keeps me company as I dig, pecking at the occasional worm or slug. Robins only stand close to me if I'm digging with a spade in the Vegetable Garden. I say 'robins' because I don't know if he/she is the same bird each year, but he/she always returns and has been doing so for decades. Maybe he/she followed us to the new garden from Limetree Farm, about eight miles away? Hm, on second thoughts, possibly not.

I used to use an old-fashioned wooden ladder to prune the limes, but lately I've noticed that winter gales are getting stronger and I'm not getting any younger. So recently I replaced it with a self-supporting aluminium ladder with splayed feet and a third, adjustable, tripod-like supporting leg. It's remarkably light to carry and the splayed feet don't sink into wet ground. It's also very stable in high winds and I feel completely safe when using it. I think it's going to extend my active gardening life by many years. The new feeling of security has transformed the way I think about the winter pleaching, which, if I'm honest, I used to rather dread. The old ladder, leaning on slimy lime bark, was prone to slip and I sometimes felt obliged to bind it temporarily into place with baler twine. I feel quite strongly that tight orange baler twine and living plants don't go happily together. But with my new tripod ladder I can now leave that horrible twine to gather yet more dust in an old dog-feed bag, deep in an abandoned lambing pen at the back of the barn.

The pleached limes shed their leaves in autumn to reveal the long, straight shoots that have grown over the summer. Some of these are thicker than my thumb and are best cut with loppers; otherwise, I use secateurs. Like most garden sheds, mine contains many pairs of cheap secateurs, which I've been given or have bought when I couldn't resist a bargain. Invariably, these are pale imitations of the best secateurs you can buy, which are made by the Swiss company Felco. My favourite Felcos have a partially revolving hand grip, which sounds rather unwieldy, and does indeed take a bit of getting used to, but once you've got the knack, you can spend an entire day pruning and not feel any tiredness in your hand. They're deeply wonderful. And when you accidentally lose them out in the border and stumble across them six months later, rusted and seized solid, you can send them off to Felco, who'll return them promptly, fully repaired, for less than the price of a cheap curry. Mr Felco, you can do no wrong.

*

Maisie used to live in Huntingdon and we have both been admirers of the Huntingdonshire style of lime pleaching for many years. Essentially, it's business-like and unfussy, with quite widely separated parallel branches, which weave into the tree alongside and grow together.[1] The knob-like bolls that produce the new season's shoots become increasingly large and knobbly as time passes. After a few decades, it's the big bolls that catch the eye and give these pleached lime aerial hedges their special character.

Equipped with my new tripod ladder, I normally start pruning the pleached limes shortly after Christmas. If the weather isn't too harsh, it generally takes me about a week to complete. I used to take the prunings down to the bonfire, but over the past few years I've changed my mind about burning garden waste. In part, this reflects my intention to do my bit towards diminishing climate change, but I also like watching what happens when one encourages wildlife. The heaps of brushwood we've piled up around the inside edges of the wood have helped to increase the breeding of hares. Ten years ago, I might have spotted a pair playing around on the meadow; these days it's not uncommon to watch a dozen or more. The meadow is rapidly becoming a hare school playground. So now I add the lime prunings to the heaps in the wood. Over the years they'll rot down, but not before they have sheltered many young hares and hedgehogs from winter winds and marauding foxes. Hedgehogs in Britain continue to be in steep decline and anything we can do to help them must be welcomed.[2]

In the early decades of the farm, it was not unusual for sheep and lambs to escape from the barn and out into the yard. Sheep are flock animals and tend to panic when they're on their own; they will dash frantically in any direction. When they got into the garden, they often did terrible damage as they rushed about in blind terror, so it didn't take us long to decide to stretch a fence across the gap between the brick wall and the barn. If we did that, escaping sheep would be encouraged to go down the drive, where we had a better chance of catching them or turning them round. We built the fence using the posts that were supporting the pleached limes overhead and I must confess it didn't look very attractive. It was a bit of a wire-and-staple lash-up and it wouldn't have won us many points for horticultural elegance. More out of desperation than inspiration, we planted two plants of a free-flowering, highly scented honeysuckle, *Lonicera japonica* var. 'Halliana',[3] in the hope that it might conceal and somehow civilise the otherwise brutal-looking fence below the pleaches. And it worked. Twenty years later, those lovely honeysuckle flowers are still looking gorgeous and they smell divine on warm summer evenings. Whenever I prune the pleaches overhead, I first take a pair of shears to the honeysuckle and cut it back severely. Within a couple of weeks it's looking better than ever, and covered with flower buds. Apart from removing the occasional rogue climbing stem, that's all the honeysuckle pruning I do for the rest of the year. It's very low maintenance. A wonderful plant.

A few years after planting the limes and the honeysuckle, we had to make some decisions about relocating the two dogs' kennels. One usually gets such decisions wrong, but we needed to put them somewhere where their furious barking would alert us and help protect both the house and the barn. The obvious place was in front of the pleaches (i.e. on the side closest to the barn). I know dog kennels are hardly an elegant feature, but ours are well built, robust and practical. I never find such things ugly.

We moved the kennels across to the pleaches over ten years ago. Today, the two blend together quite well when seen from the yard, and the honeysuckle hedge and overhead pleaches provide the dogs with good protection against north-easterly gales in winter. On the garden side of the pleaches there's a long, rather sinuous path that runs from the small lawn at the back of the house, behind the pleaches, along the rear of the barn, through a deer-proof wrought-iron gate and into the Vegetable Garden. It's a path we use quite frequently throughout the year. In the early days after moving the kennels the dogs would invariably wake up and bark if one of us walked along it, but that ceased several years ago, when the honeysuckle hedge became established. Today, the kennels are effectively hidden from the garden.

This brief story of the placement of the kennels presents a strong argument for a careful, measured approach to garden development. I concede that an underlying understanding of its structure is important for a garden's evolution, but I also believe strongly that gardeners should give themselves the freedom to plan, to improvise and sometimes even to make mistakes. Try to stay clear of off-the-shelf garden designs, unless you have the confidence to alter them extensively. I prefer to follow general principles rather than hard-and-fast prescriptions.

*

Even the tidiest of builders can leave you with heaps of rubble, and the nice people who built our house were no exception. Mark you, they'd had to contend with a very wet winter in which the wheels of fork-lift trucks, dumpers and even wheelbarrows and sack trucks sank deep into the clay-silt ground. As I said to one of the carpenters: 'It's almost as if this soil has been laid down by water.' He was a Fenman to his fingertips and, like all of his kind, he preferred his humour as dry as dust. I knew he wouldn't respond – and he didn't. 'Hm,' he growled, without looking up. Excellent.

To consolidate the dampest spots, the builders had been forced to dump in broken rubble, such as bits of cement, broken bricks and smashed roof tiles. They were kind enough to remove most of this from the front garden, when work was finished by the spring of 1995, but because of the builders' rubble the soil had completely lost its structure and didn't provide much nourishment for plant roots for at least five years – and that was with the addition of lots of sheep manure. There was also an area of tyre-ravaged soil, with lots of added rubble, between the house and the yard, but on the sunny side of the seven-foot-tall brick wall. I think the builders must have assumed that we'd put this to some practical farming use, such as an implement parking area or a pallet store, because they had made no effort to clear the rubble. We soon realised, however, that it had great potential.

I hired a mini-digger and started to scrape away at the surface, largely to prise out larger pieces of brick or tile, which we piled up in a bank alongside the drive. I then dug a wide, flat-bottomed trench, heaping the mostly rubble-free soil along the rough path in front of the wall. That path has long since been paved, but then it was made of rubble, builders' sand and gravel – not perfect, but it kept the worst of the mud off our feet during lambing. Finally, I shoved the rubble along the drive into the trench and then buried it under the topsoil I'd heaped up over the path. We now had a low raised bed with excellent natural drainage. I thought it could be perfect for asparagus – and I was right: it still is.

As you may remember from Chapter 7, we have two asparagus beds: one in the Vegetable Garden; the other near the back door. We call the flower bed that surrounds the back-door asparagus bed the Hot Garden, for the simple reason that it always seems to be hot there. Indeed, in summertime the heat can be almost unpleasant. It was the heat that persuaded us to site the washing line parallel with the path that runs alongside the narrow informal border immediately below the wall. If I have one regret about the siting of the line, it is that I sometimes get rather fed up having to disentangle flapping laundry from the branches of the fig trees at the far end. Those trees were tiny when I embedded the end-posts in concrete.

The bed at the foot of the wall faces south-west and gets baked by sunshine for most of the day. It's also quite dry because of the wall's foundations. It has been a difficult bed to plant and manage for various other reasons, which one would normally draw a discreet veil over in a book about fabulous gardens, except this book has turned out to be more warts-and-all than gosh-that's-gorgeous. So I'll come clean, as it were. Halfway along the wall is where the builders decided to site our septic tank, which has to be pumped out a minimum of once a year and sometimes twice, especially if we have visitors from London staying with us. Why is it that Londoners take two baths a day? I know the air there is rather grimy, but two baths would last me a good week, or even more during lambing when activities like sleep and bathing become rarities. Emptying the tank requires heavy-duty pipes, various spades and poles, and of course the massive cast-iron lid has to be put down somewhere. Not surprisingly, it's a process that can be quite destructive for any plants or shrubs growing nearby.

The border beneath the wall takes the biggest hit when the septic tank is emptied, so we have tended to plant it with bulbs that are surplus to requirements elsewhere – taken out of winter displays in the house, for example, or from large pots out in the garden. They're mostly bulbs that neither of us is prepared to throw away, and tulips feature prominently among them. It seems wrong to discard magnificent bulbs that cost a fortune. Sadly, even though I sprinkle plant food on them liberally, they rarely flower for a second time. Shortly after we built the wall, we planted one or two bulbs of the double snowdrops of the original and best species, *Galanthus nivalis* 'Flore Pleno'. We didn't want double snowdrop flowers out in the wood, where we were aiming for a simpler and more natural look, so we only planted them in certain flower beds around the house. To avoid crosses between the single and double snowdrops, we never mixed the two and made sure that the beds remained separated by some distance. Happily, those few double snowdrops at the foot of the wall have thrived, together with blue- and white-flowered grape hyacinths (*Muscari armeniacum*). I've always been fond of grape hyacinths. They do best when left on their own, but they can become quite invasive in richer soils, so a fairly narrow bed between a stout brick wall and a wide paved path has proved ideal.

The bed at the foot of the brick wall is also where I like to plant bulbs that I know will never thrive for long in our garden, but which I do love to see – and enjoy their scents. My favourites are undoubtedly Crown Imperial lilies, which are native to Turkey but thrive in Britain.[4] I am particularly fond of the golden variety, *Fritillaria imperialis* 'Aurora'. Crown Imperials prefer soils more freely draining than our heavy clay-silts, so they rarely survive for many years. Some find their scent a bit overpowering, but I love it – it reminds me of my childhood spent in a garden where the subsoil was chalk. Crown Imperials used to thrive there. Smells can evoke such vivid memories.

*

The Hot Garden, on the other side of the path that runs along the wall, has a feature that has proved one of the great successes of the garden and one, moreover, that was completely unplanned. For much of the year it is almost entirely self-seeded and it comes back every season in a slightly different form. It doesn't have a name yet; we just refer to it as 'the self-seeded bit near the yard' – which I concede is not very memorable. I'm sure one day we'll think of something better.

The yard in front of the barn can be a busy place at times. It's at the end of the drive and it's where delivery drivers turn round and trailers for carrying sheep are parked before loading up. It's also where all friends and visitors leave their cars before walking to the house. The large bed in the Hot Garden is the first close look that most people have of the garden. It's also where I start my tours when groups have booked a visit as part of the National Garden Scheme. So why on earth has it taken me nearly twenty-five years to appreciate this? I honestly don't know, but I suspect it might have been an unconscious reaction to those grand Georgian country houses, with their imposing avenues and elaborate front doors. We both wanted our garden to be different; to be a place that visitors discovered and where revelations were more subtle and laid-back. So maybe that is why I have resisted calling the Hot Garden what it really is: the Welcome Garden. But I'm sorry, names like that make me cringe. In my mind, it's always going to be called that 'self-seeded bit near the yard'.

You can always remove something that's very unsightly, but concealment doesn't always work. The best solutions seem to happen by accident, as we discovered when we planted the honeysuckle hedge beneath the pleached limes. So how were we to manage the juxtaposition of a large flower-cum-asparagus bed with a rather unsightly yard, where livestock trailers are turned around and where the scuffed-up surface never looks neat and tidy? It's certainly no National Trust car park.

In hindsight, I suppose we could have tried to establish something spectacular that would contrast with the workaday yard and also give arriving visitors something impressive to look at while they're waiting for their creaky old tour guide to arrive. It would have been an ideal location for one of those magnificent outdoor plant displays, such as the auricula theatre at Calke Abbey.[5] We do possess a few auriculas but the trouble is, neither of us is a collector. We don't possess enough potted plants to even fill half the splendid Calke theatre. So we did nothing about it.

We did, however, plant a few things in the Hot Garden, largely because, unlike the rest of the garden, it is very free draining. Lilacs seem to like it, as do red-hot pokers (*Kniphofia*). Somewhere we came across the pampas grass *Cortaderia richardii*, which has to be one of the most elegant of all grasses, with six- to seven-foot-tall arching flower plumes that sway delightfully in the late summer breeze. Another herbaceous plant that doesn't like to get too wet for too long is *Acanthus spinosus* (spiny bear's breeches), which we positioned near the end of the washing line. It carpets the surrounding yard surface with seedlings, which, if they're dug up before they sink a deep root, can be readily potted on. They sell well on the plant stall at our annual National Garden Scheme open weekend, in mid-September.

Rather unexpectedly, the loose material of the yard surface around its edge has proved to be home to plants of dark mullein (*Verbascum nigrum*), which formed an elegant edging to the bed in late summer and early autumn (when we open for the NGS).[6] They are a perfect end-stop and look so natural. I'd love to claim to our garden visitors that I designed the effect, but sadly I didn't. Mother Nature did it all.

To this day, I have no idea where the dark mullein had spread from. We had tried to grow it in the past, but the soil in most of the beds and borders of the main garden proved too heavy and poorly drained for it to get established. So we gave up on it. Another plant that we tried to grow, initially with minimal success – and probably for the same reasons – was the very distinctive giant sea holly, *Eryngium giganteum*, widely known as 'Miss Willmott's Ghost'. Ellen Willmott was a very well-respected gardener of the early twentieth century who lived at Warley Place in Essex and was known for her love of this plant. It was said she would spread its seeds when she visited other people's gardens and nobody was looking. Her ghost must still be around, long after her death (she died in 1934), because we noticed a few seedlings growing along the edge of the yard. By 2016, they had become well established.

The dry conditions of the Hot Garden gave Maisie a chance to grow one of her favourite perennials, the spectacular red-hot poker, *Kniphofia* 'Prince Igor', which provides a blaze of colour in high summer. It contrasts well with the dried-up leaves and seedheads of Miss Willmott's Ghost.

If you visit gardens frequently, you will often come across teams of gardeners preparing beds and borders for the next big seasonal flowering. Expired or expiring annuals at the front of the border are being replaced and larger, late-season perennials are being tied in and generally tidied up. What I like so much about the plants along the yard-edge of the Hot Garden is that they only need a good clearing-out once a year – usually in late February or early March. For the rest of the year they look after themselves, but they still manage to pull off those spectacular changes. And every year they're subtly different.

\*

We have never drawn a hard-and-fast distinction in our minds between 'indoors' and 'outdoors'. Even in the depths of winter, we are constantly opening doors and leaving the house, often only for a few moments, to collect a few logs from the front veranda, or to pick parsley from the herb bed outside the back porch. We have a small fridge (where we used to keep antibiotics for the sheep) and a freezer in the barn and we frequently nip out to collect or deposit stuff there. The pergola that we had built behind the house (by the excellent carpenter who assembled and erected the barn) is essentially a half-in-half-out sort of space. We often have tea there, and when the evenings get a bit longer it's an ideal spot for a pre-supper glass of wine. We named it the Poop Deck, not just because it has a wooden decking floor, but because it forms an integral part of the ship that is our house. In reality, of course, poop decks were on the top of the superstructure at the rear of a wooden warship. It's where an Elizabethan captain would have stood, telescope to his eye, surveying the approaching hostile Spaniards. He wouldn't have seen much from our Poop Deck, especially when the wisteria is in flower, but I think he'd have loved the scent on the air.

I love wisteria, in fact I'd almost go so far as to say it's my favourite garden plant. The variety we grow is *Wisteria sinensis* ('sinensis' means Chinese) and I don't think it can really be improved on.[7] The flowers are a vibrant pale blue or white (I greatly prefer the blue) and they come out in late spring, with a smaller second flowering in the autumn, when the slightly weaker sunshine allows the fewer flowers to retain their colour much better than in the first flowering. We have one plant that climbs across the front of the house and another that we have trained to cover the large (7 x 5 yards) pergola above the Poop Deck, at the rear of the house. I initially made the mistake of planting the wisteria over the Poop Deck in the damp soil of the Long Border, which lies immediately north of it. It grew well for two or three years, but was killed in a particularly cold, wet winter. The following spring, we put the replacement close to the house wall, where the ground is about two feet higher and far better drained. The new wisteria loved this location and in about seven years it completely covered the Poop. It flowers so freely that we have to remove the spent flowers from the decking with a wheelbarrow, rake and snow shovel. If we left them to rot where they fell, the decking wouldn't last long.

When I lived in Toronto, everyone scrupulously removed everything 'domestic' from the garden in late autumn: most potted plants, all chairs, tables, furniture and barbecue equipment. To do anything less would be insane, when temperatures outside could often be cold enough to give you frostbite. Once everything had been taken indoors, for most people their gardens effectively ceased to exist; it was far too cold to grow vegetables or salads. So life in winter was restricted to indoors. I think that this annual in-out shift made it much harder to think of the garden as an integral part of the house or home. Essentially, it was an add-on; an optional extra. I think you could probably say that a broadly similar attitude prevailed in Georgian and Victorian England, where gardens served to set off houses: they provided spectacular or picturesque settings for them. You can also glimpse this attitude in the placing of walled vegetable gardens at some distance from the house, as is the case at Holkham Hall, in Norfolk. These were places that were visited and used by maids, under-gardeners and other household staff. I suppose you could see them more as units of production for the great house. They were never a part of it.

Attitudes changed in the late nineteenth century with the rise of the Arts and Crafts Movement, when gardeners such as Gertrude Jekyll successfully integrated houses into their gardens. We still tend to view the pioneers of eighteenth-century landscape design, men like Capability Brown and Humphry Repton, as being Britain's greatest contributors to garden design; but as far as most gardeners are concerned, far and away the most outstandingly original contributions were made by Gertrude Jekyll and her followers, who realised that gardens were spaces to be lived in. They were not there just to be looked at. Most importantly, her designs treated the garden as an extension of the house; the two could not be separated. Jekyll's philosophy drove many developments in both garden design and plant breeding that took place in the decades prior to 1950.

I like to think that the evolution (I hesitate to say 'design') of our Fenland garden owes much to Gertrude Jekyll, and it probably does, as both Maisie and I admire her gardens enormously. But perhaps a bigger influence has been our love for those far-from-ordinary cottage gardens that you can still sometimes find in small towns and villages across rural Britain. Today, the united forces of gentrification and Cotswoldification are trying to replace old-fashioned, do-it-yourself inspiration. It's so sad that many people are losing the confidence to fashion gardens that aren't out of a Chelsea catalogue or a television gardening show. I love it when I see small ponds and large gnomes with long fishing rods. Thank goodness that the urge to please young children will often trump Good Taste.

Friendly neighbours who also enjoy gardening can inspire one another, and you can watch the inspiration spread to other houses and gardens in the village. I remember a wonderful series of front gardens in Guyhirn, a village beside the high banks of the River Nene, not far from Limetree Farm. Some of these gardens had wonderful stands of fruit trees and lovely flower-rich borders. One had a huge old wisteria, which scrambled along the long fence between two front gardens. It was plainly much loved by the people living on either side. It was such an improvement on those horribly divisive leylandii walls-of-darkness that were becoming increasingly popular in the 1970s and 80s. So, much as I would love to be able to say 'we owe everything to the great Miss Jekyll', the truth is that we were influenced more fundamentally by local cottage gardens. A good cottage garden is a very personal creation; it is part of the house and its owner's identity. The two cannot be separated.

# 9

# The Front Garden

*Following the Wheel Ruts • Two New Spots on the Map •
Chaos Cottage • Fences and Frames • Formal Touches •
A Very Pleasant Place*

We had long been aware that we wanted the garden
outside the front door of our new home at Inley Drove
Farm to be our version of a cottage garden. And that's how it
would turn out, but, as with all aspects of the project, when
we actually came to do the work, nothing was quite as simple
or straightforward as it had seemed at first. Some of the basic
constraints were, to put it mildly, unusual. For example, the size
and shape of the Front Garden wasn't anything like what either
of us had imagined and it certainly bore scant resemblance to
those lovely cottage gardens at Guyhirn that I mentioned at the
end of the last chapter.

The unexpected proportions of the Front Garden were
dictated by two factors, over which we had little or no control.
The first was the course of the driveway that now skirts the
house and allows visitors a rapid impression of the front of the
house as they drive past on their way towards the farmyard,
where they can park and get out. When I laid out the driveway
in December 1992, the local planning authorities hadn't decided

precisely where the house was to be positioned, although they had accepted that we needed to start work on constructing the barn early in spring 1993. So I laid out the drive in a way that I hoped would fit with how the paddocks, orchard and garden would later be arranged. I knew a dead straight line from the entrance onto Inley Drove wouldn't work. There were far too many straight lines as it was: most roads and tracks in the area followed the arrangement of the straight-sided rectangular fields, which at the time we were starting to discover were probably medieval in age. The new driveway had to curve, if only to give the house some privacy. So I decided not to attempt to survey or measure it in, as I would have done had I been carrying out an excavation. This was a decision that was made simpler because the new land lacked any obvious fixed points other than the entrance onto Inley Drove and the four corners of the field. We did possess two or three 100-foot tapes, but the distances involved were far larger. The idea of a measured-in drive, essentially to nowhere, seemed idiotic. So I made a bold decision: I would employ one of my favourite survey tools, my small, lightweight and already quite old and battered Suzuki four-wheel drive.

In the 1970s and 80s, like most archaeologists, I looked after my excavations with the help of a long-wheelbase Land Rover. They were reliable, cheap to run and never got stuck. The trouble was, they were too heavy for the wet soils of the Fens in winter: tyres were narrower in those days and the wheels would sink down to make grooves a foot or more deep. You simply couldn't take them onto farmers' fields, which you had to do if you were carrying out a survey. So I got hold of a lightweight second-hand Suzuki four-wheel drive, fitted with wider tyres. You could squash in four passengers, together with a few tapes and a box of maps; any heavy equipment, such as buckets, spades and shovels, could go in the brand-new but

incredibly cheap two-wheeled open trailer. The combination of
Suzuki plus trailer proved a massive success on digs – and for
getting about our new field here at Inley Drove.

One day in the autumn of 1992, shortly after we had
officially taken possession of the new land, I drove the Suzuki
slowly through the gap in the hedge and out onto the field,
where the new grass the local farmer had recently sown for
us was just starting to grow. I had a rough idea of where we
wanted to site the house and barn – in the highest part of the
field, which would give a little added protection if the land were
to flood. But this location could hardly be described as a hill: it
was a rise of just a couple of feet. Driving the Suzuki across the
field was a decidedly eerie experience. The field was completely
featureless, so I had to imagine everything: the house, the barn,
the farmyard, the wood and the garden. I was moving at a slow
walking pace, and in a four-wheel drive. Soon I found I was
veering to the right and travelling parallel with Inley Drove.
By now the highest point of the field was clearly visible, but
I decided to keep going straight for a few more yards, before
turning quite sharply left towards it. A few yards further on,
I stopped and got out. This was where I imagined we would
place the farmyard, with the barn on the far side, directly over
the high point.

I drove in a couple of red-and-black ranging poles to mark
where I had got to and then went round to the back of the
Suzuki to inspect the wheel marks through the growing grass.
And then I almost had a heart attack: they weren't there! I had
driven so slowly and carefully that I seemed to have made no
impression. On closer inspection, however, I could see where
the soil had been compressed by the tyres. So I took a few pegs
and canes from the surveying box and carefully flagged the edge
of the tyre marks. Overnight it rained and the next morning I
was able to follow those pegs in the Suzuki, and this time I

left good, deep wheel ruts that you could easily spot from the edge of the field. If they weren't disturbed, they'd still be clearly visible in five years' time.

\*

In Britain, the Ordnance Survey (OS) – famous for its one-inch to a mile series – reigns supreme over the nation's mapping. Its professional surveyors established a national network of benchmarks that recorded the precise height of various walls, churches and bridges above sea level, or ordnance datum as the mapmakers liked to call it. Even in the Fens, most of these benchmarks have survived quite well, although a few of the walls on which the marks were chiselled have been whacked by passing tractors or have slipped into neighbouring dykes or drains. Everyone knew when a new house or farm had been surveyed and would therefore appear on the next edition of an OS map. I won't say it was a cause for celebration, but it did make a small statement that a farm, pub or shop had 'arrived'. Indeed, many important junctions in the Lincolnshire Fens were named for the pub that once stood there. Inley Drove, for example, enters New Fen Dyke at The Gate – an old Elgood's\* pub, which has long since closed, but was known as The Gate Hangs High. The eighteenth-century painted gate that formed the inn sign reads:

This Gate Hangs High
And Hinders None,
Drink Hearty Boys

And Travel On.

---

\* The long-established Wisbech brewery.

You can see the sign in the museum at Elgood's Brewery, where you can also buy some delightful traditional ales, brewed in an eighteenth-century brewery, using Georgian vats and equipment.[1] Incidentally, the road at the other (north) end of Inley Drove, Old Fen Dyke, joins the road from Sutton St James to Sutton St Edmund at The Sun crossroads. The Sun, sadly also closed, was another Elgood's house.

Methods of mapmaking were to change profoundly in the postwar years. Modern mapping was greatly influenced by the introduction of accurate aerial photographs, a process that began in the Great War and gathered pace in the 1920s and 30s. The arrival of the internet has further transformed the way we make our maps, with digital sources such as Google Earth – which uses aerial photography, satellite imagery and other geographic data – playing a major part.[2] The result of this continuous and increasingly rapid development is that digital maps are now very rapidly updated and many of these updates are being applied to printed maps too. Maps and aerial surveys have become an integral part of modern development projects. But this was not the situation back in the early 1990s when I drove the Suzuki along the course of what would shortly become our driveway, and when, in January 1993, sixteen lorry-loads of old bricks from the dumps around Peterborough's brickworks were carefully tipped, spread and then rolled onto those wheel ruts. In the run-up to Christmas 1992, seeking clarity about where precisely we could position the house and the barn, I paid a visit to the local planning office. Here, things were to take a curious but ultimately positive turn.

I had sketched the line of the wheel ruts onto a large-scale map of the field and I had also marked in where we would like to position the yard and the barn, at the end of the driveway. The planning officer wasn't the man I had seen before, but he seemed very friendly and helpful. So I showed him the map with my sketches and he nodded wisely, as if he had seen it before. This puzzled me, but I said nothing. What I wanted was his agreement and this seemed a good start. I began my explanation of the map by pointing out the line of the driveway. To my surprise, he cut in.

'Ah, yes,' he said slowly. 'I'm quite familiar with the area and that's an old lane or farm track, isn't it?'

I certainly wasn't going to reply that I'd made it a few days ago. So I mumbled something in agreement.

'Well, you can see it from the lane alongside the field. It shows up quite clearly. You'll see it when you visit.'

I was astonished he thought I'd never visited the site of our new home. But again, I kept my peace.

'So yes, I'd certainly make use of it. And maybe I'd move the barn back just a little. That yard looks a bit cramped. You're going to have problems turning round tractors and lorries in that small space.'

I altered the map and he nodded.

'Yes, that's much better,' he agreed. So far so good. It was time to grasp the nettle.

'And the house?' I enquired as innocently as I could.

He pointed along the west side of the driveway, areas that I was planning to use as quiet pasture for sheep and lambs for the next twenty-plus years.

'I'd put it somewhere along there.'

That wasn't what I wanted. Time for an innocent but necessary ruse:

'I know you're familiar with the area, but I wondered whether you'd been there during the morning or evening rush hour?' He was looking slightly surprised, so I continued: 'Lots of people living in the villages nearby commute to work in Spalding and Peterborough and many of them use Inley Drove as a shortcut. I believe they're called "rat runs" these days...'

The term was just coming into use. He nodded sympathetically. I had a growing feeling he was a regular commuter himself.

'Oh really? In that case, I'd put the house on the other side of the drive – and you can set it back a bit, if you want.'

Result!

*

So our new Lincolnshire house had an oddly shaped front garden from the outset and the way it started to develop was certainly more haphazard than planned. For several months it was a complete mess, with deep (and very haphazard!) wheel ruts, broken bricks, roof tiles and other builders' debris. I contemplated trying to tackle the mess by hand, but rapidly abandoned the idea after a couple of days' work. I shifted lots of rubble and turned over loads of sticky clay-like soil, but seemed to be making very little progress. It was very disheartening – and really tough, back-breaking work.

It was at about this time that we were having problems acquiring a supply of water or electricity at Flag Fen, because of its remoteness. I phoned a local hire company and ordered a mini-digger. I'd never driven one before, but I knew how to work a full-size one. The man who delivered it explained what the various levers and pedals did and after about an hour of jerky and erratic movement I started to get the hang of it. The digger was fitted with a three-foot-wide toothless bucket, which was far too broad for digging a cable trench. I was about to track across to the spot on the edge of the roadway where he had dropped off two or three buckets for me to choose from, and had started to loosen the round pegs that secured the broad bucket, when something made me pause. I found I was staring intently at the bucket I was meant to be removing. I was about to give myself a stern reminder to concentrate on what I was doing and not to let my mind get diverted by other thoughts. And then it came to me: that broad bucket fitted to a lightweight mini-digger was just what I needed to clear the rubble and level off the front garden at Inley Drove Farm. The area around the back of the house was a terrible mess too. Two or three days with a mini-digger and a wide-blade bucket would soon sort things out.

I climbed back into the machine, started the engine and extended the boom and dipper – the two steel limbs of the digger. I carefully opened the bucket and slowly drew it back towards me through the rough soil, dead weeds and eroded furrows of what had been a freshly ploughed field four months ago. Carefully, I worked my way across the field to the digger buckets by the side of the road. Then I looked back at what I had done. The result was spectacular: a wonderfully flat and level area of bare earth. Spread a few handfuls of grass seed and within a few months that bare soil would be lawn.

The mini-digger was delivered to Inley Drove Farm in late March 1995 and I think the work of levelling off and smoothing out the soil around the house took about four days to complete. Shortly after the digger had been collected by the hire company, I drove slowly up the new driveway and was astonished to see a clear set of footprints taking the shortest route possible, in both directions, between the edge of the drive and our front door. It was likely to have been the postman, who in those days was an eccentric elderly gentleman whose idea of heaven was a half-hour chat about the price of eggs. I guessed he hadn't spotted that the front door didn't have a letterbox because I found half a dozen letters lying on the floor of the porch around the side of the house. In one of our lengthy conversations, I had explained that we never locked that porch's outer door. Still, his frustrated earlier diversion towards the front door had kindly provided us with the exact route of the main path through the front garden.

I found those footprints strangely uplifting: at last things were starting to progress.

I have long been interested in the way the British landscape has evolved into what we have today. One of the lessons I have learnt is that there is no such thing as an unchanging feature in the landscape. Something as simple as the relationship between a village and its parish church can alter really quite rapidly. Take the neighbouring village of Parson Drove. Here, the more recent houses of the village have slowly migrated away from the original parish church, which was built in the thirteenth and fourteenth centuries. Today, the magnificent church of St John the Baptist sits just outside the village and is cared for by the Churches Conservation Trust. There is a newer, Victorian parish church closer to the centre of the village, whose focus is the green, pub, shop, garage and school, which are all centred on a junction between two fairly busy rural roads and a large, also nineteenth-century, main drainage dyke. It's a compact landscape that has evolved rapidly in just four centuries.

When you examine the process of long-term landscape change closely, it's difficult to single out simple underlying motives for the people making the changes. They sometimes happened because individuals felt the need to display their wealth and social importance. Powerful bishops and monastic figures could make major changes to the estates and buildings under their control in the Middle Ages. Changes could be brought about by the establishing and development of a business or as a result of some family event, such as a birth, marriage or death. And often people did things simply on a whim – for no apparent reason. Working out how these people, all driven by very different motives, altered the landscape around them is what gives landscape history its special appeal. It's also what makes it impossible to abandon or retire from. I find it difficult to concentrate on a book during a daytime train journey because I want to look out of the window at the landscape flashing by. This might help explain why I so often found myself examining my motives when making changes to the developing garden, especially in those more problematical, difficult areas, such as the front garden.

Those deep footmarks left by our garrulous postman clearly demonstrated that the topsoil around the house had lost most of its structure and resilience. We also knew that the paths there would be quite heavily used, so we decided to build them as formal structures that could be maintained and repaired. We went about this as if it was an archaeological excavation. First, we marked them out with string and pegs. These were going to be formal paths, so we avoided any unnecessary curves. They looked a bit straight and stark when completed, but we knew that, within a few seasons, growing plants would blur most of the straight lines. Some of the timber we used has subsequently distorted and bent, which has also added an element of informality. The paths today look remarkably natural.

The brick wall that runs from the house to the driveway is breached by an arched gateway at its centre, which links the Front Garden to the lower-lying Pond Garden to the north. The wall provides shelter from the north-easterly gales of winter for the Front Garden and has created a wonderful environment for growing sun-loving shrubs and climbing plants. We decided to keep things simple and laid out a short path linking the gate in the wall to the straight path to the front door. The paths of the Front Garden were sunk about six inches into the soil and were made from layers first of coarse then of finer gravel, kept in place by edging boards. They have proved very durable and easy to maintain.

There's a narrow veranda at the front of the house and we decided in effect to widen it by laying out a wider path-like area alongside it that joined the main front door path to a smaller, slightly less formal path that skirted around the house to the back-door porch. This path became established while the house was being built and we thought about removing it when work stopped; but it continued to be very useful, so we decided to keep it. Today, it links the back door to the herb garden and beyond that to the Front Garden. The original path around the house was made from builders' rubble, which we partially removed and replaced with edge boards and gravel to match the paths in the Front Garden. The shaping of the Front Garden has been far from straightforward. I have outlined the histories of its various paths because they illustrate how something as simple as the layout of a small set-piece garden can be about far more than design. Indeed, the shaping of features within gardens can sometimes echo the complexities of landscape history. I still find that rather surprising; but at the same time it is strangely satisfying.

The front garden from the front door during a snowy spell in late winter 2008. The lined paths still look rather stark, but the garden's formal arrangement can clearly be seen. In high summer this is obscured by the luxuriant growth of plants.

\*

Flowers, like paintings and photos, almost always look better when they are given an appropriate frame. I nearly said 'attractive', but in fact some of the best frames are actually quite simple. Our Front Garden features both. So we will start with the simplest frame of all: a wooden gate hurdle. Ours came from Central Wool Growers depot in Stamford where we used to take our wool after shearing, which just fifteen years ago happened in late June or early July. Today, most sheep have been shorn well before the end of May. I'm fairly certain this reflects the changing climate: in recent years, the weather has started getting very warm in mid-May, or even before that – at least six weeks earlier than used to be the norm. But to return to Stamford, we delivered the wool in six huge fifty-kilo (8-stone) woolsacks, which were pulled off the trailer by two extremely fit young assistants armed with viciously sharp bale hooks. The bags hit the lanoline-lubricated floor of the old wartime aircraft hangar and were rapidly dragged across to the area where the wool was stored before being inspected and graded. Somebody then signed our delivery note and we were free to enjoy the delights of one of Britain's most architecturally important market towns. The trouble is, we rarely ventured into town on these trips because we were only too aware that we both stank of sheep, wool and lanoline. So instead we headed round to the front of the old hangar and into the CWG country store, which still stocked all sorts of locally produced farm equipment and a good selection of hurdles, which included both the more traditional Midlands-style ash gate hurdles and woven wattle hurdles.

We had thought about constructing a fence between the driveway and our Front Garden, which we'd weave using our own hazel wattles, but the bushes we'd planted out in the wood were still barely three years old, and although they were growing fast, they were still two or three years too young to be cut. So we opted instead for the traditional Midland-style ash gate hurdles, which we knew from practical experience were very strong and stood up to the weather remarkably well. You can drive them a few inches into the ground, but this encourages wet rot at the point where the wood enters the soil. A hurdle fence of this sort might last five or six years. So we decided instead to fix them to some of the ordinary rot-treated fence posts that we had in heaps around the edge of the yard, as we were then actively fencing some of the paddocks on the farm. Twenty-seven years later, the gate hurdle fence is still in good condition, although the ash wood has recently become very brittle. I should add here that fences and other garden frames should be allowed to grow old, along with the plants they support. Age can give a structure individuality: repairs and supporting props can be made to look quite elegant and unusual if they are done imaginatively and in a way that enhances or respects the plants climbing over them. Most importantly, you can't always predict how things will become wobbly or unstable and the repairs will reflect this. Plants always adapt themselves to whatever is supporting them – and they nearly always improve it. Gardening is about acquiring patience: we must learn to resist the urge always to intervene; plants need the time to adapt and respond.

There is a good example of a slightly haphazard fix and repair at the narrow southern edge of the Front Garden. At this point, the driveway is only ten feet away from the south-west corner of the house. The distance was made even smaller when, shortly before we started work on the Front Garden, I used the mini-digger to cut a drainage ditch along the east side of the drive. Before the digging of what we would soon call 'the moat', the soil in the Front Garden was impossibly wet, as that poor postman discovered to his boots' cost. The moat, which drains into the pond, rapidly proved a great success and every autumn

I check that all the pipes beneath the various paths that cross it are clear and running freely.

We didn't start work on the new Front Garden's hurdle fence along the moat for several weeks after cutting the moat. We knew, from our experience making the stock-wire fences around the various paddocks at Inley Drove, that posts driven into wet ground go in much easier and faster, which of course is great if you're doing the job using a heavy hand-held post-driver, but then, as it dries, the land shrinks away from the post, which then becomes very unstable. Always drive fence posts into dry ground. So that's what we did – and it worked.

While we were waiting for the ground to dry out, the few bulbs that we had managed to plant out in the wood and in the very young Nut Walk were almost blown out of the ground – not by the usual cold winter north-easterly gales, but by a very cool and drying south-easterly, which went with rained-out Atlantic weather systems coming in from the west. I had never experienced such winds before, largely I suspect because I had never worked in such an exposed garden. Bluebell and daffodil leaves started to shrivel up, but they very rarely dried out: a wet morning's dew or a passing light shower would soon invigorate them. But we both knew only too well that young perennials or shrubs wouldn't last long in such conditions. We would have to provide protection – and fast.

The south-westerly winds were particularly fierce at the southern end of the Front Garden, where they were intensified by a sort of funnelling effect caused by the house's southern gable end, which seemed to scoop the gales round the corner into the Front Garden – rather like a wind-powered turbine. At this point, we were starting to plant a rose hedge along the far side of the driveway, both as a screen and a windbreak. We used a variety of the North American native rose *Rosa suffulta*, which I had seen growing by the side of country roads in upstate

New York. I particularly liked its upright habit (it grows almost six feet tall\*) and its cheerful pink flowers, which still look good after early autumn frosts or heavy spring showers. I didn't want the drive-side hedge to be too tall and dominating, because that would shade out the Front Garden and cast a certain amount of gloom on the darker days of winter. Five feet may not be very tall, but it would probably be enough to enhance the turbine-like funnelling winds that were battering the south of the house.

We reckoned that a short windproof barrier from the corner of the house straight across to the hurdle fence on the edge of the moat and driveway should be enough to cut the worst of the gales. I thought briefly about buying a largish pre-prepared fence panel, as the distance to be spanned was only six feet. The width of the bed along the base of the house wall was just under two feet. We could even get a pre-made gateway to bridge the path between the new short fence and the house. That all seemed very straightforward. So I added it to our To Do List – and did nothing about it. There was so much to do elsewhere. I think we were well into June 1995 when Mother Nature decided, as She does every so often, that summer hadn't arrived after all. To emphasise the point, She whipped up a south-westerly wind that did horrible damage. To hell with nice, neat, ready-made fence panels. I spent an hour or so rummaging through a stack of old sheets of exterior plywood, pallets and things-that-might-come-in-useful-one-day and came across a slightly damaged sheet of rustic-looking, red-dyed sheet fencing, with one of its sides missing. I combined this with a leftover gate hurdle from the Front Garden fence, knocked in a few posts at either end and tweaked it here and there with offcuts of stock wire.

---

\* In our garden, it grows to this height. US and UK websites suggest it should reach about half that.

And the result? I think it's rustic perfection, which we made even more perfect (if such a thing is possible) with a short stub of panel, which spanned the narrow bed at the base of the house wall. Then I carefully twisted and shaped two long hazel rods into an arch, which bridged the path that ran round the house. For the next three or four years, I scavenged the rods from a local copse; since then, I have cut them from bushes in our own wood. Hazel loses its flexibility after a few months, and although the archway might last for a couple of years, I find it best to replace it annually, just to be safe. When hazel does decide to break, it always seems to be when we are busily preparing the garden for a booked-in group of visitors. I find it's best if I replace the hazel in early spring, at the same time that we prune the hybrid musk rose 'Daybreak' that climbs through it. The rest of the screen is covered by the main bush of the rose and by a red-flowering jasmine (*Jasminum beesianum*).

*

The Front Garden has probably been tweaked and modified more than any other part of the garden. I think this might be because it doesn't have a very strong identity; it isn't part of a larger design and can absorb alterations without creating a sense of imbalance. Sometimes these changes can be quite large. Shortly after the turn of the century, my younger brother Felix very kindly gave us a beautiful wirework gazebo, with four arches and a central dome. We originally placed it in the small room-like garden just off the Rose Garden, which we still refer to as the Dome Garden.* But it didn't really work there: it was a bit too large and formal.

---

* See Chapter 13, page 268.

A view from the Dome along the light-duty footpath across the front garden, to the free-standing wirework arch. Note the wooden sheep hurdles which had been edging the Front Garden for almost twenty-five years when this picture was taken in April 2020.

Then eventually, sometime around 2010, we decided to move it to the Front Garden. Looking back on it, this was a very strange decision, as the Front Garden was far more informal. We positioned it directly above the junction between the original (postman's footprints) path to the front door and the short footpath leading to the gateway down to the pond.[3] As the dome possessed four arches, we decided to extend the path from the pond gateway across to the other side of the main path to the front door, but this time we made it far less formal, with no supporting side boards, and lightweight paving slabs rather than gravel. It's a path that is intended to be looked at, rather than walked down. Indeed, in midsummer it becomes difficult to use with any safety, as there are so many bees feeding on the roses, lupins, delphiniums and other perennials that closely border it. Moving the dome to the Front Garden proved a huge success and also gave us a wonderful opportunity for training hardy fuchsias and clematis. The new, more informal paving-slab path soon acquired its own wirework arch, which we carefully aligned on the dome and, beyond it, the arched brickwork gateway through the wall, down to the pond. Modern wirework is wonderful, but it can require reinforcement if it doesn't have a self-supporting structure like the four interconnected arches of the dome. The single wirework arch looked lovely when we erected it, but it swung about wildly in even a moderate breeze. I thought about wires and guy ropes, but I couldn't see how this could be done safely. So I decided on the simplest option and hammered in four stout timber supports, next to the arch uprights. This solved the problem. I was surprised, however, that such a flimsy structure could be sold in the first place: I would imagine it could be very dangerous in a storm. The manufacturers should have printed a prominent warning on the box: *Caution: this arch rocks about wildly in a light breeze.*

*

As a general rule, I prefer garden features that are practical rather than purely aesthetic. Maybe that's why our pond at Limetree Farm hadn't really worked: it was more about being ornamental than anything else. It didn't provide us with edible reeds or fish and I seemed to spend a lot of my time rather pointlessly cleaning the water and pulling out great strands of fibrous (filamentous) algae. I admit, it did look quite nice, especially when roses were reflected in its clear waters, but every time I looked at it, I would invariably spot something wrong: some liner exposed or plastic plant pots clearly visible among the underwater rocks.

At first, the Front Garden at Inley Drove was a good excuse for Maisie to plant the traditional roses that we both love, such as the hybrid musk 'Prosperity' and the very old variety *Rosa mundi* 'Fair Rosamund', whose delightful bicolour flowers are clearly visible from my office window as I write this. The main path to the front door is lined with the low-growing and freely flowering polyantha rose 'The Fairy'. The point where the Pond Garden wall joins the house features the *Rosa moyesii* seedling 'Geranium', whose vibrant single red flowers are extraordinary in that they aren't damaged by rain or bright sunshine. It also has excellent hips in the autumn.

But what, you may be asking, is the practical feature of the Front Garden? Does it provide cut flowers for the house, for example? The answer to that question is yes, sometimes. But only sometimes: most of the flowers we cut for the house are grown in rows in the Vegetable Garden. The main practical purpose of the Front Garden lies in its location. Thanks to the moat alongside the driveway, it is well drained. It is also shaded from the full heat of the late morning summer sun, which allows us to grow a large range of flowers, such as peonies, which rarely do very well out in the searing summer heat of the Long Border. On warm summer mornings, we open the front door to allow the cooler air into the house, bringing with it the delicious scents of Maisie's traditional roses and the occasional wren, bumble bee and red admiral butterfly. All are welcome. As the day warms up and the sun starts to shine more directly on the back of the house, we shut the front door and close the upstairs curtains, while opening the windows. In the afternoon, during the main heat of the day, we close all doors and windows. We had had Inley Drove Farmhouse built using a timber frame, and had also made sure the house was well insulated. These decisions were taken partly to save on winter fuel, but were also a response to the challenge of global warming. Our highly insulated roof and walls will really come into their own during Britain's increasingly hot summers. This arrangement means that, on hot summer afternoons, we can keep the house cool by drawing the curtains and closing all external doors and windows. Then, around six o'clock in the evening, we open everything up again. Nothing is quite so pleasant as a cool drink on the shady veranda in late summer and autumn. The scents from the Front Garden can be almost overpowering. And many a hamburger has been overcooked on the barbecue because I have become lost in the sights and smells of the garden, whose main purpose is (and was) what front gardens have always done best: to serve the house of which they are an intimate and pleasurable part. That garden has become one of our dearest friends.

# PART III

## *Inley Drove Farm:*
## *The Garden Grows*

# 10

# The Long Border

*Positioning the Border • The House and the Pergola Ends •*
*Planting the Long Border • Nurseries or Garden Centres? •*
*Of Weather and Weeding*

T he Long Border dominates the map of Inley Drove Garden.
Our visitors enjoy it hugely and its maintenance is a major
activity throughout the gardening year. I hate to think how many
long-handled shears I have worn out when tidying up its edges.
Maisie and I knew we wanted to have a substantial double
border when we moved out of Limetree Farm, because the long
single border there didn't really work. This was largely because
it lacked focus and we agreed that having a double border with
parallel beds would have been a much better layout. So it was
always going to happen, but strangely it hasn't dominated our
thinking about the new garden. One reason for this is that it
has been subject to constant change and modification, as we
will see with the feature we call 'the Squint', which cut through
a small part of the back of the Long Border – an alteration
that was successfully hidden behind an attractive golden shrub
(*Physocarpus opulifolius* 'Dart's Gold'), planted at the back of
the border.

In the late autumn of 1993, we laid out the boundaries of the
Vegetable Garden, having previously decided on the location of

the new barn. Following the sale of Limetree Farm in the spring of 1994, we decided on the precise location of the new farmhouse at Inley Drove. All three – house, barn and vegetable garden – were carefully aligned with each other and were positioned to sit comfortably within the landscape (such as it then was!). By this time, we had also laid out and planted the eight-acre outer wood, together with the Nut Walk and Orchard. With these principal elements of the new project firmly fixed, it became possible to plan the basic structure of the larger garden.

We were always aware that the hedge around the Vegetable Garden was going to be a very substantial feature, because winter winds at Inley Drove would inevitably be a big problem. At the same time, we knew that too much direct summer sunshine can also limit the number and variety of plants one could grow. So we decided to align the new double border directly beside the long side of the Vegetable Garden, thereby taking advantage of its tall hedge for summer shade. This looked quite impressive when we pegged it out on the ground, but we both felt that it would probably lack impact. We needed something more spectacular. So we decided to extend it past the barn and just beyond the proposed gable end of the house, which would provide a large area of deeper shade in the afternoon and evening. The border was now some 230 feet long. If nothing else, its length alone was impressive. Initially, we did have some doubts about it, but these soon vanished as we realised how the new border would link the veg garden, barn, yard and house together. It would also provide a focus for the surrounding garden and meadow. As time has passed, we have found that this strong central feature has enabled the individual components of the rest of the garden to develop identities and characters of their own.

\*

Gardens aren't just about viewing, strolling and admiring. They're also about daily life: walking through the rain to pick sprouts or sitting outside on the Poop Deck with a quick cup of tea. But even during the course of ordinary life the garden needs to have form and shape; it must continue to give pleasure, to make the day more pleasant. We knew that many of the beds and other features would be most frequently seen from the back of the house – whether we were indoors, on the Poop Deck or on the small lawn outside the kitchen, scullery and dining area. The Long Border just misses this area, clipping its northern edge. There were times when I worried that we had missed an opportunity to make a more direct connection between the Long Border and the back of the house, but the layout has turned out better than we could have imagined. Visitors to the house always want to go out and view the garden and, like many country people, we rarely use our front door. So people usually head out through either the back door (especially if it's a wet day and they need to put on boots), or through the French doors out onto the Poop Deck. They can then stroll through the paths and small beds between the house and the barn, but invariably they end up in the Long Border – where they generally stand, immobile for a moment, looking right and left. This surprise encounter with the garden's most spectacular feature always makes a big impression. When we were pegging out the Long Border, which we did exactly as if we were doing an archaeological trench, with wooden pegs, nails and vast quantities of string, it didn't seem to be *that* spectacular, despite its extraordinary length. Admittedly, at that time we were viewing it without tall hedges or any plants, but even so it seemed to us to lack impact. I can't remember where Maisie had read it – possibly in Christopher Lloyd, whose books she can practically recite by heart – but in the past, apparently, some garden designers increased the visual impact of avenues and borders by very slightly altering their shape. So in the autumn of 1994 we did a little bit of judicious string tweaking and edge digging, and now our border tapers very slightly from the house to the pergola end. The house end is about three feet wider than the pergola end. I thought that this effect would only be appreciated from the wider, house end, but over the years it has slowly dawned on me that it actually works in both directions. Indeed, in some respects the view from the pergola end is slightly better, partly because the massive pale oak seat at the house end stands out so sharply from the dark yew hedge behind it; but also because the scene is enhanced and enlivened by the golden-leaved dawn redwood (*Metasequoia glyptostroboides* 'Gold Rush') that stands in the Long Border facing the entrance into the garden from the front of the barn and has now grown into a substantial tree.

A view of the Long Border, taken from the first floor of the house in November 2006, a few months after the construction of the pergola covering the Poop Deck. The border edges have yet to be cut.
Note also the heavy reliance on self-seeded hardy annuals, such as the upright, dark-leaved red orach (*Atriplex hortensis*).

We moved into the Inley Drove house late in 1994 and during the first two months of 1995 I spent a lot of time sitting in a large Hy-Mac digger making good some of the deep ruts and pits left by the builders. The ground at the back of the house looked a bit like a First World War battlefield, with trenches dug for the phone line and water main, both of which were originally connected to our temporary kitchen in the barn. We extended them out to the house quite late in 1994. There were also several big heaps of soil that had been removed to make space for the large reinforced concrete slab on which the house is based and to provide foundations for the two brick walls. I used this soil to shape the small raised lawn directly outside the kitchen window, at the back of the house. I deliberately mixed in a certain amount of sand, gravel and general builders' rubble, and now this raised lawn and the beds around it have developed light and well-drained soils that (touch wood!) remain flood free, even in the wettest winters.

While I was working with the digger around the back of the house, I used its extended boom and dipper (I think someone told me it had once been owned by a drainage contractor) to slope the side of the pond nearest to the house. So now the lawn in the Pond Garden dips into the pond in a more natural-looking way. I knew this would encourage reed growth, but I don't mind that. We're in the Fens, after all, and the principal reed around the edge of the pond has been the native British yellow flag iris (*Iris pseudacorus*), which gave the site at Flag Fen its name.[1] Sadly, in the last ten years the pond has been invaded by the non-native New Zealand pigmyweed (*Crassula helmsii*), which has proved extremely difficult to control.[2] I have no idea how it found its way into the pond as I haven't bought any aquatic plants; but my main concern now is that it doesn't escape into the surrounding ditches and dykes.

In the early days at Inley Drove, two of the principal challenges that faced us were poor drainage and heavy soil – neither of which made the task of planting a large double border any more straightforward. By the summer of 1996, however, the Long Border was becoming better established. Planting of the hornbeam hedges was continuing and the earlier lengths, especially those around the Vegetable Garden and the parallel beds of the Long Border away from the house, were now about shoulder high and far more visible. The single row of black poplar tree cuttings that ran along the north side of the small meadow (which was used for grazing by our rams, or tups, and came to be known to this day as the Tup Field) had been planted a year ago and were now starting to grow again and with extraordinary vigour – as fast as healthy willow.* It was clear to both of us that the combination of trees and hedges would soon dominate the end of the Long Border, which urgently needed a focus. We briefly toyed with the idea of buying a statue of some sort, but they were either too small or too expensive and, besides, bathing modest maidens cast in concrete soon lose their appeal when splattered by the colourful droppings of birds that have been feeding on red rose hips or blackberries. It didn't take us long to decide that what we needed was a timber pergola bridging the end of the border. It could be planted with climbing roses and clematis that would contrast with the surrounding trees and hedges. It sounded ideal, but there were problems.

The pergola was built in the summer of 1996, following quite a wet winter and spring. We were well aware that this was the wettest end of the Long Border and the soil was very heavy, which explains why it dried so hard. Digging the holes for the

---

* I describe the planting of black poplar cuttings in Chapter 14, pages 289–95.

posts was very difficult in such hard ground, but I knew the pergola would be more stable if the posts were firm.* Eventually, we got it finished and the pergola now spans the entire width of the Long Border: to the right, a wide mown path leads into the Vegetable Garden. About five years ago, we had to erect an ironwork gateway to prevent muntjac deer from raiding the growing winter vegetables. To the left, the pergola leads into the Hay Meadow and the Serpentine Walk. Despite my efforts to fix the uprights solidly into the ground, successive winter floods and gales eventually caused it to lean to one side in a rather precarious fashion. So about ten years after its first construction I had to carry out a major rebuild, which relies quite heavily on sloping posts that reinforce the uprights along the pergola's non-border wall. Happily, this has been overgrown by a clipped hawthorn hedge, which effectively screens the buttress posts. I keep my fingers crossed every winter, but so far the reinforced pergola remains standing, proudly upright.

*

Before we could start doing any planting in the Long Border, we had to decide what sort of border it was going to be. In some respects, this was quite an easy decision, simply because of its scale and size. Purely herbaceous borders (i.e. ones containing no permanent plants such as roses and shrubs) have to be cleared out and thinned, in many cases annually, and then, of course, replanted. It's very labour-intensive work and we knew we couldn't spare the time. I do like a good herbaceous border, but they require reliably flood-free land and a good reserve collection of plants that will allow change from one year to the

---

* We saw in the previous chapter how important it is not to drive or sink posts into soft ground.

next. Rose beds are very attractive, but a large double border composed entirely of roses was a rather daunting prospect. So we decided, without much discussion, that we both wanted a mixed border filled with all sorts of garden plants, ranging from small trees down to bulbs.

For most of their length, the two parallel borders were backed by a tall hornbeam hedge, which had to be clipped at least once a year. This required a narrow access area running along the back of the border, which needed to be available in later July. It couldn't be blocked by large shrubs or small trees and prickly roses would require very careful positioning. We also recognised that borders require unifying themes if they are to be anything more than a mixed bed of various plants. We both agreed that the length and scale of the parallel borders would be what united them. Ideally, your experiences as you walked along the border would be ones of changing scale and contrast: the sight and scent of the plants in the bed alongside you, compared with the changing perspective of the double borders ahead of and behind you. None of this would be possible unless the planting of the borders was coherent. We knew that a random hit-or-miss approach wouldn't work.

The basic rule when planting the borders was quite simple: taller plants at the back, shorter ones at the front. This might seem obvious, if only to avoid concealment, but it's a rule that can so often be applied too rigidly; in such cases, the border planting can look 'stepped'. I like it when taller plants spread towards the front, giving a more 'coastal' effect of promontories that protect and partly conceal embayments in which more delicate low-growing plants can flourish. Sometimes, parts of the Long Border in high summer can remind me of the slightly mysterious north Cornish coast near King Arthur's Tintagel.*

---

* See my book *Paths to the Past*, Chapter 7 (Penguin Books, 2018).

The taller plants in the Long Border include the normal (green) Indian bean tree (*Catalpa bignonioides*), a more golden version, '*Aurea*', and one with distinctively speckled leaves (*Catalpa speciosa* 'Pulverenta'). Another, more purple, variety that also grows well in the Long Border is *Catalpa* x *erubescens*. Rather surprisingly, we have found that junipers grow well in our garden. Two tall, narrow trees of the North American *Juniperus scopulorum* 'Skyrocket', which we planted shortly after erecting the pergola, now frame – perhaps 'proclaim' would be a better word – the entrance into it from the Hay Meadow. Another, more spreading, juniper (*J. chinensis* 'Blaauw's Variety') grows well in the border and helps to provide much-needed shelter for birds and wildlife in winter. Other permanent taller shrubs include scented white-flowered philadelphus, and *Viburnum sargentii* 'Onondaga'. More recently, we have planted the golden leaf willow (*Salix udensis* 'Golden Sunshine') and *Physocarpus opulifolius* 'Dart's Gold', both of which thrive on the wetter ground at the centre of the border.

We wanted the Long Border to appear quite rural and informal, but we knew that this would also require a degree of advance planning. In gardening, informality has to be achieved: it doesn't just happen. So Maisie came up with a basic colour scheme that worked from the outset, twenty years ago, and has needed very little tweaking since. At the house end of the border, the plants have darker foliage and the flowers are all bright colours. Towards the centre, flowers are mostly darkish reds and pinks and the general impression is of warmth. By way of contrast, the two beds leading up to the pergola are cooler, with blues, yellows and pale colours predominating. While she was developing this colour scheme, Maisie was also reading Gertrude Jekyll, who suggested distances were enhanced or exaggerated when you looked from dark to light and from warming colours, such as reds, towards cooler hues, like blues and yellows. And it does work. In those rare summer moments when we have a chance to sit on the large seat in the afternoon shade of the house, the pergola can seem a mile away.

Herbaceous plants, including a variety of taller asters (mostly our own seedlings derived from the blue *Symphyotrichum laeve* 'Calliope' and the pink *Aster novae-angliae* 'Andenken an Alma Pötschke'), inhabit the back of the border. Lupins seed freely through the border and the trick is to weed out those hybrid plants that have started to acquire rather lacklustre, muddy-coloured flowers. Towards the front of the border we have many stands of hemerocallis, especially 'Hornby Castle', 'Marion Vaughan' and 'Golden Chimes'. These start to grow in mid-spring and flower in early summer at a time when the main border display is still gathering strength. More ground-cover-style plants include blue geranium seedlings of what we bought as 'Johnson's Blue', but almost certainly wasn't. But we don't mind: the varied seedlings are lovely and it seems to find its way everywhere. In those areas of the border where warm colours are needed, the tallish, bright-red flowers of the unimproved native Russian *Lychnis chalcedonica* can be very striking. It's also quite an easy plant to remove and control. Other plants that seed freely and are now an established part of the garden are *Alchemilla mollis*, which is shade tolerant and easy to control; it also blends with almost anything – very useful. The border also features the bright black-centred yellow-golden flowers of a rudbeckia with an impossibly long name (*R. fulgida* var. *sullivantii* 'Goldsturm'). This plant seeds quite freely also, but is easy to control and soon forms large clumps that grow about two to three feet high and look very well at the front and in the middle of the border.

Managing the Long Border has at times been quite difficult, especially in the early years before root systems and land drainage improved. Some plants that we initially admired because of their vigorous growth have subsequently proved to be invasive thugs that we still struggle to eliminate. Of these, it's the two very different irises, *sibirica* and *ochroleuca*, that I most regret not being able to grow any more. The tall *Molinia* grasses, which are supposed to prefer drier conditions, do very well with us and produce numerous seedlings, some of which have proved worth growing on, and replanting. The border is at its best from May to the first harder frosts of November. Recently, the season has started to creep into December, probably a symptom of climate change. As a general rule we try to avoid cutting back herbaceous plants in the autumn, because birds love to feed on their seedheads. I know this means we acquire numerous seedlings, but I don't care. I think feeding birds in such an intensively farmed landscape as the Fens matters very much more.

*

Over the years, we have gradually given up buying our plants from large garden centres. For the past two or three decades they have been aiming most of their products at the owners of smaller gardens and urban patios, where miniature or dwarf varieties are much in demand. But on a more positive note, the recent Covid pandemic has seen a very welcome rise in the popularity of gardening – especially vegetable growing – and this has encouraged the growth of smaller, locally based nurseries and plant shops. Local suppliers of this sort tend to be staffed by their owners, their friends and family, all of whom are interested in gardening – and are happy to talk. Increasingly these days, staff in some large garden centres are simply doing a job. And this takes me back to a wonderful gentleman I mentioned in Chapter 3, when discussing our first Fenland garden at Limetree Farm.

'The Major' was immensely knowledgeable, and the garden where he ran his business was wonderfully old-fashioned. The unrestored walled garden at Holkham Hall, close by the coast in north Norfolk, was full of atmosphere in the early 1980s when we first started visiting. The large Victorian glasshouses below the tall surrounding walls were pleasingly run down: the paintwork needed restoration and much of the woodwork was looking decidedly tired, but they still seemed sound; nothing was about to collapse. Certainly, The Major and his assistants seemed perfectly happy as they bustled about their daily business, carrying pots or dragging hosepipes with watering-can-style sprinkler heads. In the mid-1980s we often visited on Sundays, because Flag Fen had yet to open on weekends and we were still frantically digging during the week. The Major took Sunday mornings off (presumably to go to church) but he would open the walled garden promptly after lunch and I can well remember walking up to the greenhouse, where he kept his cash, a couple of reference books and various other useful bits and pieces.[3] On most of our Sunday visits, his wife would be standing at a bench, busily potting up new plants for sale. I should add that by the 1970s – and certainly by the 1980s – ceramic pots had been replaced by plastic. One day in the near future, I'm going to have to hire a large skip to get rid of our surplus plastic pots.

I don't want to sound like a moaning oldie, and I'm well aware that the internet has transformed many aspects of our lives, probably for the better. I do, however, regret the effect it has had on normal, everyday conversation. Today, you visit a garden centre and everyone is doing a Google search to find out more about the plants they have in their trolleys – and of course that's very sensible and perfectly reasonable; but it also means that nobody gets to speak to the assistants who work there, many of whom may be trained or trainee horticulturalists. I also find that information I read on Google doesn't stay with me for long, whereas when The Major told me something it somehow engraved itself permanently on my memory. Doubtless it was the anecdotes that came with the wisdom that made them so memorable. I forget what shrub it was that his dog used to love rubbing against, but it didn't live very long – the shrub, that is.

Over the years we must have bought hundreds of plants from The Major, many of which we took with us, either as plants or cuttings, to Inley Drove Farm. We generally made our expeditions to buy plants in spring and autumn, largely because in the 1980s and 90s the north Norfolk coast was growing in popularity and second homes – often very large ones – were being built everywhere. The process continued into the new century and towns like Burnham Market acquired local nicknames such as Chelsea-on-Sea, because the familiar mud-spattered Land Rovers were rapidly being outnumbered by large, shiny four-wheel drives (inevitably dubbed Chelsea Tractors). In summertime, pubs, restaurants and shops within about ten miles of the coast became very crowded and impossibly expensive. I can remember chatting to one of The Major's helpers who lived just outside the second-home zone, who said she avoided places like Burnham Market in July, August and September. It's so sad when locals feel excluded from the places where they have grown up.

The Major retired shortly after we moved into Inley Drove Farm, but by then we had discovered three more superb nurseries in north Norfolk, in or near the villages of North Creek, South Creek and West Acre. The last one is closest to King's Lynn, which I still consider a local town, despite it being in a different county. The nursery at West Acre sits within the park of a substantial country house, somewhat smaller than Holkham Hall (as indeed most houses are). The West Acre walled garden is well protected against strong sea breezes and has proved to be a superb spot for growing unusual shrubs and other garden plants.[4] The nursery was well established when we discovered it in the mid-1990s. The staff are very friendly and helpful and are all experienced gardeners. The timber shed where you take your purchases to be paid for contains a good selection of well-thumbed reference books.

We were both rather worried when in 2010 rumours began to circulate that the house and park at West Acre had been purchased by a new owner. I had visions of the park being sold off for lavish holiday homes and was hugely relieved when I discovered that the new owner was none other than the artist Antony Gormley. I've been a bit of a fan of Gormley's ever since we drove close by his famous Angel of the North sculpture. And about fifteen years ago, I was lucky enough to meet him in the flesh at a college reunion dinner in Cambridge.

I was sitting in the body of the dining hall with various old friends, when we all rose to our feet to welcome the Master and his guests to High Table. I love a good bit of medieval ritual and this was cracking. Then the friend who was standing on my left gave me a painful jab just below the ribs. He was much shorter than me, so I was relieved he had aimed high. He whispered something to the effect that the tall thin man beside the Master was the well-known artist Antony Gormley. After dinner, everyone adjourned to the Master's lodge and there I introduced myself to the great man. I told him that I wrote books and was currently researching *The Making of the British Landscape*. He was very interested in landscape history, so I promised to send him a copy. A year or so later, the hardback was published. The cover picture is a superb photo, taken at dawn, of the Angel of the North.

The new landowner at West Acre has been a great support to the plant nursery, which now boasts a café in one of the old garden buildings. Little has changed out in the park, except for the appearance of one or two reclining male figures fashioned from square blocks of metal.

*

The longer I spend in the garden, the more convinced I have become that what I am doing is a reflection of the lives we are all living. During my years of professional archaeology, I made many, many friends, but, sadly, a few enemies too. Now, I don't know whether this implies that I have divine powers, but I'm slowly realising that all the people who opposed me, and what I stood for, have gone. For ever. Of course I prefer the divine explanation, but it's also possible that these people opposed me because they belonged to an earlier generation that did and saw things rather differently – which leads me to think that if there is an Afterlife, it must be a very disputatious place: a bit like Parliament, only worse.

Human lives are relatively short: 'three score years and ten'* is our official allowance, but plants are rather different. Obviously, trees such as yew and oak can live for hundreds, even thousands, of years, but how old are those stinging nettles with the long yellow fibrous roots that creep along hedgerows and into gardens, where they have continued to thrive, despite being dug into and chopped by frustrated gardeners' spades over countless generations? My point is that gardening enemies can be far more persistent and harder to control than their equivalents in human life. I always found it simpler to ignore the people who said rude things about me. But how do you turn your back on a gardening enemy, such as perennial stinging nettles or – far, far worse – ground elder?

---

* The Bible: Psalm 90 verse 10.

We had ground elder (*Aegopodium podagraria*) in my parents' gardens in Hertfordshire, when I was starting my gardening life. In those days, weedkillers were relatively crude and were best confined to paths and areas where you wanted nothing whatsoever to grow. So I controlled the ground elder by persistent digging and the scrupulous removal of even the tiniest traces of root – and it sort of worked. Creeping stinging nettles (*Urtica dioica*) were a bit less persistent, but I never really got on top of the smaller-flowered meadow bindweed (*Convolvulus arvensis*); that defeated me completely: its roots penetrated far too deep. I suspect that one reason why the Hertfordshire gardens were so full of persistent weeds was the simple fact that they had been worked as gardens for hundreds of years, back to the Middle Ages. Our first Fenland house at Limetree Farm had some fairly persistent weeds, including creeping nettles and bindweed, but I suspect that quite a lot of this was due to the incompetence of the previous owners. I shall say no more.

Our experience of dealing with persistent weeds came in very useful when we were setting up the Lincolnshire garden, although it played no part in our selection of the place or its setting. That was entirely based on where we wanted to be and its landscape setting. We did know, however, that Inley Drove was an old road and the hedge that ran alongside it had been there for more than two centuries. The dyke that accompanied the hedge was lined with ivy and boasted a thriving population of brambles, bindweed and creeping stinging nettles, but – glory be! – no ground elder. I suspect this was because the surrounding fen would not have been drained in Roman times, when ground elder was introduced to Britain as a salad crop and medicinal herb.[5] As a general rule, ground elder doesn't occur in very rural settings.

Weeds and their movement from the boundary hedge into the main body of the garden played an important part in the way we arranged the garden at Inley Drove. However, it wasn't, as perhaps I've been suggesting up until now, a simple matter of 'them' and 'us': weeds aren't enemies to everyone. Those invasive creeping stinging nettles, for example, are an important source of food for wildlife, particularly for tortoiseshell and peacock butterflies.[6] The ivy that cloaked the bottom of the dyke alongside the hedge is often portrayed as an enemy of trees, although of course there is an old country saying that 'Ivy never killed a healthy tree'. We didn't want ivy to spread into the more formal beds and borders, but we were quite relaxed about it finding its way into the wood. Over the past two decades, it has spread into some of the less formal tree screens (especially the massive black poplars) and hedges around the paddocks. I can remember reading that ivy, which flowers in late autumn and winter, is an important source of nectar for many insects, but I had no idea that this would be something one could actually witness. On warmer, sunny days, even in the depths of winter, certain ivy-rich areas of the wood come alive with insects. I used to think this was solely due to the appearance of aconites and snowdrops, but flying insects are just as common in those ivy-carpeted areas, where snowdrops don't thrive.

We noticed another rather strange and completely unexpected relationship between a supposed 'weed' and man's best friend: dogs. I've long known that dogs sometimes eat grass if they require more roughage to digest their food, but our two dogs, Pen (the Labrador cross) and Baldwin (the Jack Russell) now appear to select twitch, or rhizomatous couch grass, a horribly invasive weed that gave us a great deal of trouble at Limetree Farm. Over the years, I've got quite good at differentiating twitch from other grasses; I am now absolutely convinced that Pen and Baldwin know where it grows and often stop their morning walks to enjoy a few tasty mouthfuls shortly before their breakfasts.

We carefully positioned the more formal parts of the garden in a way that allowed me to mow a quite wide barrier of lawn between them and any potential source of invasive weeds. A reasonably closely mown lawn is an effective barrier against most unwanted ground-spreading plants. But here I must sound another warning about the dangers of mowing too closely.

Indeed, if we British have an abiding horticultural sin, it has to be our inability to raise our mowers' blades. We're particularly good at cutting the grass carpet-short immediately before a hot, dry spell. To make matters worse, we scrupulously catch all the mowings and tip them into a foetid heap at the bottom of the garden. These untended heaps are extremely acidic and certainly don't count as compost, but they're out of sight and out of mind. For a few hours, the freshly shorn lawn looks neat and the mown stripes stand out boldly. But very soon the grass loses its freshness and starts to wilt. Those close-cut leaves can't retain any moisture and so the grass doesn't benefit from any morning or evening dew. Passing showers, which have been the lifeblood of our garden during the searingly hot summer of 2022, when I was still writing this book, have little or no effect on such closely cut grass, which rapidly turns brown and either dies or becomes dormant. The survival of a lawn in such circumstances will largely depend on the type of grass. We chose native species that are quite resilient, but few can survive a severe drought for more than four to six weeks. Consequently, I don't mow our lawns at all during hot, dry weather and I don't care if lawn weeds start to flower. You can always pull them out and some can be dealt a fatal cut with every gardener's secret friend – a sharp penknife. Now, I'm aware that my gardening records are a bit disorganised, but I do try to record rain accurately. Sadly, I don't note down when I've mown the lawn, which I normally do once a week, if it isn't too hot or dry. Today is the last day of July and I don't think the mower has been used since mid-June, when we last had an appreciable fall of rain. Our grass may not be looking very neat, but at least it's staying a good shade of green.

# 11

# The Birch Grove

*Chapters in a Book • Early Birches • The Glade • Birch Grove •*
*Open Days • The Serpentine Walk*

We are living through strange and often threatening times.
Just over a week ago (I am writing this in July 2022),
the Met Office warned us to expect a very warm spell over
the following weekend. A few days later they increased this to
an unprecedented Red Warning for Sunday and the following
two days (17–19 July). The Fens, including our garden, were
included within the area of the Red Warning. The Sunday and
Monday were very warm, but bearable. Then came Tuesday,
when the heat was quite unlike anything I had ever experienced.
We recorded 40 degrees Celsius, and at RAF Coningsby, not far
away at the edge of the Lincolnshire Fens, the all-time highest
British temperature record was reset at 40.3 degrees Celsius.
But life had to continue. I will never forget the strange, sticky
sound of tractor and trailer tyres driving down local lanes
where the tar had melted, as they carried home loads of freshly
harvested barley.

I have never been in any doubt about the reality and pressing
urgency of climate change. I first learnt about post-Ice Age
warming as a student in the mid-1960s, when new research

233

based on pollen analysis, seabed cores and other sources of reliable information was clearly demonstrating how natural conditions have been growing warmer. Of course, it wasn't a regular process: mini 'Ice Ages' occur from time to time, but the underlying steady rise in sea levels was very apparent, and certainly affected the way we understood and interpreted the Fenland sites we were excavating. However, it wasn't until later that I became aware of just how sharply the pace of climate change altered in the years leading up to 1850, when the effects of early industrialisation and the massive increase in the burning of coal could be measured in temperature and rainfall records.

Over the past two decades, I have been able to learn a great deal about post-industrial climate change and its effects on the landscape, but it is only in the past ten or so years that I have realised how rapidly the process is accelerating. If we take the ten highest recorded temperatures in England, seven of them occurred in the twenty-first century and, of these, five were post-2014.[1] Fiercely hot days cause serious problems in most domestic gardens, where any recent plantings are increasingly threatened by scorching and drying out. These plants have to be temporarily sheltered from sunlight (I use dark green horticultural mesh), but above all they must have their roots kept wet – and in hot summers, water is always in short supply.

One of the things Maisie and I have noticed when strolling through large, well-visited public gardens is the extent to which borders are planted with new flowers more than once a year. In winter, this usually involves dividing up and reducing perennials, but sometimes the head gardener will introduce an entirely new planting scheme, often based on a specially commissioned design. Currently, exotic grasses are frequently being used in so-called carpet bedding schemes, which require constant maintenance. In many public gardens, bulbs and smaller bedding plants are inserted in early spring and late summer to provide additional interest at the front of the border in summer and late autumn. This style of gardening, with regular replanting and digging, inevitably makes the soil more susceptible to drying out and, as a consequence, plants have to be watered far more frequently. In heavier soils, such as the clay-silts at Inley Drove, new plantings have to be watered daily during warm spells; even so, in the recent record heatwave I lost many newly planted-out brassica seedlings and I fear our early Brussels sprouts may not be ready until December. That's a grim thought: what is Britain coming to?

Initially, we decided on a minimal replanting strategy for all the borders at Inley Drove, simply because we couldn't spare the time ourselves and didn't have the money to hire in help. We thought we could freshen up the borders with a few bought-in bedding plants from local garden centres, but it didn't work: most of the new plants looked artificial; they simply didn't blend with the rest of the borders. Maisie still buys a few bedding plants to go in her pots, which have become something of a feature in the more formal parts of the garden. It's fine for displays in large pots to contrast with the beds around them. For some reason, the bright flowers in the pots enhance the slightly more restrained blooms in the border: the trick is to get the colours to blend or contrast (even to clash!), but in a sympathetic way. However, Maisie's colour sense is remarkable. Even more extraordinary, she can remember the precise colour of a flower, or a pot, when we are away from the garden. So when she buys a bedding plant, or even a pot of paint for me to retouch some ageing garden furniture, I can be absolutely confident that it won't clash with the plants and flowers surrounding it. You will be unsurprised to hear that she has *complete* control of all planting in the formal parts of the garden: the Long and the Short Borders, the Front Garden, the Pond Garden, the Rose Garden and the Dome Garden. I can make suggestions, but she doesn't have to accept them – although it's not often she rejects an idea entirely.

Neither of us is keen on the idea of borders or gardens that are 'purely' for roses, perennials, shrubs or bulbs. Our Rose Garden, for example, is largely given over to roses, but not entirely. We find that clematis go well with roses; so the rose beds are enhanced by four large iron obelisks, all of which carry clematis. I think they work very well, because sometimes rose gardens can seem rather flat and one-dimensional – the horticultural equivalent of a stamp collector's album. So we applied these principles of plant-mixing to the Long Border. For most of its length, the Long Border is backed either by a tall hornbeam hedge or the gable end of our house. In these areas, it didn't really matter how high shrubs grew, provided they didn't interfere with the annual hedge cutting in late July. The golden rule was not to plant thorn-covered roses so close to the hedge that they interfered with the hedge trimmer. In the decades when I did the hedge trimming, I had absolutely no compunction whatsoever about slicing away at roses whose thorns would otherwise threaten my eyes or the skin at the back of my neck (a particularly sensitive area, I find).

Every season when the summer heat starts to increase, we try to interfere less. This year (2022) has been incredibly hot and I haven't yet mown the lawn in July – and I doubt if I will in early August, to judge by the Met Office website predictions. An uncut, slightly shaggy-looking lawn absorbs night-time dew and short summer showers very much better than recently mown grass. We talk about 'blades' of grass, as if somehow they weren't alive, but it's easy to lose sight of the fact that lawn mowing is about slicing through living *leaves*. Box hedges can look terrible if they are trimmed on hot summer days. In effect, they've been mown, and being evergreen their leaves react very quickly, often curling up and dying.

In hot, dry weather, we even cut down on hoeing and heavy-duty weeding. We are also getting better at catching and storing rainwater, a task that was much easier in the recent past when we still had a large unused sheep dip, which must have held hundreds, even thousands, of gallons. When visiting young children started to take an interest in it, we decided, not without regret, to fill it with rubble. After a short period of reflection, we had both decided that an improvised lid didn't seem sufficient to protect a child's life, so it had to be filled in. We try to confine our watering of the garden to cloudy days, early mornings or late evenings, to get the maximum soil penetration and minimum evaporation. We try to avoid it, but can anyone honestly claim they have never watered a much-loved plant that's wilting in the sunshine?

*

Some gardens tell specific stories about certain times and places. A good example is the superb complex of eighteenth-century gardens at Stowe, in Buckinghamshire.[2] Gardens of this sort are best appreciated if you do some research in advance. Websites run by various tourist operators will tell you a certain amount, but they tend to be bland and oversimplified. Very often the garden's true history is more complex and in it, the personality – the humanity – of its creators can be seen in great detail.[3] As gardens go, Stowe is so complex and so vast (some 400 acres) that I tend to think of it as a landscape rather than a garden.[4] Gardens like Stowe and another favourite of ours, Wrest Park, not far away from us, in Bedfordshire, were intended to astonish and impress. They were also about conveying political and historical messages – and of course their grandeur proclaimed that of their rich or noble owners.

Our woods, paddocks, house, barn and garden occupy a 17-acre field. Even if you add in the three neighbouring medium-size fields we have bought over the past twenty years, our total land holding is just over 50 acres – a mere one-eighth the size of Stowe. Some of the views at Stowe extend beyond the home estate, where they 'borrow' (and slightly modify or 'improve') certain prominent features in the landscape. These views were intended to impress, and there is no doubt that they succeed. Our garden lacks the area to create such views, but we have been able to construct some smaller-scale – though still impactful – features that visitors seem to enjoy. The Long Border, which I described in the previous chapter, is particularly impressive in later June, when all the old-fashioned roses are in flower. The Hay Meadow is very different, but just as impressive, with its vast array of cowslips, snake's-head fritillaries and meadow buttercups. At certain times of the year I think it covers thirty acres, not merely three! But with the best will in the world, even these two features don't trumpet the garden owners' grandeur. Indeed, our garden doesn't have any message to proclaim; instead, it is about encouraging certain feelings and moods in us – its owners – and in our friends and visitors. This can best be seen in the many walks and paths that have come into existence over the years. Each one of these has developed a character and atmosphere of its own, which can be soothing, exciting, or even slightly humorous, depending on one's mood and, of course, the weather. (Too many gardens are designed to be seen only on warm, sunlit days in summer.) But let's start with a walk that emerged slowly from among a group of young and rapidly growing birch trees.

\*

For some reason, it seems to be much easier to lay out straight rather than curved or sinuous paths. This is certainly true when you're planning a layout on paper, but it isn't always the best way to do things. Since we moved away from the idea of grand designs and shifted to a strategy of gradual development on the ground, curved paths and beds seem to have appeared everywhere. The earliest of these paths, which we later named the Serpentine Walk, runs through a small group of birch trees, which we planted in a triangular space formed by the meadow and the east end of the Long Border. In the pollen record of post-Ice Age Britain, birches were among the first trees to grow in the vast empty spaces left behind by the retreating glaciers. Initially, the bare rocks, pebbles and sand were host to moss, ferns and grasses; soon they would be joined by flowering plants and shrubs; and then by birch trees. Eventually, and if conditions on the ground were right, this open scrubland would gradually be superseded by the ash, oak, elm and beech of our now familiar mixed oak woodland.

When you learn about a subject, such as prehistoric botany, it's strange the way it can colour or even override your practical knowledge and experience. My years as an archaeologist had so fixed in my mind the notion of birch trees as primary colonists of thin, dry and not very fertile land that I dismissed them when considering what trees to plant at Inley Drove. Then one day, probably in early 1996, I made one of my many visits to the superb Holme Fen Nature Reserve near Whittlesey, a few miles south of Peterborough. The water table at Holme Fen is only just below the surface and yet birches were thriving all around me in a luxuriant wood. If birches were thriving here, I pondered, surely they would do well at Inley Drove Farm?

There are very few species of border plants that haven't suffered from the introduction of gaudy garden varieties, some of them quite ugly, in my view. Roses are a prime example, the worst offenders having garish, scentless flowers and foliage that is highly susceptible to fungal diseases. With the possible exception of some flowering cherries, trees have generally fared rather better. Indeed, improved varieties of birch have retained the native tree's lofty elegance and subtle colours. Some of them, it must be said, have stridently white bark, but this looks fine in early winter when a grove of leafless birches can provide brightness and contrast at an otherwise dreary time of year. The recently planted winter gardens at Anglesey Abbey, near Cambridge, use birches very effectively.[5]

A view of the Serpentine Walk through the Birch Grove, taken a week before Christmas, 2010.

The roofed seat in the Round Garden in midsummer. The seat is covered by a variety of large-flowered clematis and scented roses.

The Glade Garden, looking towards the Serpentine Walk.
This picture was taken in early October 2015 and the leaves of the alder, *Alnus incana* 'Aurea', have started to turn gold.

The Glade Garden in early April 2018, a year of heavy rainfall and flooding. The Round Garden, in the background, was positioned on a substantial roddon and has escaped serious floods.

The Serpentine Walk in mid-winter, with freshly cut edges, around 2010. The entranceway through the roses, on the right, leads into the Round Garden.

A general view, taken from the roof of the house in July 2005, showing the extent of the Long Border. The Small Border can just be seen running parallel to it, bottom right.

A view of the Long Border in early July. The rose in the foreground is 'Geoff Hamilton'; behind it, to the left, is the tall shrub rose 'Bloomfield Abundance'.

A view along the Long Border in late October, looking towards the house end. *Metasequoia glyptostroboides* 'Gold Rush' is on the left, and *Euonymus europaeus* 'Red Cascade' in the foreground.

A view along the Small Border with a double spread of *Hemerocallis* 'Hornby Castle'. *Metasequoia glyptostroboides* 'Gold Rush' can be seen to the right of the house.

In late autumn the asters come into full flower in the Long Border. *Symphyotrichum lateriflorum* 'Black Prince' has a compact clump-forming habit that suits the edges of borders.

The yew hedge and oak seat at the north-west end of the Long Border.

Part of the Rose Garden in late May. Note the pink rose 'Cornelia' behind the box hedge, which is already showing some signs of heat stress.

A sunset view of pollarded red-barked willow *Salix alba,* var. 'Kermesina', near the pond.

A springtime view down Chicken Lane towards the wood and the Black Poplar Walk. Note the profusion of white and pink blossom, mostly from sloes (blackthorn), bullaces, wild plums and damsons.

A view along the Black Poplar Walk in early November, when most of the poplar leaves had fallen. The poplars are on the right.

The Serpentine Walk and the Birch Grove lie immediately behind the tall hornbeam hedge that protects the northern edge of the Long Border from the biting north-easterly winds of winter. This was one of the earliest lengths of hornbeam hedge and was planted in the winter of 1995/6. This part of the garden is far away from the old hawthorn hedge that protects the northern edge of the garden and was subjected to truly fearsome winds. Early in the spring of 1994, the windproofing that I had put in place to protect the Vegetable Garden was blown out of the ground by a severe gale. The newly planted hornbeam hedge along the north side of the border ran parallel and quite close to it and was intended to provide yet another line of defence. Seasonal gales are a potent enemy, and they will find a weak point in anything less than a robust and multilayered defence.

Although we knew that the two parallel hornbeam hedges we had just planted along the north sides of the Long Border and the Vegetable Garden would provide protection from the routine north-easterly winds, they would not protect against the very fiercest gales. To do that, we required what was in effect a miniature wood, but one with a thicker than normal understorey that would lift the wind and allow the trees to raise it even higher, above the Long Border, the Vegetable Garden and the various borders and beds behind the house. The young hornbeam hedges were having trouble getting established; strong saplings that had put their roots down were surviving, but we were losing smaller plants in long spells of dry, breezy winter weather. It was quite a challenge: we needed protection to establish the protection – if you see what I mean.

At the time we did this work, I was serving on an English Heritage committee that was looking into the protection of surviving Second World War invasion defences. These were first built in 1940 and were strengthened in 1941 with several layers of defences-in-depth.[6] The idea was to absorb the force of an attack. At Inley Drove, it was clear that we needed to find fast-growing, wind-resistant trees or shrubs to plant in the more exposed places along the southern edge of the meadow. And what could be better for that purpose than that well-known fast-growing primary colonist tree I had seen at Holme Fen?

In the winter of 1997, we were still planting lengths of the many hornbeam hedges that have become an important unifying feature of the garden at Inley Drove Farm. The nursery that had supplied us with three-year-old bare-rooted hornbeams also offered plants of the native silver birch, *Betula pendula*; so we bought three of them. I admit I was rather sceptical about these bare-rooted birch trees. But I shouldn't have been: once planted – and assiduously kept wet – they started to grow lustily. By the end of the first season, they had doubled in size.

*

At its centre, the Long Border passed through a damp and slightly lower-lying part of the field that used to flood regularly after heavier spells of winter rain. It was an area that never seemed to dry out properly. During the winter of 1994, I discovered that in the 1960s the entire field had been underlaid by a series of parallel land drains, about twenty feet apart. These were made from thousands of foot-long four-inch fired-clay pipes, placed in a trench about three feet below the surface. No attempt had been made to cover the gaps between each short length of pipe, which lay in the ground edge to edge with its neighbours in the line. Of course, it was this slight gap that allowed water to seep into the drain. These pipes were often buried in a layer of sand and gravel, which also encouraged water to seep into the drain from the surrounding soil. In the winter of 1999, a contractor jet-cleaned our land drains, working from their outfalls in the side of the dyke that runs along the eastern side of our field. Once unblocked, they worked very much better and have been flowing freely ever since. Happily, this dyke is maintained open and in good condition by the local Drainage Board.

Clearing out the land drains made a huge difference, but even so, the damp patch at the centre of the Long Border remained stubbornly persistent. So we decided to plant three alders there. We knew from many visits to places like Holme Fen that alders thrived in the wet, and we were aware from examples we had planted at Flag Fen that their shallow root systems effectively dried out the soil. We had intended to plant the native alder (*Alnus glutinosa*), but in one of her many catalogues Maisie had come across the golden alder, *Alnus incana* 'Aurea', which the catalogue recommended as being suitable for 'difficult sites'. It sounded perfect. We planted three trees in the dampest area and they were soon thriving. The golden colour of the leaves remains consistent throughout the summer months and intensifies in autumn. The bark of twigs and young branches is red, as are the catkins in spring. Our trees are now over twenty years old and are almost fully grown. I would guess they are less than half the height and size of the native alder, which has turned out to be perfect for their position: you can appreciate them in their entirety and they don't throw too much shade over an area where two varieties of geraniums provide different episodes of ground cover in spring and early summer.

The first to flower is *Geranium pyrenaicum* 'Bill Wallis',[7] which flowers in April and May with lovely pinky-purple flowers.* The second floral carpet is *Geranium palustre*, which flowers (with us) in June and July. Both geraniums seed quite freely, but don't appear to be invasive. They are far less aggressive than the much larger-flowered *Geranium psilostemon*, which has spread through most of the borders and has to be removed equally aggressively to prevent it taking over the entire garden. It's never a task I enjoy, as its rich purple-pink flowers are particularly attractive and don't seem to fade in even the hottest summer sunshine.

The garden around the three golden alders quite quickly developed its own distinctive woodland-like character. We have tried to enhance this with careful plantings of the smaller-flowered species *Hemerocallis* and daffodils such as *Narcissus* 'Hawera' and *Narcissus jonquilla*. The latter is a native of Spain and Portugal, and is otherwise known as the jonquil or rush daffodil – a name that might explain why it thrives in such a damp spot.

\*

Over the years, The Glade has developed its own distinctive character, but remains an integral part of the informal woodland garden that has developed on either side of the Serpentine Walk that now winds its way through the many trees of the Birch Grove. Rather to my surprise, the three birch trees we had planted as part of an effort to fend off the relentless winter winds that were threatening the Long Border and the Vegetable Garden – and even the hedges we had planted to protect them – did indeed rise to the challenge. They didn't grow narrow

---

* We cannot be certain that the 'Bill Wallis' we bought is precisely the same as the standard variety, which I gather can be quite variable. Ours flower a bit earlier than the standard variety – as described in books and on the internet.

A view along the birch-lined Serpentine Walk in late May, 2009.

and thin, as we had feared, but instead bushed out, while still growing vigorously upwards.

After we had planted those first three native British birches, we went in search of more exotic varieties, including the elegantly drooping *Betula pendula* 'Dalecarlica', and a personal favourite, the purple-leaved *Betula pendula* 'Purpurea', which looks magnificent from the paths within the Hay Meadow when the dark pink flowers of the old cultivated rose *Rosa* 'Morlettii' are in bloom around its trunk.* You can smell its fragrance in the air, or 'on the wind'. Close to, the flowers don't seem quite so fragrant. Birch trees and roses grow and look well together. Next to the purple birch, on the edge of the meadow, the small dark-red flowers of *Rosa moyesii* can be seen high among the branches of another birch. Every year, the sight of those red roses flowering so high up is a source of surprise and

* Introduced in 1883.

amazement. I love to point them out to visitors, who invariably gasp in astonishment. One year, a lady's hat fell off when she spotted them.

The path that wends its way through the birch trees now looks sinuous and very natural, but it came into existence by accident. We needed access around the slightly boggy ground of what became The Glade while we were planting a fringe of tough wind-resistant shrubs along the edges of the Birch Grove. These included *Rosa rugosa* and various dogwoods (*Cornus* sp.). We found *Rosa rugosa* particularly useful, as it was so tough and wind-resistant, yet its wrinkled leaves (hence the name *rugosa*) and large flowers always looked fresh and healthy. It grows wild in East Asia, where it is often found near sandy beaches – hence its tolerance of gales.[8]

*

As the garden grew, Maisie and I wondered if the time might be right to risk opening it to wider view. So on Sunday 22 June 1997, we opened Inley Drove Farm for the National Garden Scheme (NGS). I thought the people at NGS would probably suggest that we should delay any opening for a few years, but after a visit and a good long discussion they decided to accept our offer, as there were then very few gardens opening for the NGS in southern Lincolnshire. In those days the garden still resembled an open field in the winter, but the trees were now large enough to provide screens when the leaves were on them. So although the winter winds were still bad, in summertime the belt of woodland along the northern boundary was starting to provide a degree of shelter. The hedges around the Vegetable Garden were just starting their fifth year of growth, so they were almost as tall as a person. Many of the other hedges we had planted were only two or three years old, but in summertime you could clearly see they were marking out boundaries and borders. So visitors could get some idea of the garden's overall form and layout, even though many of its features were still in their infancy. But there were problems, too.

When you visit a well-known public garden, you will probably find that the lawns, paths and borders have been edged with specially made iron or steel strips. Older or less visited gardens often use wood for edging, as we would – slightly clumsily, perhaps – in the Front Garden at Inley Drove. But the owners of most private gardens don't bother with border edging at all; like us, they simply cut the edges of lawns and paths. (I use a sharp, crescent-shaped spade to recut lawn edges every other year or so.) The trouble was, at this early stage in the life of our garden, the hard work of setting up and laying out the new garden hadn't yet allowed us the time to dig out edges at all, let alone to cut them neatly. So most of them were marked out with canes and string. The lawns were kept back by hoeing or the use of a small Rotavator, set very shallow, or even (dare I say it?) by the occasional use of weedkiller. It wasn't perfect, I know, but the borders and paths stood out clearly and the garden looked tidy and organised.

Certain plants, such as lupins and a few roses, were now well established and helped provide a colourful display. To our relief, the opening seemed to have gone very well. People said nice things about Maisie's cakes. One of the great benefits of opening the garden to visitors was getting to meet other keen gardeners in the area, all of whom had seen our piece in the NGS's famous annual publication, the 'Yellow Book'.* Over the next few years we would visit many of their gardens and what we learnt from them would have a significant influence on the way that Inley Drove developed. It was instructive

---

* I discuss the NGS further in Chapter 15 (page 309).

to see how other people dealt with the special problems of Fenland gardening. And we were to encounter one of these the following year.

In April and July 1998 there was very heavy rainfall, leading to widespread flooding. Suddenly, all structure vanished and the garden became a soggy mess. The lawns continued to grow and of course weeds were the first plants to recover. I still don't know how we managed to repair the damage for the open day in June, but somehow we did. And it was a huge success. Even so, the preparations were a cause of considerable stress: the last thing anyone wanted was for our visitors to be welcomed by a sea of mud and expiring plants.

There was more heavy rain in July, but by then we had committed to reopening on 21 June 1999. Despite the rain, our second opening in 1998 had gone surprisingly well; doubtless we were helped by the rodding-out of the land drains a few months earlier. We agreed to two more open days, both in late June 1999 and 2000 (when Maisie's large collection of historic roses would be in flower). Sadly, it poured with rain for the second of these, in 2000. So we decided not to open the garden for a few years to see how we could improve drainage. I'm in no doubt now that it was a sensible decision, although it felt very much like a defeat at the time.

*

In the Birch Grove, what had started life as an effort to fight the gales was rapidly developing a character and identity of its own. As the birches continued to be planted from 1997 to 2001, the now rather sinuous path through the young trees acquired the name 'the Serpentine Walk'. At first, this was a bit of a joke between Maisie and myself, a not very subtle parody of the pompous-sounding names one comes across in the gardens of stately homes, but eventually it stuck. So now we have to live with it. The joke is on us. At the midpoint of the serpentine curve, we laid out a small round garden, which we planted with old, highly scented roses. Some of these have done quite well, but others haven't thrived in the increasingly deep shade cast by the growing birch trees. Facing the entrance into the circle is an elegant covered wooden seat, where we often sit on warm summer afternoons, sipping tea to the rustle of birch leaves that are now high above our heads.

The path into The Glade is on the other side of the Serpentine Walk, directly opposite the entrance to the Round Garden. Originally, this area was home to some large bushes of the white hedging *Rosa rugosa* 'Alba', which you can still buy very cheaply from hedging nurseries. It's a good, reliable, wind-resistant plant with large and attractive scented white flowers. In more formal parts of the garden, we tend to favour the double flowered and even more highly scented variety *Rosa rugosa* 'Blanc Double de Coubert'. As time passed, The Glade ceased to be windy and, as we have seen, wet-loving geraniums and other plants started to thrive there. However, these changing conditions didn't suit the white *rugosa* roses, so we removed them. We realised just how much moisture the *rugosa* had been removing from the soil when seedling geraniums rapidly colonised the ground as soon as they were gone. Today, The Glade has a very special and rather gentle woodland atmosphere.

The very wet years of the transition from the twentieth to the twenty-first century led to us planting even more hornbeam hedges, around the Dome and Rose Gardens. These hedges have the most extraordinary root systems, which drain the soil but don't inhibit the growth of other plants. In this they differ from birch trees, whose shallow, often surface roots can even discourage cyclamen, which can normally grow anywhere parched, dry and shady. The entrance from the meadow into the Dome Garden is crossed by the Serpentine Walk, which at that point becomes the Long Walk. This is quite an important junction and is marked by a high arched entranceway through the hornbeam hedge. Unfortunately, you can't really see this from the main path through the meadow and into the wood beyond, so we drew attention to it by planting a pair of *Betula utilis* var. *jacquemontii*, West Himalayan birches with particularly bright white bark, which peels off very easily. I'm not a huge fan of very tidy gardens, but I do detest it when litter is dropped. Unfortunately, I am always mistaking the thin white bark of *Betula utilis* for litter, especially when it gets a bit wet and muddy. These two white-bark birches have grown very well together and now form a prominent feature.

Up until the end of our first five years of NGS open days, we confined alders and birches to the Birch Grove and the Serpentine Walk. Very shortly afterwards, in the late summer of 2001, we were having a holiday in the Scottish Borders, where there are some absolutely superb gardens, including the Botanic Garden at Dawyck, 26 miles south of Edinburgh.[9] Their fine collection of trees embraces many rare and unusual species, including some massive, centuries-old evergreens. However, we were both struck by a variant of a wet-loving tree that we knew would thrive at Inley Drove Farm. This is the cut-leaf alder (*Alnus glutinosa* 'Laciniata'),[10] a version of the native common alder that was first identified in France around 1800. On our return home we came across a less rare but equally striking wet-loving birch tree that occurs quite frequently in the United States, the river birch, *Betula nigra*. As its name suggests, it thrives in wet ground. We were particularly struck by the tree's pale brown papery bark, which doesn't lie flat on the trunk and always looks interesting. We planted the two unusual wet-loving trees next to each other at the pond end of the Rose Garden. They look splendid together and always remind me of the gloriously diverse, rain-fed landscapes of the Scottish Borders.

We reopened the garden, this time for the whole weekend, on 17/18 September 2016. Six seasons later, it is quite clear to me that people's attitudes to gardens are changing subtly. Visitors certainly enjoyed and admired the Long Border and other structured features of the garden, but they found the less formal parts very appealing too. More than once I recall visitors describing the Birch Grove and the Serpentine Walk as 'tranquil' or 'peaceful'.

We find this part of the garden a source of great comfort too, but for a more melancholy reason. In the late 1990s, we worked closely with Dr Dave Coombs, a leading expert on the Bronze Age, who was studying the spears, daggers and other metalwork our excavations had uncovered at Flag Fen. Many of his students from Manchester University came to Flag Fen to gain experience of wetland archaeology. We used to stay with Dave and his wife, Jenny, at their Manchester home, and over the years we became the closest of friends. Tragically, Jenny then developed breast cancer, which ended her life all too rapidly. Somehow, Dave kept working and delivered his superb report on the metalwork, which English Heritage published in 2001, in the first comprehensive volume on Flag Fen.[11] A few years after Jenny passed away, Dave found he had cancer too, and soon he had joined her. Dave and Jenny's house in Manchester was in a charming tree-lined road, named Birch Grove.

# 12

# Paths for Play and Reflection

*The Stamford Gap* • *A Little Surprise* • *The Need for Squints* •
*Another Little Surprise*

Ever since I was a child, I have delighted in coming across secret places. In an ideal world I would love to have built a Gothick temple, replete with secret chambers and dripping water, perhaps not quite on the scale of the superb Crystal Grotto at Painshill, Surrey, but large enough to impress.[1] One disadvantage of a Fenland garden is that features sunk more than a few inches below the ground surface rapidly fill with water in winter. This means that our built garden features have to be above ground and less in your face; sometimes beautifully restored eighteenth-century temples can seem just a little bit too Georgian. I also like garden features that cause surprise and then curiosity and finally, of course, delight. Two features in our garden are worth mentioning because they both appeal to children. Both are based on Maisie's ideas, which often have a humorous edge to them. I love it when a youngster discovers one of them and then looks everywhere for his or her parents, who are then dragged back to see what he or she has discovered. I'm pleased to say that the parents' delight is genuine when it is revealed to them by their excited child, who looks so proud and cannot conceal the broadest of smiles.

The first of these two constructed surprises is at the house end of the Long Border. The terminal feature here is a large oak seat (big enough to seat four people), which is surrounded on three sides by a tall yew hedge, surmounted by a carefully clipped topiary acorn on a pedestal. Everything about this feature is intended to draw your gaze to the centre; towards the seat and the acorn above it. Many visitors, young and old, reach this point and then naturally sit down. The border stretches ahead of them and just a few paces away from them are paths and stretches of grass leading off in different directions. But to head back down the Long Border would be to retrace their steps, which would be an offence against our principle of No Turning Back. Now, I concede we might have allowed ourselves this small infringement of a non-binding self-imposed principle, but that surrounding yew hedge gave Maisie her clever idea.

During our early years at Inley Drove, in the late 1990s, we were invited to lunch with an elderly gentleman who lived in a large old house on the edge of the Fens, just east of Stamford. In many ways, it was like stepping into a pre-war novel. Our host was wonderfully old-fashioned and eccentric. I particularly remember his extravagant tie-pin and well-starched high collar. The house was in a state of cluttered decline, but it still managed to retain a certain rural elegance. I particularly remember a massive blue-flowered wisteria that covered the rear of the house and whose flowers were clearly visible through the ground-floor windows. Outside in the garden we could see an elderly gardener working beside a wooden wheelbarrow – at least, that's what I remember, although it seems scarcely credible that in the late 1990s even eccentric elderly country gents would still have used such things. After lunch we decided to take a stroll in the garden, or what was left of it, because huge areas had been allowed to revert to elderberry/hawthorn scrub. We left the house through the French doors at the centre of the back of the house and paused for a moment while our host put his coffee cup on a rather flimsy-looking wooden table, which looked in urgent need of a coat of wood preservative. I looked around me.

All things considered, the maintained parts of the garden were still in remarkably good condition and the gardener who kept it so neat was still out there, hard at work. One particularly prominent and well-maintained feature was a tall yew hedge, which bounded the garden along one side. You could see the carefully graded tiles of an old Collyweston limestone roof beyond the hedge.* As if reading my mind, our host told us that this was where the gardener – I can't remember his name, but let's call him Old Jake – lived, or rather resided; I suspect the house belonged to our host's estate, or what little was left of it. Then something rather remarkable happened.

Old Jake had been tending the border that edged the far side of the large lawn behind the house. He looked at his watch, I glanced at mine: it was about four in the afternoon. He then placed all his tools in the barrow. As he did this, he spotted us standing by the house. He raised his hat and our host gave him a slow but gracious nod. Under his breath, he muttered to us: 'Four o'clock sharp. Jake'll be off for his tea.' Jake was too punctilious a gardener to leave his tools and barrow cluttering up his master's lawn, so he started pushing them towards his house. I glanced at Maisie and she at me. We were rather puzzled: he seemed to be aiming the barrow straight at a solid wall of yew hedge. The next thing we knew was that he had

---

* Collyweston slates are quarried near the village of Collyweston in Northamptonshire, close to the border with Lincolnshire (and not far from Stamford).

passed through it – as if by magic. Neither he nor his barrow seemed to have touched the hedge. I glanced at Maisie, who was frowning; she was obviously puzzled too. I was about to ask our host what had happened when the phone rang and he hastened indoors to answer it.

We could hear him talking quite animatedly and we didn't want to overhear something that might later prove awkward, so we headed across the lawn, towards the spot where Jake had seemed to vanish through the hedge. When we got there, we found a narrowish, wheelbarrow-wide gap in the hedge, which had been cunningly concealed from the main house by being set within a gently reversed curve. There were no sharp corners. It had clearly been carefully planned and executed. And it certainly worked. Maisie produced a pocket tape measure and made a rapid sketch in the back of her diary. Doubtless now we'd have taken photos on our phones.

*

A week or so after the incident of Jake and the disappearing wheelbarrow, I found myself trimming the young yew hedge surrounding the large seat at the end of the Long Border. Until very recently, I used to do all the hedge cutting myself. You might suppose that this fairly monumental task (there are well over a hundred yards of hedges at Inley Drove Farm) was far more demanding once the hedges had all grown up, but in actual fact it took just as long to trim them when they were only two or three feet high. The short hedges were more seriously damaged by a misplaced cut and the amount of bending was very hard on the back. At least when you're cutting an eight-foot-tall hedge, you get to stretch upwards. Working with a powered trimmer can be hard too, especially when the power unit (a two-stroke petrol engine) was quite heavy. Today, with

PATHS FOR PLAY AND REFLECTION

battery technology improving so fast, electric-powered hedge trimmers are very much lighter and easier to use and you don't have the constant worry about cutting through the power cable – something that somehow I've managed to avoid.

Earlier that year, we had been making efforts to tidy up the small garden that lay between the brick wall at the northern end of the Front Garden and the pond. This garden, which we have called the Pond Garden, doesn't get a lot of light and has proved quite difficult to plant. In the late 1990s we hadn't yet planted the stepped golden *Lonicera* hedge that is now such a commanding feature of this area.* So the back or north side of the young yew hedge was still subjected to cold north-easterly winds in winter. I laid my clippers down and Maisie handed me one of two insulated plastic mugs of tea, which we used a lot in those days when we didn't feel the need to sit down. So we stood and sipped. She mentioned our trip to Stamford and the disappearing gardener. Then she said she'd been thinking about it. For a moment, I was slightly horrified: she wasn't contemplating a wheelbarrow-sized gap in the yew hedge I had just been clipping so carefully, was she? I was about to mention north-easterly gales. But Maisie had already thought about them. 'I wondered whether it might be fun if we put a narrow gap, not in the back of the hedge, but on the short side, nearest the house. It would be completely out of the wind.'

I could see what she was getting at, but a slot through the hedge at that point would take you into a shady flower bed. Maisie had already thought of that: 'Yes, but a few carefully placed stepping stones are all you need to avoid the bulbs and take you across to the path from the gate through the Front Garden wall – and then down to the pond. I know it's a bit unusual, but I don't see why it shouldn't work. I think it's certainly worth a try.'

---

* *Lonicera nitida* 'Baggesen's Gold'.

257

The concealed narrow gap through the yew hedge around the large
seat at the north-west end of the Long Border.

I looked across at the short length of hedge she had mentioned and yes, I did think it was possible. It would only involve digging up two yew plants, and a little bit of careful clipping could effectively hide the gap from anyone standing in the Long Border. Then all we had to do was buy half a dozen paving stones.

The large yew hedge around the oak seat at the end of the Long Border had been mature for many years when I got the chance to witness just how successful the hidden gap had become. Heaven knows we all needed cheering up in that ghastly first Covid summer of 2020. Eventually, the restrictions on socialising and meeting people were lifted and we were able to welcome one of our nieces, together with her husband and young son. Both the niece and her partner were professional gardeners and it was a pleasure to show them round our garden, even if some of the maintenance was doubtless below their very high standards. During a quiet moment when we weren't strolling around, I was standing in the Long Border chatting about this and that to our two visitors. As we chatted away, I noticed that their six-year-old son was sitting at the centre of the large oak seat with the massive yew hedge behind him. He looked completely at ease, as if he always sat on something large enough to land a small aircraft. Maisie was standing to one side telling him something and he was listening with rapt attention, unsmiling and with slightly furrowed brows. One got the impression that whatever she was telling him was very serious.

After a few more words of explanation, Maisie headed across to the three of us. We were now watching her and the little boy intently as we stood, four or five paces away, in a neat row at the centre of the border. She stood at one end of the row, also facing the little boy on the seat, then turned to us and announced:

'We are now going to witness something truly remarkable. In a few moments I will tell you all to close your eyes. Then I will call out the magic word. After three seconds you can open them again. OK?'

We nodded dutifully. The little boy was sitting motionless, his eyes firmly fixed on Maisie, who now paused for a few moments to allow tension to build. Then she drew a deep breath and addressed both the audience and the performer:

'Right,' she announced. 'It is time to perform the magic trick.' She turned towards us.

'Close your eyes!' We all did as we were told. There was a short pause before she proclaimed portentously: 'ABRACADABRA!' I counted a fairly rapid three seconds, and even so I was the last of us to open their eyes. I immediately looked at the bench: the little boy had completely vanished. There was no trace of him anywhere. My niece was smiling, but was also looking a bit puzzled. Was there just the tiniest hint of anxiety behind her gaze? Then Maisie issued her command for a second time:

'Close your eyes!' This time there was no pause before she again proclaimed: 'ABRACADABRA!' When I opened my eyes, the little boy was back in the centre of the seat, smiling broadly. He was very proud of himself. I glanced at Maisie: I could see she was very proud of him too – and that magical hidden hole in the yew hedge.

*

I love it when I'm strolling through a garden and catch a glimpse of something unexpected, which makes me divert from a walk that is otherwise pleasant, if perhaps a little predictable. Historically, garden designers were very good at offering people tantalising glimpses of mysterious ruins, or strange-looking towers, often in 'borrowed' landscapes, some distance from the actual park or garden. I cherish such features and always enjoy it when I come across them. Rousham, in Oxfordshire, has a particularly well-preserved example.* The trouble is, the Fens around the Wash are just a little flat, and if you want to 'borrow' part of a distant landscape, it does help if you can see it – a process that is made much simpler if you have a conveniently placed hill or mound nearby. If our garden was situated within ten miles of Ely, I am sure that somehow we'd have engineered several exciting glimpses of that spectacular 'Ship of the Fens', dominating the surrounding landscape from its hilltop site. I suppose we could possibly make something out of our neighbours' barns and grain silos a mile and a half across the fen, but we'd have trouble hiding or disguising the dust, the tractors and the combines at harvest time. No, we both knew that the answer had to lie closer to home: within the garden itself.

There are several places within the garden where visitors are offered views of alternative routes or paths to follow. Sometimes these views are deliberately limited or framed by an arched hedge or a gateway through a wall. It's an old trick, but deliberately limiting a view is a simple but effective way of giving it added appeal: if you can see only *part* of the view, you invariably want to find out more. Having said that, I have visited gardens with rather superior, know-it-all types who, when I enthusiastically suggest that we should go through the gate to discover what lies concealed beyond it, will say rather disdainfully: 'Oh don't bother, Francis: it'll be yet another replanted avenue of limes leading up to a Temple of Diana, or an Orangery' – both of which would delight and excite me. One of the great things about growing a bit older is being able to rediscover enthusiasm and a measure of naivety. So nowadays

---

* I discuss Rousham at the start of Chapter 14, page 283.

I'd open the gate and explore the delights that lay on the other side, leaving Old Grumpy standing on his own. I was never much good at being sophisticated.

When you reach the pergola end of the Long Border you may be tempted to turn right, up the gentle slope of the roddon 'hill', towards the Vegetable Garden. Sadly, that option has been taken away by the necessity of installing a double iron gateway to prevent muntjac and roe deer from finding their way into the veg garden, where they have done a lot of damage. This gate is always kept closed unless it's an NGS open day or we are expecting an advance-booked party of garden visitors, usually for the NGS. So visitors usually turn left towards the meadow, which does look very appealing, being framed by the pergola, the hornbeam hedge and the massive trunks of the line of black poplars that run from the Long Border to a small pine copse. We sometimes erroneously refer to this as 'The Pinetum', which it certainly isn't, as it contains only two species of commonly occurring trees: Scots pine, *Pinus sylvestris* (six trees) and western red cedar, *Thuja plicata* (two trees). A real pinetum should include a large and very choice selection of unusual conifers.

If you had been tempted to turn left towards the meadow, you would have passed the entrance into the Serpentine Walk, which can be seen curving its way through the many trees of the Birch Grove. So now you have to decide: meadow or Birch Grove – or maybe even the darkness of the pine trees at the end of the gently curving line of black poplars. It's nice sometimes to be spoilt for choice.

When you reach the end of a garden feature like the Long Border, you expect to have to make choices. But the appeal of 'borrowed' views is that they often come as a surprise. The Old Vicarage Garden at East Ruston, in Norfolk, is probably our favourite modern country garden. I particularly like the way its owners use succulents and other semi-hardy plants, taking advantage of the slightly warmer coastal effect that we also benefit from at Inley Drove Farm. The garden is also well known for its unexpected 'borrowed' views of the north Norfolk coast,[2] which include intriguing glimpses of the spectacular red-and-white-banded Happisburgh Lighthouse, maybe a mile away to the east. It is a remarkable and spectacular building, the oldest working lighthouse in East Anglia (built in 1790) and operated today entirely by local people.[3]

At Limetree Farm we had a distant view of a very attractive parish church across open fields and it proved quite straightforward to make this view an integral part of a path around the outside of the garden. But there were no such distant churches, nor indeed striped lighthouses, at Inley Drove. So we decided to make our unexpected view not from something 'borrowed' from the surrounding landscape, but from a pre-existing feature within the garden itself. Various possible subjects, such as rose arches, pots of plants and even urns, suggested themselves to us from time to time, but we rejected them all after a period of reflection. Eventually, we hit on a solution to what was becoming something of a growing, frustrated obsession (at least for me, if not for Maisie). I really did want our visitors to enjoy a surprise as they strolled through our peaceful country garden, but the way it happened certainly took *us* by surprise.

*

I blame it all on the highly skilled surgeons at the Queen Elizabeth Hospital, King's Lynn, who in the autumn of 2017 very kindly fitted me with a replacement joint for my left hip. My hip had been hurting for several years, but in 2015 it had become too painful to allow me to cut our main hedges. It's a job that requires lifting a heavy powered hedge cutter and climbing up old wooden ladders precariously balanced against nothing very fixed, firm or stable. Today, I'm much more careful and always use a triangular aluminium ladder, whose stability is truly miraculous. For the three years from 2016 to 2018, we used the services of various contract gardeners who said they specialised in hedges. All these people insisted on working for a fixed price, which they specified in advance, and then rushed the job to meet their self-imposed deadline. We tried in vain to explain to them that we weren't interested in speed and that the quality of the hedge was our main consideration. But our words fell on deaf ears; they didn't want to hear. It was like telling a pub landlord that all beer is disgusting, or a vicar that God doesn't exist. And then, in 2020, we came across Jason, who turned out to have been born and brought up in Sutton St James, the village of the parish that includes Inley Drove. He now lives and works in north Norfolk, where he makes most of his highly informative and practical YouTube gardening films.[4] Jason has turned out to be a godsend: he's confident and experienced and knows a great deal about gardening; having said that, he listens closely to what we say and has been able to put some of our more improbable suggestions into practice. He works fast and efficiently, always tidying up very carefully behind him.

When Jason first started cutting our hedges, in 2020, the restrictions of the first Covid lockdown had just been lifted and we all stood at a respectful distance. It was a very strange experience, made a little easier to deal with by the fact that Jason was wielding a large powered hedge trimmer, which nobody in their right mind would want to approach too closely. Before Jason started work, we decided to check all the hedges for potential problems. I was carrying the long board with a gallows-like side piece that I had made a few years previously as a height guide for the main border hedges. I had shown this to the people who had last cut our hedges and they weren't at all interested. Jason wasn't surprised.

I thought the hedges had grown a bit taller, and indeed they had: in places, Jason had to lower them a good deal. They had also become too wide, but I was doubtful about cutting the sides back too drastically. If we had yet another very hot, dry summer, such radical surgery could kill them, so we decided to hard-trim one side at a time. The other side would be lightly clipped and its green growth should ensure that the hedge survived any dry weather. They also wouldn't look too terrible when we opened the garden to the public for the NGS in mid-September.

Some of the archways and entrances through the hornbeam hedges had been very poorly shaped by the contract cutters. An arch looks horrible unless it is evenly shaped and balanced, but many had become lopsided or slightly twisted. By and large, we tend to favour rounded coverings (Norman-style, in terms of church architecture) for our hedge entranceways as this shape seems to suit the way that hornbeams grow. But I also sometimes prefer a flat, Stonehenge-style lintel if I'm trying to achieve a room-like feel for the area enclosed by the hedge. A flat green lintel, level with the top of the hedge, emphasises continuity and the wall-like feel of the hedge.

One of the gaps in the hedges was just off the Long Border, close by the curved double-hedged mown path from the centre of the border into the Rose Garden. The gap that concerned me accommodated a slightly curving narrow path to The Glade via the rear of the Long Border. Like other slightly awkward paths, this one had come into being because it was needed, especially in wet weather in the early days of the garden when The Glade was liable to flood. But now we didn't use it so much and we were discussing with Jason whether we should close the gap in the hedge, and if so whether we would also need to buy a larger, potted hornbeam to fill the space. Jason, who had been standing in the gap as we were talking, then moved out to assess the problem from a distance. I don't think either Maisie or I had ever stood in that precise position on the Long Border before, and as Jason moved away from the gap, we both caught a direct view of The Glade, straight through the curve of the narrow path. It looked amazing as the late summer sunshine heightened the colour of the golden alders against a glimpse of the Serpentine Walk and Round Garden in the background. The contrast with the more formal layout of the Long Border could not have been greater. That narrow path provided a tantalising view of another, more natural, woodland world. Maisie and I exchanged glances. We knew exactly what we had to do: we must straighten the curved path and shape the hedge to draw the eye into The Glade. I must confess, it did look a bit odd when we had finished. But it really worked – and Jason agreed. The feature that we now refer to affectionately as 'the Squint' had been born.

As a footnote, I'd like to add that last year (2021), during our NGS open weekend in September, I found myself watching as a family of four were walking across the Long Border towards the curving hedged path leading to the Rose Garden. They had almost passed the Squint when, to my unconcealable delight, the youngest child, who was walking a few steps behind his parents, suddenly shouted out. Then he ran forward, grabbed his father's hand and led him back to the Squint, which he pointed out proudly. It was almost exactly the reaction I had hoped for – only even better.

# Rooms and Cells

*Garden 'Rooms' • The Dome Garden • Dylings •*
*The Rose and Domeless Dome Gardens*

When we were in the early stages of laying out our new garden at Inley Drove Farm, we were initially drawn to the idea of 'rooms' – that is, areas of a garden enclosed by tall hedges. The idea of room-like enclosed spaces within gardens goes back a very long way. Indeed, the careful arrangement of the gardens at the large Roman palace at Fishbourne, near Chichester, West Sussex, undoubtedly reflects the layout of the building, with many straight paths, hedges and 'rooms'.[1] I would suggest the 'rooms' of Britain's earliest known formal garden are more genuinely room-like than all the later examples.

By the mid-1990s, all archaeologists were very well aware of Fishbourne, which had been so superbly excavated by Barry Cunliffe back in the 1960s. Barry published an excellent book on it in 1971, which Maisie and I had both read.[2] As an example of modern archaeological excavation and research, Fishbourne is still widely regarded as one of the best; but as an inspiration for a garden, it didn't appeal to either of us. It was too rigid, Roman and formal. We were seeking something a bit more anarchic: we knew we had to have structure, but layout shouldn't dominate everything. We wanted our garden to be more fluid, more accommodating and even a little mysterious.

We searched widely for inspiration. Maisie came across many references to Sissinghurst Castle in the rural Weald of Kent. The site itself goes back to the Middle Ages, but its post-medieval history hasn't always been very inspiring, and it slipped into quite rapid decline following the Civil Wars of the mid-seventeenth century. In the following century, the castle (actually a house) was used to house prisoners captured during the Seven Years' War with France, and in the nineteenth much of the house and its outbuildings were demolished. Eventually, it was placed on the market in 1928 for just £12,000, but it attracted no offers until, in 1930, it was bought by the writer (and lover of Virginia Woolf) Vita Sackville-West and her husband, Harold Nicolson.

Nicolson concentrated on the garden's layout and structure; Vita was more concerned with its plants and their arrangement. Within less than twenty years, it was widely recognised that the gardens they had created at Sissinghurst were among the finest in Britain. Sackville-West wrote a regular column for the *Observer* and Sissinghurst opened to the public for the first time in 1938. Following Vita's death in 1962, Sissinghurst was donated to the National Trust. Today it is one of their most popular properties, with some 200,000 visitors a year. Nicolson and Sackville-West's approach to their task had been uncompromising in that the garden came first: it has a structure of its own, but it respects its surroundings and is in harmony with them. The garden is particularly celebrated for its imaginative use of 'rooms', which were subtly planted by Vita Sackville-West.

We visited Sissinghurst in the mid-1990s and were hugely impressed by the garden's overall layout and gentle maturity. It had a charm all of its own. We also found the unusual story of the creation of the Sissinghurst garden inspiring at a time when we were planning our own garden. You could imagine the empty field at Inley Drove as a blank canvas, compared with what confronted Nicolson and Sackville-West in 1930: the remnants of an ancient park, gardens, house and outbuildings. At the time, we were feeling rather daunted by the project we were starting at Inley Drove. There were many things that worried us, but the long timescale involved in transforming an empty field into a sheltered garden was a particular concern. We both knew quite a lot about the development of prehistoric landscapes, where a supposedly rapid change might take place over a few centuries – if you were lucky. Woods and forests didn't just appear: first there were a few scrubby shrubs, then colonising pine and birch and finally mixed woodland, complete with oak and/or beech. Our work at Limetree Farm had shown that gardens could be developed much faster than natural woodland, but we still didn't realise just how rapid that change could be. So our visit to Sissinghurst, where Nicolson and Sackville-West had created such a magnificent garden in less than twenty years, was a heartening experience for both of us.

Sissinghurst was one of the gardens that confirmed our ideas about routes, paths and journeys with 'no turning back'. Our visit to Sissinghurst was a day of discovery and exploration, which we both enjoyed hugely. Only one thing disappointed us. Before we journeyed down to Kent, we had been completely won over by what we had read about Vita Sackville-West's garden 'rooms'. But the reality didn't live up to expectation: the much-praised White Garden was frankly rather drab. Some of this may be down to the style of gardening favoured by the National Trust in the 1990s, which was much more conservative and formulaic. Today, on-site gardening staff are allowed far greater freedom than they were thirty years ago. As a result of our visit, we decided not to go for tightly enclosed 'rooms'; instead, we would opt for something less confined and more connective. If you were desperate for a house-like analogy, I suppose you might call them 'corridors' or 'passages' – but I'd much rather you didn't. There was, however, one exception to our decision about 'rooms', which we found we had created and seemed to have appeared on the scene more by accident than design. And I'm so glad we allowed it to materialise. On hot summer days, its tall hedges provide much welcome shade from the sun and when the winter winds start to blow in earnest, it's to the Dome Garden that we retreat with our warming mugs of tea.

*

The Dome Garden at Inley Drove Farm is remarkable because there's no sign of anything remotely dome-shaped. It acquired the name because it was home to the wonderful wirework dome that my brother Felix gave us on my sixtieth birthday, in 2005. It stood at the northern entrance into the more formal garden areas, from the meadow, but as the hornbeam hedges that ran close by it gradually grew taller, the dome seemed to shrink. We had realised it was beginning to lose its impact when we made the decision to extend the outer hedge and thereby completely enclose the small garden that had been gradually developing behind it.

Five years after we had been given the dome, the outer areas of formal garden were still being developed. Every year I would find myself planting a few more hornbeam hedging plants and getting out the sharp, sickle-shaped spade I use to cut new border edges. Inevitably, you have to change things to accommodate the garden's gradual growth in maturity. At the same time as we were extending the hedges around the site where we had originally positioned the dome, we were also reassessing the Front Garden, which was starting to acquire height around the house (mostly roses and wisteria), and the wall that ran from the house to the drive. This had been built to cut winter winds, which were now largely baffled by the oaks and ash trees in the wood beyond it, to the north-east. This shelter meant that the wall could be given a thick blanketing cover of large-leaved ivy and pyracantha, which greatly increased its height and impact – especially in the autumn when the pyracantha ('Orange Glow') lived up to its reputation as a 'firethorn'. In wintertime, the thick covering of climbing plants on the wall provides a welcome refuge for dozens of sparrows and wrens, whose morning calls through the bedroom window liven up our early waking moments.

In 2010 we decided to move the dome into the Front Garden to provide some much-needed height at the centre. But although it had vanished, it had left its name behind. We tried calling its former home the small garden, even the hedge garden, but they didn't work. It had become the Dome Garden and that's how it has stayed. Meanwhile, we're learning to live with earnest visitors asking us, while pointing at the map: 'So am I here?' 'Yes,' I reply and then rapidly add: 'But there's no dome. If you want to see that, it's in the Front Garden.' Nine times out of ten they stay put; they're quite happy to stroll through the domeless Dome Garden, which becomes more and more room-like with every passing season. If I believed in such things, I could imagine the spirit of Vita Sackville-West looking down with quizzical approval.

The Dome Garden has taken longer to find its final form than any other part of the garden. This is partly due to its location near the centre of everything, where it has to contend somehow with conflicting influences of formality, as in the Long Border, extreme informality, as in The Glade, and the openness of the Meadow, just a short distance to the north. Its shape and layout, however, remain simple. As garden 'rooms' go, it is remarkably house-like. It is roughly square and about 12–13 yards wide; its 'walls' are formed of tall clipped hornbeam hedges with three doorway-style entrances in the north, south and west 'walls'. The north and west entrances are just wide enough to allow me to mow the lawn with our ride-on mower. Most visitors enter the Dome Garden through the southern entrance, which leads from the curved hedged walk that links the centre of the Long Border to the Rose Garden. The Dome Garden has become quite an intimate, reflective space, and the narrow southern entrance helps keep crowds out, even on popular days when we open for the National Garden Scheme. The feeling of privacy is enhanced by what has become quite a large golden evergreen *Thuja orientalis* 'Aurea Nana', planted at the centre. Even if there are other people in the 'room', they are usually hidden behind this dense central shrub.

The garden at Inley Drove Farm includes quite a few seats, chairs, stools and benches and, as the years pass and its owners grow older, it will probably acquire quite a few more. The simple iron double seat in the Dome Garden is positioned against the southern 'wall', and over the past five or so summers the clipped hedge behind it has gradually crept forward, providing it with a roof and side walls. The roof gives much-needed shade in summer. Hornbeam, like beech hedges, retain their dead brown leaves through the winter and the narrow side walls make for very effective draught excluders. I still can't decide whether or not the Long Border is actually modelled on the straight Bronze Age droveways we excavated in Peterborough back in the 1970s. Sometimes I think it is; at other times I think my memory is playing tricks. The same can be said for the seat-within-its-hedged-niche in the Dome Garden. Its position, at the centre of the wall facing the main entrance into the 'room' from the open world of the Hay Meadow, precisely recalls the arrangement of seats and probable altars within Neolithic stone houses such as Skara Brae in the Orkney Islands. I visited Orkney several times in the 1990s and the following decade while carrying out research for books and filming television documentaries, and these extraordinary sites made a deep impression on me. So is the Dome Garden a hedged Skara Brae? Maybe – or maybe not. I can't decide.

One advantage of having restricted spaces in a garden – such as 'rooms' – is that they tend to concentrate scents and smells. Maisie and I have always adored the different scents of a garden. In fact, Maisie won't buy a new rose if she can't get to smell it in advance. A few years ago, a group of blind people visited the garden, and as they were having a cup of tea after their walk, they enthused about the richness and variety of scents they'd encountered. It was fascinating – and rather moving – to listen to them as they discussed the different scents like another group of flower enthusiasts would have compared blooms. Sometimes the scents in the Dome Garden can be astonishingly strong, but you can always tell what time of year it is. Spring smells nothing like autumn, but don't ask me to define either of them. They're just very different.

The area that became the Dome Garden had always been difficult to manage, largely owing to its poor drainage. I used to think this was an entirely natural phenomenon, and a reflection of the fact that some of the soil was slightly more clay-rich and was a few inches lower-lying than the silty ridge that runs along the better-drained north side of the Dome Garden. I'm now convinced that although my observations about the soil's changing height and texture are undoubtedly correct, these features of the garden landscape are not, as I had once assumed, entirely natural. As so often happens when one examines Fen landscapes closely, we can detect clear signs of interference by the hand of man.

*

One of the reasons we chose the land at Inley Drove was that it seemed to be free of archaeological remains. Setting aside the fact that we both excavated sites and studied archaeological finds for a living, and therefore wanted our new home to be somewhere to escape from work, we didn't want to damage any ancient remains when we started to build the house and lay out the garden. But I suppose we should have known better, because we were both well aware, from years of study and research, that there are, on average, significant archaeological remains in every square quarter-mile of Britain. The main exceptions to this rule are fairly obvious: higher mountains, areas of primeval forest, lakes and marshes. I was well aware that the Fens around the Wash had been drained and occupied from at least the Middle Ages, but we couldn't spot anything suspicious on aerial photos and there were certainly no finds in the ploughed topsoil, when we first walked over it, or since then, when digging the Vegetable Garden, for example. So the chances of coming across any archaeological features *in situ* seemed very slight indeed.

I first started to have doubts about a dozen years ago (*c.* 2010) when the young trees in the wood were starting to mature. Maybe it was the effect their growing root systems were having on drainage close by, but the ten-yard-wide strip of open grassland between them and the deep drainage dyke that formed the eastern boundary to the field began to reveal different patterns of grass growth. These were most evident in early summer, especially in dry years. At first, I assumed that some strips of darker green growth revealed where the ground had been disturbed during the laying of short clay pipes in the early 1960s. These pipes, which were laid end to end without any attempt to join them together physically, formed subsoil land drains, about three to four feet below the surface. They drained into the deep dyke and had remained hidden for several decades, before I had the good fortune to discover them after some very wet winters when we first opened the garden to the public in the years around 2000. Some were still flowing and needed little attention; others were blocked. Today, after a good jetting-out, they all work very effectively. But the land drains didn't coincide with the darker areas of grass growth, which were six feet or so wide. And this pattern of growth certainly wouldn't fit with the way the clay pipes were laid, which was probably done using a very narrow machine-cut slot. Those parallel marks looked for all the world like the remains of an old ridge-and-furrow field system, though Inley Drove was hardly a place where I would have expected to find them.[3]

The system of ridge-and-furrow was used across large areas of central and eastern England in the Middle Ages.[*] It was an important element of the medieval open field system of farming, which centred on a parish-based manorial court that organised the rent of land among the various families resident in the parish. Like most modern vegetable gardens, the big open fields controlled by the manorial authorities were used in a way that ensured land was rested and wasn't overexploited. The parish and village of Laxton in Nottinghamshire is the only place in Britain that still uses the open field system and we have visited it many times.[4] The open field system at Laxton differs from the 'grain plain' agri-deserts that are now such a sad feature of East Anglia and the east Midlands, since the village, the access roads

---

[*] It is the result of ploughing with a non-reversible plough.

and the fields themselves are surrounded by trees and abundant hedgerows (as were the villages of the medieval Midlands). The big fields may have been open, but there was still plenty of cover for birds and wildlife.

The low-lying and often flooded land around the Wash could be managed quite effectively using a system of parallel shallow drains and low banks. While most of the ridge-and-furrow fields of the drier Midlands were used for arable crops, the Fenland dylings were frequently used to provide wide ridges of dry grazing for sheep. Essentially, they were shallow ditches that channelled surface water into deeper dykes. Dylings proved to be very useful and effective and there is evidence to suggest that some continued to be maintained and used as recently as the nineteenth century, just a few miles away, near Holbeach.[5]

Over the years, I have been able to identify the dead straight, parallel dyling ditches that run across our garden and the fields on either side. There are about eight beneath the garden and about twenty, or more, if you include the fields on either side. You can see two of them very clearly on the drone picture, where they show up as dark parallel marks through the pasture that borders the farm, to the south. They are running precisely parallel with the drainage dyke that borders the house and garden to the south – which may also once have been a dyling. I think my next project must be to map them all more accurately. Isn't it fascinating how something as substantial as a system of ancient drainage ditches should vanish from human memories so rapidly and so completely – only to be rediscovered by a curious gardener?

*

As the hornbeam hedges gradually established themselves, their roots started to drain the beds and borders alongside them. One of my early worries was that this would stunt the growth of herbaceous plants at the back of the Long Border, closest to the hedge, which was not at all what we wanted. We needed tall plants at the back and short ones at the front. To my immense relief, the hedge roots seemed to have the opposite effect: they encouraged the growth of the taller roses, grasses, asters and other perennials along the back of the border. I was beginning to realise that our heavy soil is far more moisture-retentive than we first appreciated and the plants we needed to grow in the border would not have thrived without help from the hedge roots. I suspect that many would have died, as actually happened in one or two very wet seasons, when the hedge plants were still quite young.

It's a happy coincidence that the Dome and Rose Gardens, both of which feature many tall hornbeam hedges, were positioned in one of the wettest places at Inley Drove. I now realise that it coincides with one of those filled-in dyling ditches, which retain dampness long after other areas have cracked and baked in the warm summer sun. It's also quite a low-lying area. I suspect that back in the Bronze Age, around three thousand years ago, it would have been a shallow pool in the tidal mudflats that are still such a commanding feature of the Wash foreshore. It would have been the sort of spot where you'd have found hundreds of marsh samphire plants (*Salicornia europaea*), just as you do around the Wash today. Every Friday in June, July and August, I buy Wash samphire from the excellent fishmonger's stall in Long Sutton market. It's one of the seasonal delights of living so close to the sea – the others being cockles, brown shrimps, oysters and mussels. I particularly like mussels when they're cooked with our own onions, shallots and garlic… But I digress: this book is about gardening, not gastronomy.

By another happy coincidence, the Dome Garden, which is completely surrounded by tall hornbeam hedges, was positioned in the dampest area of all. It took some time for the hedge plants to get established, but once they had got going, they grew like rockets.

As the Dome Garden became more enclosed and sheltered, I found that it had begun to acquire an unconsciously soothing or tranquillising atmosphere. It was something that I felt myself, but it was also something I noticed when I was showing people around the garden. When they passed through one of the doorway-like gaps in the surrounding hedge and entered the enclosed space, they would pause and look around them. Quite often they would take a few silent steps towards the centre, where a hand would touch and feel the *Thuja* without the head appearing to take any notice. Invariably, they would turn to me, smiling. I could see the garden was starting to soothe them.

A view of the Dome Garden showing two of the doorway-like entrances through the surrounding hornbeam hedge. The right-hand entrance faces out onto the meadow; that to the left (partially hidden behind an aster in this view), leads directly into the Rose Garden. Part of the central golden *Thuja* can be seen at the edge of the frame, to the right.

They were clearly more relaxed and happy. I can't remember experiencing such a feeling of release and relaxation anywhere else, until about ten years ago when Maisie and I stayed at the holiday flat in one of the post-Dissolution buildings at Mount Grace Priory, near Northallerton, North Yorkshire.[6] The flat is in the service wing of the early seventeenth-century country house that was mainly built with stone taken from the ruins of the disused monastic buildings.

I first began to get interested in the medieval monastic world when I started filming for *Time Team*, which featured several episodes filmed at abbey and priory sites. The late Mick Aston, the co-founder of *Time Team*, knew a great deal about them and was very enthusiastic, which I can remember I found a bit odd as, like me, he was a convinced atheist. He regarded the monastic buildings of the Middle Ages as a tribute to the people who built them, rather than to any supernatural force. I sort of share that view, but I have to say I find places like Ely Cathedral do inspire feelings that somehow extend beyond the here and now. Some might describe them as numinous;* I prefer to acknowledge their existence and enjoy the experience when I visit buildings like Ely and, rather unexpectedly, a restored monk's cell at Mount Grace.

The Carthusians were the only solitary order of monks in medieval Britain and they spent their days as hermits, living and working in 'cells'. The order dated to the years following the Black Death of 1348 when there was a move towards 'piety and strict living'.[7] Before visiting Mount Grace, I had always supposed that medieval hermits lived very austere lives in hovels and caves. But the Carthusian monks were rather different, as is shown by one of their 'cells' that was authentically restored by the priory's modern owner between

_____

* A word derived from the Latin *numen*, meaning deity or divinity.

1901 and 1905. The restorers had done a superb job and had captured the spirit of what it would have been like to have lived as a Carthusian hermit. The 'cell' was in fact a compact lodging with two rooms on the ground floor; one was a large living room, with a substantial fireplace, the other a smaller space with a bed and provision for prayer. Food was prepared in the priory kitchens and was passed into each cell's living room through a purpose-built hatch, next to the front door into the main cloister. Food was mainly vegetarian, but it also included fish, and drink came in the form of water and beer. I can think of worse diets.

Upstairs, above the living room and sleeping space, was a large room where the monk could carry out his trade, such as preparing manuscripts, binding books and weaving. Immediately outside the 'cell', and enclosed within the same tall outer wall, was a garden almost exactly the same shape and size as our Dome Garden. It had been beautifully planted with medicinal and culinary herbs, flowers and tightly trimmed box hedges. The scent was delightful, as was the soft sound of water from the small stream directly behind the enclosing wall. I paused for a few moments to take it all in. At home in the Lincolnshire Fens, the 'peace of the countryside' can sometimes be quite deafening, as RAF fighter jets perform combat aerobatics and vast tractors slowly grind their way through flat arable fields. Happily, there was none of that here: just the gentle sound of the stream and the lovely scent of herbs. As I stood there, I realised I was starting to experience that same sense of tranquillity and deep calm that I so often enjoyed in the Dome Garden at home. But here I was in the small garden attached to a medieval monk's cell; you can visit so many distant worlds in the privacy of a garden. I have revisited that monastic moment many, many times while kneeling and weeding or just standing, surrounded by tall, rather severe and austere tightly clipped hornbeam hedges. I have never experienced the monastic life, but I do know that the discipline of those solitary hours, while hard at work gardening, can be profoundly liberating.

## 14

# Walking the Walk

*Starting Points • The Nutless Walk • Chicken Lane •*
*The Black Poplar Walk • Dioecious Catkins*

Good gardens are all about temptation: succulent raspberries, glistening red apples, heavenly perfumed roses and various delights of scent, colour and taste. But there are other forms of temptation too. Take simple curiosity – what lies hidden behind that tall screen of Jerusalem artichokes? – or something perhaps with a slight hint of mystery, such as the mouth of a dark tunnel of trees or bushes with no light visible at the end.

One garden that has raised temptation to an art form is Rousham, just west of Bicester. During our early years at Inley Drove, we made quite frequent trips to Oxfordshire for family reasons. It was a long drive and we would try to break the monotony by visiting gardens along the route, among which Rousham was one of our favourites. Designed first by Charles Bridgeman and then by William Kent, who started work there in 1738,[1] it is one of the best-preserved early eighteenth-century gardens. Rousham has an extraordinary atmosphere: formal and carefully structured, yet still rural and very relaxed. At Rousham, we discovered that walks and paths only work if you can tempt people into them.[2] And that isn't as simple as it might at first appear.

The area of the Inley Drove garden that was close to the house was inevitably more adversely affected by building work than elsewhere. For jobs that involved trenches – such as the burying of power cables, phone lines and water mains – we hired a mini-digger, which I drove myself. We dug out the pond to take run-off from the house roof and carefully landscaped the soil removed from it into a low bank that ran alongside the drive. On top of this bank we planted cuttings of the red-barked willow *Salix alba*, var. 'Kermesina', that we found in the Cambridge Botanic Garden and which we had grown so successfully at Limetree Farm. Within less than ten years, these vigorous young trees were threatening to shade out the young orchard. So we decided to pollard them. It was a purely practical decision made by two people who loved their apples, but it proved to be a huge success from a purely visual point of view. Visitors to the garden in late autumn, winter and spring are now greeted by a superb display of young orange-red bark as they enter the drive and the colour is vividly enhanced by sunlight. Nothing, but nothing, looks quite as spectacular as their glowing bark in the low light of an autumnal setting sun. Even now, after years of enjoyment, those trees almost move me to tears.

By the time we first pollarded the willows around the pond, the Nut Walk had started to mature. It had roofed over and was becoming tunnel-like. Slowly, we shaped its entrance from the Pond Garden and carefully placed one or two shrubs nearby to funnel people in from the Long Walk that bounded the Rose Garden to the north. These shrubs included the richly scented autumn- and winter-flowering *Viburnum* x *bodnantense* 'Dawn', which we knew loved our heavy soil. You can sometimes detect their distinctive scent when you're halfway along the Nut Walk on a mild winter's evening.

For about ten years the Nut Walk proved a huge gardening success, with large yields of hazelnuts and a profusion of snowdrops and aconites in winter, but as time passed we noticed a few, rather strange, changes. There didn't seem to be quite so many snowdrops, and a light scattering of nuts, all still quite green, began to appear on the ground in August. Something was going on.

*

As disasters went, it was quite gradual – a bit like climate change, and possibly not unrelated to it. No branches collapsed; the bushes continued to thrive; in fact, the crop of cobnuts probably grew larger. The trouble was they all lay on the ground, in July and August, still unripe and green – and if you picked one up, you would find it empty, with a neatly bitten hole through the shell. It had been lunch for a grey squirrel. I can't be absolutely certain when grey squirrels moved into the garden, but they certainly hadn't visited us during the first ten years of our lives at Inley Drove. In fact, I think it's fair to say that in those days squirrels were generally quite rare in the open, arable fens. You'd see them in old urban and country parks, and in churchyards, but not out in the fen. I suppose it was the replanting of hedges and projects like the Farm Woodland Scheme that provided the habitats they had previously lacked. So, trying to look on the bright side, you could see those tens of thousands of discarded unripe nuts that every year carpet the ground beneath the Nut Walk as a sort of symbol of success. It's just a shame it wasn't the native red squirrel.

Again, trying to feel positive, as the garden has matured, wildlife has returned – and in larger quantities than either of us could possibly have imagined when we began the project back in 1992. When I take the dogs for a walk, especially in the late afternoon, it is not unusual to spot a dozen hares in the meadow.

Cock and hen pheasants sometimes stroll among them, and I've also noticed that we are now losing fewer snake's-head fritillary seedheads to hungry pheasants. I wonder whether those hares enjoy seeing them flower as much as we do, and resent it when the pheasants peck them off. Very rarely we might spot a rabbit, but hares and rabbits don't mix much; I much prefer to see groups of graceful native hares than those hopping bunnies that were introduced to Britain by the Romans.[3]

In theory it's possible to stop birds and squirrels from stealing nuts by spraying them with a special chemical intended to deter casual grazing. The trouble is, it has to be resprayed after heavy rain and it's not a job I enjoy much. The stuff is quite smelly (one of the reasons it provides protection) and it covers everything with a fine whiteish-yellow coating. Nor did it always work very well, but that might well be because I got fed up with respraying it after a series of quite sharp late-summer thundery showers. The other way around the problem is to wait until the rate at which the squirrels are removing the nuts increases (which means the nuts are likely to be ripe), and then to pick as many as you want as late as possible. If you pick the nuts *before* the squirrels start their plundering, the nuts almost certainly won't have much, if anything, beneath the shells. But do beware: squirrels are unbelievably cunning. I suspect they know that I am planning a rapid raid and at least once I've walked out to the Nut Walk with a large basket, only to find that every bush has been stripped. All around, you can hear the sound of rumbling stomachs and contented sighs.

The squirrels also raid our bird feeders, and there are times when I wish I could wipe them off the face of the earth: 'furry rats', I've heard people call them. Yes, like rats, they are rodents, but so too are guinea pigs, hamsters, beavers, red squirrels and dormice – and I wouldn't like any of these to suffer in a campaign to exterminate grey squirrels. And anyway, it was us Brits who introduced them to Britain from North America, in the 1890s.[4] When I worked at the Royal Ontario Museum in Toronto, the park near the museum was heaving with grey squirrels, but there were also black ones, which were very striking and elegant. Had I been introducing North American squirrels to my Victorian country house park, I'd definitely have chosen the black in preference to the grey. Over the years, we've decided to put up with our huge population of grey squirrels and I've long ago got rid of that horrible chemical solution.

But now I have a small confession to make. I know one is supposed to be very opposed to grey squirrels, but every morning when I look out of the kitchen window at the Poop Deck, with the bird feeders hanging from the pergola overhead, I can usually see one or two grey squirrels. Every once in a while they'll stop trying to pinch bird food from our expensive squirrel-proof feeders and will look across at the house. I know that rodents aren't supposed to be able to smile – but when I see them in the low sunlight of early morning, I sometimes wonder. Despite all the problems they cause, they can be *very* endearing.

Our supply of nuts has massively declined since grey squirrels became so well established, but there is more to the food that a garden can produce than apples, pears and cobnuts. So now I want to take you to the third path linking the house and garden to the wood and paddocks that surround them. The third path into the wood runs in a south-easterly direction from the Vegetable Garden and farmyard behind the barn. The yard was always busy when we still kept sheep and it acquired a huge muck heap when we cleaned out the barn after lambing, in March and April. Today, it accumulates garden compost rather than sheep manure. The yard remains a home to chickens, who love to feed on the worms and insects in the muck heap. With bellies full, they often like to take a post-prandial stroll along that third path down to the wood, which we had no alternative but to name Chicken Lane.

*

Many farms in lowland Britain have very clearly separated fields and gardens. Today, this is made more evident by the increasingly vast size of the fields around them, which so often begin to resemble featureless 'grain plains'. In such situations, the farmhouse and garden can seem like an oasis in a vast desert, but in the less intensively farmed uplands, fields, farms, woods and lanes blend together to form a harmonious, and for me at least, very soothing landscape that we were keen to replicate at Inley Drove Farm. So we were at pains *not* to separate the farm and its fields from the wood and the garden. Sadly, we weren't blessed with those beautiful drystone walls that are such a fabulous feature of the Cotswolds or the Yorkshire Moors, and livestock has to be controlled somehow. So we had no option but to use fences made from posts and stock wire. While these don't exactly look inviting, they do work, are wildlife-friendly (moles and hares can readily pass through them) and can quickly be hidden within a hedge or a tall growing stand of nettles.

When we first fenced the paddocks around the house and barn, they looked more than a little stark. The posts were all a uniformly bright green colour (owing to their anti-rot preservative), the stock wire positively gleamed in the sunshine and the whole assemblage – fences, gates and buildings – looked thoroughly unnatural. The route from the yard and muck heap down to the wood appeared particularly uninviting. We decided we needed a track or lane at this point because the field alongside it was where we planned to keep our rams, when they weren't 'working' with their ewes. We knew from bitter experience that rams needed to be widely separated from their ewes and that a single fence wouldn't be enough: if they could see their ewes they would smash their way to them, even if they injured themselves in the process. That is why the Tup Field (in this part of England, rams are known as 'tups') is surrounded by hedges and why we decided to plant hedges along both sides of the lane to the wood, which would later become Chicken Lane. Most of the hedges on the farm were planted with hawthorn, blackthorn and other native hedging plants, but the parallel hedges on either side of the straight lane from the yard to the wood felt very much like part of the garden. So we thought we'd try something a bit different.

Winter can confer its own very special magic. This is a view down Chicken Lane on 19 December 2010. Hoar frosts can be almost snow-like in the Fens around the Wash and this one was no exception.

Archaeologists frequently find themselves collaborating quite closely with specialists in other related disciplines, and in the mid-1990s Maisie found herself working with a palaeobotanist at the Pitt Rivers Museum in Oxford. While they were together one day, Maisie told him about our garden and the projected new hedge. His ears pricked up. He was clearly very interested. A day or two later, Maisie returned home with the news that he had agreed to supply us with a collection of small plants of the various forms of wild plum that are native to Britain. He was aware, as were his colleagues in Oxford, that hedges were then being ripped up at an appalling rate with a devastating effect on biodiversity.

So he was keen to do something – however small – to slow down what many of us could see was an approaching environmental disaster. It also helped that the Fens were in the heart of what was rapidly becoming an industrialised farming landscape. If a few 'islands' of environmental sanity could be established, they would help the region recover when (and if) politicians ever decided to do something substantial and practical to reverse the environmental decline. I can remember as a final-year student at university in the late 1960s driving my illegal car to a party, where the only record being played was the Beatles' *Sgt. Pepper* album. The party had been in a converted water mill and while I was driving home I had to pull over and scrape a mass of dead insects off the windscreen. I did a similar trip the other day and my windscreen remained entirely clean. As a gardener, I find the 60 per cent decline in UK insects over the past twenty years one of the most worrying of all environmental statistics.[5]

In the heat of high summer, Chicken Lane is a cool, delightfully shaded tunnel. In springtime, its wild plum blossom is one of the garden's big features. It looks lovely, and smells sweetly on the air from within the tunnel, but in some respects the white blossom is even more spectacular when viewed across the Tup Field, where it forms a floral ridge rather like the roof over the platforms of a miniature King's Cross or St Pancras station. In their early years, the actual fruit – the sloes, damsons, bullaces and wild plums – were less prolific than they have been in the past decade or so. Maybe this reflects the garden's seemingly quite healthy insect population. I hope it does. Our wild plums make excellent jam and of course there is only one real use for sloes: sloe gin. I prefer to drink ours when it is over three years old, but I have to limit myself, as I'm sure it's highly addictive.

From later summer, the ubiquitous grey squirrels and other animals like to feed on the ripe plums that litter the ground inside the Chicken Lane tunnel, whereas birds usually feed on them from the safety of the branches high overhead. I'm secretly rather delighted when I see crows, blackbirds and starlings having a good feed on sloes because I know they often swallow them whole – stones and all. Then they fly off. I'm aware it may sound a bit strange, but I like to think of them as our environmental warriors. Let me explain.

Most of our neighbouring farmers have an environmental conscience and have planted trees and hedges. Many have done this simply because it's the right thing to do and not as part of any government countryside enhancement scheme, or suchlike. Keeping livestock – mostly cattle and sheep – has become more popular locally than was the case when we moved to Lincolnshire in the early 1990s and this had undoubtedly led to many environmental improvements. But there are still one or two farmers who remain solely arable and they prefer large open fields without any trees, since they often get in the way of those increasingly vast sprayers. And this is where my environmental warriors play their part. We tend to think of bird poo as something irritating to be hastily removed from a car windscreen, but sometimes it's quite brightly coloured and contains small seeds of plants like blackberries or even sloes. I also understand that the process of digestion actually helps the seeds and berries in the poo to germinate when they land on the ground. So those birds standing on the edge of treeless fields and dykes quietly digesting bellyfuls of sloes from Chicken Lane are actually helping to establish natural hedges in the sadly rather unlikely event that certain farmers will cut down on their use of Roundup and other herbicides. One can only live in hope.

*

The planting of Chicken Lane was quite carefully planned, but other successful garden features came about in a more haphazard fashion. Perhaps the most spectacular of them all is the Black Poplar Walk, which follows the western edge of the wood and then links the meadow to the brink of the large drainage dyke that runs along the southern edge of the property. Chicken Lane crosses it midway, as it joins the main footpath through the wood.

I'm reasonably sure that our original intention was to plant an informal field-style hedge where the massive black poplars now stand, but for some reason it never happened. It was also about this time, in the early/mid-1990s, that we began what I can only describe as our 'affair' with black poplars. This began as a purely academic interest. At the time, people were becoming increasingly aware of the rapid decline of trees and woods in the English countryside, largely owing to agricultural intensification, and certain species seemed to be faring very badly, especially the native black poplar (*Populus nigra*), which is now widely regarded as an endangered species.[6] Black poplars are very fast-growing, large trees that do best in open wet landscapes. Not surprisingly, they were very widespread in the Fens, but over the past century or so have largely been replaced by the tall, fastigiate* Lombardy poplar (*Populus nigra* 'Italica'), which is now the preferred windbreak around the apple orchards in the Wisbech area. Poplars cross-pollinate quite readily, so it is hard to find black poplars today that do not have traces of Lombardy poplar in them. The branches of hybrid poplars tend to be more upright and the lower boughs don't dip down towards the ground, where they can root and form new trees.

In the Middle Ages, the massive trunks of unhybridised black poplar trees were used to form the distinctive, curving floor-to-apex 'blades' or beams of so-called cruck barns.[7] The tall trunks of the native black poplar are well known for being gently curved to deflect the prevailing wind. Our trees all curve to the north-east and they would have made excellent cruck blades – and that's after barely twenty-five years of growth. In the Middle Ages, many trees were grown with the specific intention of using their trunks and branches for crucks and beams. It was all carefully managed: people didn't just wander out into the forest with an axe, on the off-chance they might spot a good tree to use in a barn. Timber would also have been a crucially important resource for use on the farm as hurdles, and of course as logs for domestic hearths. Woodland was a valuable communal asset and was treated as such, with clear rules about who could cut what timber, when – and how often.

We planted dozens of hazel bushes in the wood, which we used to cut back to harvest rods for use not just in our garden, but in those of neighbours too, as rose or bean supports. But we had no intention of ever harvesting or using wood from our black poplars. We were both too keen to see how they would grow – and how fast. We planted two rows of them, one along the route from the meadow to the brink by the drainage

---

* Fastigiate trees grow tall and narrow.

dyke forming the garden's southern boundary. The trees were planted along the field boundary instead of a hedge, with a gap at the centre at the junction with Chicken Lane. A shorter row of black poplars was planted along the north side of the Tup Field, in one of the wettest parts of the garden, where they have thrived.

We had learnt a great deal about black poplars from books, so we knew they were very fast-growing, that they would probably lean away from the wind and that their lower branches might dip down. But reality never precisely coincides with what you read in books. For a start, their growth was extremely rapid and very much faster than we had expected, especially given their rather uncertain beginning. Conversations with nursery staff and others who were used to propagating trees left us in no doubt that the best way to plant them would *not* be to root them first and then dig them in; if you do that, especially in a dry year when the ground is still quite hard, the roots will often get damaged and the soil won't pack around them tightly enough to retain moisture and provide support and stability for the young growing tree. Most people we spoke to were in little doubt that trees such as willow and poplar, which root very readily, are best planted as unrooted twigs shortly after Christmas or very early in January, when the days are short, dark and often quite wet. The best twigs were ones that had been broken off the trunk of a young sapling, preferably from the upper part. We had to break them off, leaving the 'heel' intact. The 'heel' was a flattish, saucer-like widening where the young side branch joined the trunk; its wood felt distinctly harder, but apparently leaving the heel intact discouraged fungal infection from spreading into the cutting from the ground, while also encouraging the formation of new roots.

One day at the very start of January 1995 I found myself heading down Chicken Lane, which was then just a double row of tiny plants in their spiral plastic hare protectors. I was walking awkwardly because one hand was holding a heavy homemade metal dibber, while the other held plastic tree guards and a bundle of stout bamboo canes. So the actual cuttings, which I had just carefully removed from a young sapling, were in the back pocket of my jeans. I think it must have been those 'heels' that were making my bum feel so uncomfortable. Still, I didn't have very far to walk. I paced out the distance (five yards) between the twenty-five trees, and for each of them I dropped a cane, a tree guard and a cutting. It didn't take long to insert them into the ground (I hesitate to say 'plant' them, as somehow one doesn't plant rootless twigs). I squashed the soil around each cutting as best I could, but I remember it felt distinctly dry and not very easy to compress and mould. That didn't worry me, as we were certain to get rain at any time. Early January is invariably wet at Inley Drove – except, it would seem, in 1995. Eventually, I was forced to take a watering can to them, because I didn't want any young roots to dry off. A few days after I'd watered the twigs, I noticed that some of the leading leaf buds were starting to expand. That was a good sign – and the weather gods took notice too, because it started to rain. I was so relieved. I checked all the plastic tubes, fully expecting a significant proportion to have failed, but to my amazement they were all showing signs of life.

*

I always like discovering new words, even if in my old age I then can't remember them. So I was delighted, when doing my background reading for the black poplars, to discover that they were 'dioecious'. Incidentally, my computer's spell-checker was only aware of the adverbial form of the word, 'dioeciously'. Dioecious means that black poplars have male and female flowers in separate trees. Those flowers are in the form of catkins that are produced early in spring. The male flowers are red and rather less fluffy than the downy white female ones. The book I read warned about the female catkins and the mess they can make in springtime; I also read somewhere that female poplars were planted in the streets of Moscow some time ago and that the mess their catkins leave on the ground is still horrible.[8] We didn't want to make the same mistake in our garden, so most of our trees are male. The red male catkins are very tidy, but for the sake of biodiversity we had to have one female tree. She is three from the meadow end of the Black Poplar Walk and, indeed, her white catkins can look a bit untidy – if not a full Moscow Mess. And yes, I can imagine what a lot of them would look like. I also don't think they would actively enhance the subtle yellow flowers of the delicate Tenby daffodils we planted beneath the trees.

I'm not a great fan of the cheap-and-cheerful large sacks of various hybridised daffodils that you can buy in certain nurseries that are 'suitable for naturalising'. In my experience, they don't interbreed and blend together when planted out in open grassland; instead, they look like what they are: a job lot of daffs, of different sizes, shapes and colours – many of which clash. So I've always chosen what I plant and I usually go for what are supposed to be the commonest native British daffodil, *Narcissus pseudonarcissus*.[9] They look gorgeous in the meadow and have a lingering scent on still, calm days. Nobody is absolutely certain that daffodils are native in Britain; I'm not aware that their bulbs or pollen have been found on pre-Roman sites. But I can't say it worries me much: if they're not native, they certainly should be. Another supposedly wild native British variety is the smaller and very much more elegant Tenby daffodil (*Narcissus obvallaris*), from Wales.[10] I'm very fond of them and I can understand why they were so popular in

Victorian times – so popular, indeed, that demand for *Narcissus obvallaris* came close to wiping out their natural habitat. But they have been better conserved since then and are now bred commercially. I decided to plant Tenby daffs in the long grass within the Black Poplar Walk, where they brighten up the deep shade, except in that one limited area below the female tree, where those white fluffy poplar catkins dominate the scene. Half an hour with a leaf rake soon clears the fluff.

The Black Poplar Walk has undoubtedly proved a great success. Much of it – especially the dramatically drooping lower branches and the dark tunnel-like effect – has been unplanned. But there have been unanticipated problems too. I don't think anyone predicted the sharp rise in spring and autumn storms and gales, brought about by climate change, that have hit the open, flat landscapes of the Fens particularly hard. Two of the trees of the Black Poplar Walk were actually snapped in half – something I had never seen before. Branches, especially those looping lower ones, are often damaged in gales, but most of the gently bending main trunks have survived.

The named storms of recent years have worried me a bit. I think it's partly because as long-term sheep farmers we have learnt not to name sheep – especially lambs. Nowadays, we only refer to them by their farm registration numbers. But when we started our small flock, back in the early 1980s, things were rather different.

I recall sitting down to a roast lamb supper in Limetree Farm with a visiting colleague from a Dutch university. He was a charming man and we were all feeling particularly relaxed, thanks to the several bottles of wine and strong Belgian beer he had brought with him. Maisie had surpassed herself in the kitchen, and though I say so myself, the sprout tops and roast potatoes were outstandingly delicious. I can remember leaning back in my chair, raising my glass and declaring:

'Well, let's all drink to Jacob. He has done us proud!'

Our Dutch friend looked up from his plate, clearly rather puzzled:

'And who he, Jacob?' He paused. 'A farmer?'

'No,' I replied without any thought, 'he was the lamb: a Jacob ram, which I castrated. He does taste good, though, doesn't he?'

Our friend didn't reply. Far from looking happy and well fed, he rose hastily to his feet and staggered to the outside toilet, at the back of the house. I felt terrible: it hadn't been my finest hour.

# 15

# People and Gardens

*Getting Grounded • Perceptions and Realities •*
*Vanishing Snowdrops • The National Garden Scheme*
*• The Tea Team*

Creating the garden has been a mirror on life and even the writing of this book has taught me many lessons. It has not been like the preparation of an academic report, where you carefully seek to integrate the views of everybody associated with the research and eventually produce what you hope will be a balanced account of what may well have been a demanding project. In this book, as well as telling the story of the creation of a garden in the Fens, I have tried to capture what it is that motivates gardeners to do what they do. Is it an art, or is it a craft? Frankly, I couldn't care less, because it's both and neither; it's something that some lucky people are born with and others acquire through life – and both are equally valid.

Gardening snobbery exists and I detest it. Is a beautifully laid-out and managed allotment plot necessarily 'inferior' to an Arts and Crafts country garden or to a Rococo labyrinth? No, they are just different and should be judged for what they are. I once visited some reconstructed prehistoric houses in

central Europe that were built during the Nazi era and had
originally been intended to illustrate their unpleasantly racist
view of the remote past. But they worked as reconstructions
and their setting was, in effect, a picturesque water garden.
Who am I to say that the men and women who carried out the
work would have all necessarily shared the fascist views of the
people who employed them? So yes, garden designs are very
much about their designers, but through time they will change
to reflect the thoughts and work of the people who love and
maintain them. I use the word 'love' here because I mean it.
I don't know how many times I have chatted to gardeners –
both professional and amateur – in famous English gardens.
As they discuss the garden, you can nearly always spot that
gleam of real affection for the place where they spend so much
of their time.

All gardeners carry their ideal garden in their heads and in
my experience it changes in size, shape, style and character,
depending on what they're doing or thinking about. Sometimes
it's an arrangement of pots on a patio, at other times it may
be a bit grander: maybe a rose bed or a border. Of course,
you are always free to change your mind and agonise about
your current project. During the early days at Inley Drove, I
endured sleepless nights while my mind wrestled with flooding,
dead cabbage plants and a hedge that refused to grow. It was
frustrating because I knew what I wanted – the vision was clear
in my head – but it just wouldn't become reality. And when
it did, it was very different from what I had first imagined.
Still, it was none the worse for that. Soon, the garden we had
created, with all its flaws and compromises, had completely
replaced all the mental pictures I had conjured up during those
hours I spent wide awake contemplating an impossible vision
of perfection. Incidentally, I deliberately used the term 'we
had created' because I was referring not just to myself, but to

Maisie and also to Mother Nature: her soil, her rain and her unexpected surprises.

Garden designers have always been very good at making their customers pay for their visions of perfect gardens. The great Lancelot Brown would famously stress a particular garden's 'Capability' for improvement. A little later in the eighteenth century, Humphry Repton would present potential clients with one of his famous 'Red Books', which would describe and illustrate his vision for their garden.[1] Modern garden designers use digital techniques to achieve the same goals. It seems to me that such gardens will only really come to life when their owners decide to become involved, to get down on their hands and knees with a trowel and a weed knife. I don't think that Brown or Repton would have objected to this, as they had people very much in mind. In those days, there was also a clear distinction between a grand, show-style display garden and an inhabited space lived in by real people and wildlife. In the more recent past, artist-designers, like Gertrude Jekyll, certainly appreciated that gardens were designed creations, but they were also places where life carried on – hopefully enhanced and made more peaceful by beautiful surroundings.

Today, I think it's hands-on gardeners who are becoming increasingly aware that their gardens are about reality; that you can best cope with the many problems inherent in the modern world if you are grounded. When and if a nuclear war happens, you won't find many gardeners in underground shelters. I've no wish to die slowly, many months later. When the bomb goes off, I'll be in my vegetable garden surrounded by my pea and bean friends, carefully threading them through hazel twigs, pulling out weeds and chewing gently on a few baby spring onions. When you are working in a garden, you are concentrating on what you are doing. You are who you are; you're being true to yourself, but it would be a huge mistake to assume that your perception of what you are doing is the only one that matters – which was something that was brought home to me by the writing of this book. It has taught me so much, not just about gardening but about people too, especially the person nearest and dearest to me. It is time to talk about Maisie.

*

I am very aware that this book reads as if I had had nearly all the ideas and then done most of the heavy spadework that made them reality. Sadly, nothing could be further from the truth. Maisie planned and executed many areas of the garden, including the Long and Short Borders, the Rose Garden, the Long Walk and the Dome Garden. These were all places where the plantings were more formal, with arrangements of perennials, roses and shrubs.

I freely confess that in *A Fenland Garden* I have written about *my own* perception of a garden we created and developed together. And that perception is very different from Maisie's. We both have very firm and clear ideas, some of which we share, but others remain personal.

Maisie is very much better at what I think of as 'flower gardening' than I am, partly – I suspect – because, like many men, I don't have a very reliable sense of colour: I often get blues and greens confused, and have a hopeless memory for hues. Maisie, on the other hand, remembers the subtlest shades with absolute precision. I have absolutely no idea how she does this, but I have never known her mismatch two flowers. I'm also not very good at remembering plant names and varieties – a failing that has got rather worse as I've grown older. Maisie, however, has a fantastic memory for such things and only very rarely has to check whether she was right, on her smartphone.

So readers might have noticed that I haven't lingered over the different asters in the Long Border, nor the many scented hybrid musk roses. Instead, I have spent more time describing the wood, the Hay Meadow, the Serpentine Walk, Chicken Lane and those areas where the plants are less formal and where bulbs and wildflowers, such as cowslips and primroses, are a main feature. All in all, Maisie has been remarkably tolerant of my account of the garden at Inley Drove.

Gardens are about contrasts, and I believe the fact that Maisie and I have concentrated on our own favourite areas of the garden has enhanced their effectiveness and impact at Inley Drove. I love the way, for example, that the Long Border, with its abundance of different coloured flowers, ends in a timber pergola, which runs along the side of the small meadow where we graze our rams when they're being kept away from the ewes. Similarly, you leave the informality of the birches in the Serpentine Walk and pass through a doorway-like opening in the tall hornbeam hedge to find yourself in the room-like enclosed space of the domeless Dome Garden. Formality and informality are woven together, and both are the better for it.

This integration of formal and informal mirrors life in the country. In the 1990s, when I drove past the local parish church during a Sunday service, the vehicles parked outside the graveyard usually included mud-spattered Land Rovers, maybe even an old tractor and quite a few ageing bicycles. Today, congregations are smaller, but I'm glad to say some cars are still quite well caked with mud. But you can be sure that their drivers, both then and now, will be looking very neat and tidy.

The contrast between formality and informality changes with the passing of the seasons. In winter, the formality of the borders declines as the perennials die back and roses start to lose their leaves. Some gardeners like to cut their borders back in late autumn, but we prefer to leave seedheads in place, as they're an important source of food for birds over winter. So the whole garden looks a bit informal in December and January. Then the first bulbs appear and the different parts of the garden start to acquire fresh identities. The informality of many country gardens enables these changes to be displayed very effectively, which is something that Maisie and I have long appreciated. It is something we try to enhance, as we both enjoy the changing seasonal contrasts. In a strange way, they bring our different areas of interest together. A good garden should be as much about the relationship of different people, as of plants.

*

Readers may recall I had quite a lot to say about snowdrops in Chapter 4. Snowdrops were one of the big successes of our move from Limetree Farm to Lincolnshire, and we planted hundreds of them when we laid out the new wood at Inley Drove Farm. They were arranged in small groups of two or three bulbs in the hope that they would grow into eye-catching clumps, which happened in just two or three years – very much faster than we had expected, but then snowdrops seem to love our clay-silt soil. Soon, squirrels and other scavengers discovered them and new clumps started appearing everywhere. And they all thrived. Snowdrops must now cover three or four acres of the wood, although what I'd hoped would be a spectacular display has been rather spoiled – perhaps diluted would be a better word – in certain areas by hundreds of oak, ash, maple and hazel seedlings, which I might have discouraged in the past, but which today are needed to replace the many mature ash trees afflicted with dieback. That disease is just one of many problems that are affecting gardeners today. Other painful realities of modern life are also catching up with us.

Dog walking has become an important part of my life. No two walks with our much-loved dogs Baldwin and Pen are ever the same, even if their excitement over finding deposits of bird poo can become a little bit wearing. That aside, dull moments when out dog walking are almost unknown. By 2020, we'd been taking the dogs for two or often three daily outings, for as many years, and it sometimes felt as if they were exercising us – which is probably true too. One day in early March, I was following the dogs along a path in the wood, towards the edge of a large spread of snowdrops. A few minutes later they suddenly both stopped, standing rigid, their heads down, with nostrils flared and quivering. I knew at once that this was no ordinary scent; they didn't usually get this excited – not even at the prospect of heron poo.

I crept up to them, my eyes on stalks. I expected to spot a muntjac or roe deer, but nothing was moving in the undergrowth – not even a hare, or squirrel – and the ground was clear of any fresh droppings. So what was it that was holding their attention? They seemed to be staring at some holes where squirrels had dug up a few snowdrops – or at least, that's what I thought. Quietly, I looped their leads around a young tree and took a closer look. And yes, the dogs were right, there *was* something odd about those holes. They were fresh, yet I couldn't spot the telltale scratch marks that burrowing squirrels usually make in our heavy clay-silt soils. The surface of the ground was also strangely clear of bulbs: squirrels are certainly energetic, but they aren't particularly tidy and they always leave dozens of bulbs, many half-chewed, lying on the surface. Then I saw something that gave me a chill. Some of the more freshly dug holes seemed to have been cut with a narrow-bladed spade. Even the lumps of soil around them had at least one straight edge. As I dropped to my knees to take a closer look, I spotted an almost empty plastic lemonade bottle sticking out of one of the holes. Now there could be no doubt whatsoever: those snowdrops had been taken by human thieves, not squirrels. I was about to pick the bottle up, when I stopped. It was now evidence for a crime and I mustn't touch it. So I left it alone and took several photos with my mobile phone.

I walked back to the house and told Maisie about what the dogs and I had discovered. She was making a pot of tea at the time, so had one or two other things on her mind, but I was still slightly surprised that she appeared to show no emotion at what I had to say. I even thought I detected a hint of disbelief.

'You do think it was robbery, don't you?'

She looked at me as if I was mad.

'Of course I do.'

She paused. 'It's just that everything now makes sense.'

I knew Maisie was good at sorting out problems, but this time she had made Sherlock Holmes look incompetent. She could see my astonishment.

'No,' she smiled. 'But now I know why that man turned up last week.'

I didn't know about this. She continued:

'I think you were at the market, but a youngish bloke knocked on the back door and said he'd just retrieved his dog out of the wood and had noticed all the snowdrop bulbs. He said they needed thinning and he offered to do it for us and give us a price for them.'

'What did he offer?' I asked.

'Oh, he didn't say, but he did give me a phone number.'

'And you didn't phone him?'

'Of course not,' she replied. 'There was something a bit creepy about him. And I didn't believe that story about his dog.'

I confess the snowdrop thefts didn't come as a complete

surprise. Every spring, the gardening press carries stories about raids on snowdrop woods and gardens. A few of these are local crimes by individuals, but the majority appear to be the work of larger networks ultimately linked to the bulb trade. I was reasonably certain that the theft of our snowdrops was a case in point. One reason I was fairly sure this wasn't a casual crime was that the thieves were clearly aware they were stealing pure-bred native snowdrops, *Galanthus nivalis*. We didn't want any fancy hybrids in the wood when we planted them, as we were trying to achieve a simple, natural look – and the thieves were plainly aware of this. The pure native snowdrop sells for good money from specialist dealers, whose adverts can be seen in the back pages of a few highly reputable gardening journals.

We reported our theft to the Lincolnshire police, who sent us an officer – I will call him PC Harry – who specialised in rural crime. PC Harry knew all about the illicit bulb trade and was in touch with colleagues in Norfolk, another county where professional snowdrop-stealing is a major problem. We gave him the phone number that the creepy visitor had given Maisie and later he told us that it was real, although he was being careful about saying much more. It was clearly a sensitive matter.

We also learnt from PC Harry that our bulbs would have been quickly sent to Holland, where their actual source could be concealed; they would then be sold on to specialist bulb sales, supposedly 'clean', where they were bought by dealers in Britain, some of whom would doubtless have known about their dodgy history. The nice rural crime policeman visited us several times and we had at least three separate raids on the snowdrops in March 2020. On each night-time visit, they must have removed a small van-full of bulbs. Over the course of the three March raids, they certainly took many thousands of bulbs.

A few weeks later, PC Harry told us that the plastic bottle had revealed traces of DNA, which we hoped would eventually help them pin down the person responsible. Sadly, it was to prove a forlorn hope.

Just as Harry had predicted, the following year, in early March 2021, the raids resumed. But this was during the height (or depths) of the Covid pandemic and world trade wasn't exactly thriving. PC Harry visited the scene of the crime but found no new evidence. In February 2022, we thought it would be a good idea if we phoned PC Harry for advice about setting up a night-vision camera, in case the raids started for a third time, but we got no reply. Eventually, we contacted someone who said that Lincolnshire Police were organising a new Rural Crime Team. I think we may have tried phoning one or two numbers, but without any success. I can remember feeling very apprehensive when I took the dogs for their woodland walks two months later, but to my surprise there was no more frenetic sniffing and no evidence of more raids. I spoke to a friend in the plant nursery world and he reckoned that after the implementation of the final Brexit trade deals, people from the UK no longer had unrestricted access to Dutch bulb sales. I've always regarded Britain's leaving the EU as an appalling mistake, but in this one particular instance I can't help thinking it seems to have worked in our favour. Back in the wood, I cannot bring myself to fill in those horrible holes. I can't make myself deliberately remove good evidence for such an egregious crime. I also know that, given time, the bulbs and the wildlife will do it for me. It's now October 2022, just eighteen months after the last raid, and I can report that the natural process of recovery is already well under way.

As I watched the snowdrops and the woodland slowly recover from the damage those thieves had inflicted, it struck me that a collector of paintings, jewellery or antiques could never fully recover from such a loss. They would always look on the thieves with loathing. But it's rather different in a garden. The snowdrop-stealers caused us great heartbreak and anxiety and we felt that something profoundly intimate and personal had been violated by what they did. But that was over a year ago. I cannot pretend that the pain has gone completely, but I don't think it will linger very much longer and this is because we both have more important and positive matters to deal with. For some ten years now, our garden has joined thousands of others in a wonderful scheme that allows us to raise large sums of money for charity.

\*

Shortly after we first met, in the mid-1970s, Maisie introduced me to the annual Yellow Book produced by the National Garden Scheme (NGS). The Yellow Book listed hundreds of gardens, which were not necessarily managed by the National Trust, English Heritage or other huge landowners. I won't describe them as 'ordinary' gardens, because none of them were at all ordinary: they were, and are, unique and very special places, and they belonged to gardeners in hamlets, villages, towns and cities right across England. They even included a few gardens attached to remote rural farmhouses.

We opened our young Inley Drove garden as part of the National Garden Scheme on a Sunday in mid-June 1997, just four and a half years after starting work on it (in the winter of 1992–3). I can still remember the excitement I felt when I saw pictures of our garden published in The Yellow Book. Looking back on it, I am slightly surprised that we were accepted by the county organiser, Sally Grant, who still keeps a motherly eye on us for the NGS. She has very high standards, but I am also aware that she has always been on the lookout for younger gardeners and unusual projects. Sometimes, older people's gardens can become a little too neat, controlled and similar. It's good to inject new ideas and maybe even sometimes a hint of iconoclasm.

June can be a very wet month in the Fens and several of our open days were spoiled by heavy showers. It didn't help that in those early years I was still laboriously cutting edges to the various beds and borders. I always cut the edges quite deep in the hope that they will act as temporary drains, which they do; but the rains that hit us on the days leading up to our opening on 18 June 2000 were truly exceptional. Most of the garden was completely flooded and I don't think we received many visitors at all – just a few faithful friends who wanted to support the NGS and who'd have turned up if the skies had been spitting fire and brimstone. The result of all this was that, very regretfully, we both decided we couldn't continue opening for the NGS until we had done more work on the garden's drainage.* We also knew it would take a few years because much of the drainage 'work' would actually be done deep in the ground by the expanding root systems of the many trees, shrubs and hornbeam hedges that formed the main framework of the garden.

We were both surprised by the speed with which those shrubs, trees and hedges grew. I was certainly aware that, even using powered trimmers, the task of cutting back the hornbeams was taking longer every year. By the time they could be considered mature – in about 2015 – it was taking me six full days to cut and clear away the clippings. So in 2015 we approached Sally and told her that we'd like to open the garden for the NGS the following year. Maisie and I had discussed the time of year we would open, and although we agreed that the garden looked spectacular in June, that was when everyone chose to open

* This work had started a year earlier in 1999, when land drains were given a first clearing with a pressure water jet.

their gardens – for the same reason. Maisie really understands old-fashioned roses and their pruning, which can encourage a strong second, late summer/early autumn, flowering. The sun's rays are less powerful later in the year, and so the flowers retain their colour better in their later flowering. And, what's more, their scent can linger in the slightly cooler air of an early autumn evening.

Maisie has always been very partial to asters and over the years she has built up a fine collection of some of the taller varieties that one used to see so often in gardens of the 1950s, 60s and 70s. Today, you can't find these varieties in garden centres; instead, the plants you are offered are shorter-stemmed and very persistent in their flowering. They look good in pots and at the front of borders, although I find their colours can be a bit strident. They also lack the subtle shifts in colour that can be seen on those plants that spring up from time to time as a result of cross-hybridisation. These hybrids can look a bit muddy and ordinary, but sometimes Maisie discovers one that really works, with good colour and flower size. I suppose if we were more commercially minded, we'd offer them to a nursery, but we don't. Instead, we give them to our gardening friends, who are always giving us plants. We also sell them at the plant stall on our open days for the NGS. Experience has shown that all varieties of plants sell very much better on the plant stall if they are also looking good out in the garden.

The garden looks wonderful in the early autumn, so we agreed that the 2016 opening would take place in mid-September (we chose the weekend of the 17th/18th). We also agreed that opening for a single day, as we had done before, was in effect placing all our eggs in one basket. So we decided to spread the risk over the two days of the weekend. We also knew from experience (and I checked the detailed day-by-day rain records I keep) that September, unlike June, is one of the

The Tea Team, ready for action in 2018. The team are (from left to right): Mark, Nigel, Rachael and Jessie. Mark and Rachael are wearing the then newly introduced National Garden Scheme yellow aprons.

driest months of the year. We have opened for a weekend in mid- and late September every year since 2016 and so far (touch wood) we haven't had a whole day ruined by rain. We opened during the two Covid summers of 2020 and 2021, when most of the visitors were advance-booked parties. It worked quite well, although inevitably numbers were slightly down.

In 2020 we raised £1,056, which was quite considerably below our average, but it was also a very happy and memorable occasion. For a start, we weren't allowed to sell tea and cakes the traditional way in teacups and saucers, with slices of cake on plates. So the Tea Team came up with a system where visitors could buy pre-bagged slices of cake from a stall at the edge of the Vegetable Garden. We placed groups of four bales of straw in the Tup (Ram) Field nearby and visitors – especially young families – were invited to sit on them while enjoying their cakes. Many of them, being farming folk, also brought Thermos flasks of tea with them. I don't think I've ever seen so many people having such a good time in the Tup Field. Small children were everywhere. It was lovely to see families relaxing after so many months of heightened tension and a growing sense of crisis, which sadly still hasn't completely gone. It was good to think that much of the money those pieces of cake had raised would be going towards nurses, many of whom worked within the NHS – whose survival is so vital to Britain's future. Even that year, when so many houses and gardens had to be closed because of lockdown, the NGS managed to raise an astonishing £2.88 million for its charities.

*

Opening our garden for the NGS has given us new inspiration and focus. Gardening is still a hobby – and, I dare say, a bit of an obsession too – but it's now a hobby with point and purpose. I know only too well that the sum isn't vast, but in the third year affected by Covid, in 2022, we managed to raise £2,353 for the various charities supported by the NGS. Most of this came during the open weekend in September, but several hundred was contributed by advance-booked groups, which we welcome from May to September.

The NGS was set up in 1927 by a Miss Elsie Wagg, who was a keen gardener and a council member of the Queen's Nursing Institute.[2] It proved highly successful and pre-war garden owners who supported it included Winston Churchill and Vita Sackville-West.[3] But the NGS isn't just about the rich and famous. One of the things I like best about it is the huge selection of gardens it has to offer. Locally, we can visit small town and suburban gardens, together with rural cottage gardens and country house gardens. There's even a tiny but absolutely perfect bonsai garden, not to mention a slightly larger one that features model railways.

After the Second World War, in 1949 the NGS came up with a yellow cover for its annual catalogue of open gardens, which soon became known universally as 'The Yellow Book'. Apparently, the colour yellow was supposed to symbolise post-war regeneration. It certainly signalled a change to a rather different, largely flower-based style of gardening, but I think we should also acknowledge the important role played by Dig for Victory campaigns in both world wars.[4] These were also intended by government to be morale-boosting, which they certainly were, but at the same time they produced hundreds of thousands of tons of fresh vegetables, which didn't have to be imported through mine- and submarine-infested seas. Lawns and flower beds were routinely dug up to grow food, which must actually have been quite difficult for many people. I can certainly sympathise with someone who has to grub up a lovingly planted front garden and replace it with rows of leeks and potatoes. Still, gardens are flexible places and if the soil is kept in good order they can grow almost anything.

After the war, the NGS broadened its scope, becoming the key funder of Macmillan Nurses, who have so far received over £17 million. In 1996, they announced they were supporting Marie Curie Cancer Care, and in 2013 Parkinson's UK became a permanent beneficiary. Inevitably, too, the NGS is supported by the great and the good across the country, but for me inspiration doesn't come from members of the Royal Family or other celebrities, however worthy they may be, but from those men and women you have the pleasure of meeting on their NGS open days. They may be slightly awkwardly wearing floral dresses or neatly pressed trousers, but take a look at the hands holding the teapot or cake slice: they'll have short nails and rough skin – maybe even a scab or two. It's a very small price to pay for such a great way of life.

If you have a smaller garden, there's a limit to the number of people who can visit at any one time, so you can probably ensure an adequate supply of tea and cake with just one or two, probably family, helpers. Our garden, however, is somewhat larger and dozens of visitors can be concealed within its hedged beds and borders, woodland walks and shrubberies. Then they miraculously appear, expecting tea and cakes at the entrance to the Poop Deck at the back of the house. It's as if they had been summoned by bells, and it happens sometime around four o'clock. To meet the challenge of the teatime rush, over the years we have developed a small but highly efficient Tea Team. This team is composed of men and women who all have specific tasks, but are also perfectly capable of doing other things if required. Not surprisingly, the vast majority of people in the Tea Team are archaeologists, who are used to working in all conditions as part of small integrated digging teams. One or two local people, also used to working within small teams on farms, can be very helpful too.

A retired professor of archaeological conservation provides considerable expertise and experience when it comes to the slicing of cakes into portions of precisely the same size. To some, she is known as the Portion Controller – and in case you were thinking what I suspect some of you might, she is small, petite and certainly not Fat. A few years ago, we bought a large urn that provides us with an abundant supply of boiling water, which allows us to keep at least two large teapots full of perfectly steeped tea (not too brown and not too watery) at those busiest of times. This urn is largely manned by the director of a large contractual archaeological unit – and you stay well away from him when he's carrying a freshly filled teapot. Many of the members of the Tea Team bring with them several home-baked cakes when they arrive. In the past, these were usually provided by the ladies, but in the past two years the men have also stepped in, usually with fruit cakes or loaves of bara brith (a fruity Welsh tea bread). For some reason, they seem to stay clear of fancy icing and decorative sugar carrots.

I relish the atmosphere within the Tea Team when the pressure is really increasing. It's like being on an excavation in that final week before the land must be returned to the landowner for development – and inevitably somebody discovers a pit filled with prehistoric coins, or a burial wearing an intricate necklace. Gardening is similar to life in the Tea Team. It's all about being true to yourself and your friends while enjoying the moment. I love it.

A view from behind the tea table on the Poop Deck on an NGS Open Sunday afternoon, in September 2021.

# Acknowledgements

First and foremost, I must acknowledge the constant help and support I have received from my wife, Maisie, who is a far better plantsman than I shall ever be. The two gardens discussed in this book were joint projects in both design and execution. I would also like to acknowledge her help, support and input in the preparation of this manuscript; her many plant notebooks were constantly referred to.

Although I have been able to discuss and describe the garden at Inley Drove Farm freely, I have decided that it would be wisest not to reveal the precise name or location of our first Fenland garden at 'Limetree Farm'; but it was indeed in the Cambridgeshire Fens, west of Wisbech.

I am particularly grateful to Professor Susan Oosthuizen for some very useful references and information about dylings, which I used extensively in Chapter 13.

When it comes to the practicalities of real gardening, I owe a huge debt of gratitude to Linda Ireson, Jason Groom, Liz Pye, Jessie Githiri, Charles and Katie Collishaw-Doubleday, Nick Baalam and Obie Smith – many of whom are also key members of the Tea Team. Sally Grant has been very helpful as our regional organiser for the National Garden Scheme.

In the early days at Inley Drove Farm, we received much useful help and advice from Reinhard Biehler, the founder of Baytree Garden Centre in Spalding. Today, we also spend much time at Jersey Cottage Nursery at nearby Moulton Seas End, where the founder and owner, Steve Foster, and his son Jo have given us much advice on unusual plants. The third local nursery that has long been an important part of our gardening lives is within the walled garden at West Acre Gardens, near King's Lynn.

I'm grateful as ever to the team at Head of Zeus: Richard Milbank, Aphra Le Levier-Bennett, Ellie Jardine and Clémence Jacquinet. Thanks are also due to Sam Marshall for her beautiful jacket image.

# Endnotes

## Chapter 1

1　www.gov.uk/government/publications/national-curriculum-in-england-history-programmes-of-study
2　Maisie established an early example of a Young Archaeologist's Club at Flag Fen. For more information about YAC, go to: new.archaeologyuk.org/join-a-yac-branch/
3　www.earthmoversmagazine.co.uk/digger-man/view,when-british-excavators-ruled-the-world_346.htm
4　Francis Pryor, *Excavation at Fengate*, Peterborough, England: The Third Report (Toronto and Northampton, 1980), fig 18, p.27.

## Chapter 2

1　David Hall, *The Fenland Project*, Number 10: Cambridgeshire Survey, The Isle of Ely and Wisbech (East Anglian Archaeology, Report 79, Cambridge, 1996), p. 186.
2　Ibid., p. 182.
3　I discuss salterns in *Scenes from Prehistoric Life: From the Ice Age to the Coming of the Romans* (Head of Zeus, London, 2021), pp. 206–222.
4　www.greatdixter.co.uk/the-nursery
5　I think this is the same as 'Chermesina Flame': www.rhs.org.uk/plants/297507/salix-alba-chermesina-flame/details
6　C. Fox, *Pattern and Purpose: A survey of Early Celtic Art in Britain* (National Museum of Wales, Cardiff, 1958).

## Chapter 3

1 I describe the construction of the Mere in *Flag Fen: Life and Death of a Prehistoric Landscape* (Tempus Books, Stroud, 2005), pp. 26–9.
2 For a fine example at Great Paxton, visit: www.charlievincetreesurgery.co.uk/single-post/2016/06/29/Pruning-Pleached-Lime-trees-in-Great-Paxton
3 This was also the nursery that supplied us with the hedging plants for our Lincolnshire garden: www.hedging.co.uk/acatalog/Index_Hedging__Trees__Shrubs___Conifers_1.html

## Chapter 4

1 https://assets.publishing.service.gov.uk/government/uploads/system/uploads/attachment_data/file/722179/FWS_summary.pdf
2 W. G. Hoskins, *The Making of the English Landscape* (republished by Penguin Books, Harmondsworth, 1970), p. 86.
3 Ibid., pp. 195–6.
4 I have also discussed Darwin and the Sandwalk in *Paths to the Past* (Allen Lane, 2018), pp. 2–7.
5 See https://powo.science.kew.org/taxon/urn:lsid:ipni.org:names:64496-1
6 www.walsinghamvillage.org/about/walsingham-abbey-grounds-and-friary
7 www.plantlife.org.uk/uk/discover-wild-plants-nature/picking-wildflowers-and-the-law

## Chapter 5

1 Arne Maynard, *The Gardens of Arne Maynard* (Merrell, London, 2015). Guanock House is featured on pp. 254–71, with excellent photos by William Collinson.
2 Like the one at Rievaulx Terrace, Yorkshire: www.nationaltrust.org.uk/rievaulx-terrace/features/the-ionic-temple-at-rievaulx-terrace
3 She is photographed by Valerie Finnis pouring a cup of tea at Ashton Wold, in Ursula Buchan, *Garden People* (Thames and Hudson, London, 2007), pp. 74–6.

## Chapter 6

1   Joan Morgan and Alison Richards, *The Book of Apples* (Brogdale Horticultural Trust, Kent, and Ebury Press, London, 1993). An enlarged edition, *The New Book of Apples*, was published by Ebury Press in 2002.
2   This may well be due to the use of agricultural insecticides. See: www.theguardian.com/environment/2022/mar/01/bee-harming-pesticide-thiamethoxam-uk-emergency-exemption
3   https://en.wikipedia.org/wiki/Norfolk_Biffin
4   https://en.wikipedia.org/wiki/Ribston_Pippin
5   https://ahdb.org.uk/news/consumer-insight-why-uk-consumers-spend-8-of-their-money-on-food
6   Published by Mitchell Beazley Publishers, London, 1978.
7   www.shuttleworth.org/explore/swiss-garden/
8   www.hindringhamhall.org/
9   One such settlement is at Star Carr in Yorkshire, which I discuss (with references) in *Scenes from Prehistoric Life*, pp. 40–56.
10  www.rhs.org.uk/plants/79628/i-corylus-maxima-i-kentish-cob-(f)/details
11  www.rhs.org.uk/plants/325170/corylus-maxima-nottingham-cobnut-(f)/details

## Chapter 7

1   It's very clearly explained with good diagrams in Tony Biggs, *Vegetables, Royal Horticultural Society's Encyclopaedia of Practical Gardening* (Mitchell Beazley, London, 1980), p. 20.
2   Ibid, pp. 38–9.

## Chapter 8

1   For a wonderful introduction to pleaching and the artistic creation of hedges, see: Jake Hobson, *The Art of Creative Pruning* (Timber Press, London, 2011).
2   www.bto.org/our-science/monitoring/hedgehogs
3   www.rhsplants.co.uk/plants/_/lonicera-japonica-halls-prolific/classid.1679/

4 www.rhs.org.uk/plants/7383/i-fritillaria-imperialis-i/details
5 https://ntcalkeabbey.wordpress.com/
6 https://en.wikipedia.org/wiki/Verbascum_nigrum
7 https://en.wikipedia.org/wiki/Wisteria_sinensis

## Chapter 9

1 For a photo of The Gate, see: www.flickr.com/photos/brighton/3640116491
2 https://en.wikipedia.org/wiki/Google_Earth
3 https://pryorfrancis.wordpress.com/2020/07/17/a-tour-around-inley-drove-farm-garden-in-june-and-july-2020-part-2/

## Chapter 10

1 https://en.wikipedia.org/wiki/Iris_pseudacorus
2 This illustrates how difficult it can be just to control: www.nationaltrust.org.uk/claremont-landscape-garden/features/combating-crassula-at-claremont
3 The Holkham Hall greenhouses have recently been beautifully restored: www.holkham.co.uk/thomas-messenger-glasshouse-restoration-success/
4 https://westacregardens.co.uk/
5 https://en.wikipedia.org/wiki/Aegopodium_podagraria
6 www.wildlifetrusts.org/wildlife-explorer/wildflowers/stinging-nettle

## Chapter 11

1 https://en.wikipedia.org/wiki/United_Kingdom_weather_records
2 www.nationaltrust.org.uk/stowe
3 The history of Stowe is described in detail, with magnificent illustrations by John Martin Robinson, in *Temples of Delight: Stowe Landscape Gardens* (The National Trust/Pitkin, London and Andover, 1994).
4 For an excellent discussion of the topic in general, see Tom Williamson, *Polite Landscapes: Gardens and Society in Eighteenth-Century England* (Johns Hopkins University Press, Baltimore, Maryland, 1995).

5  www.nationaltrust.org.uk/anglesey-abbey-gardens-and-lode-mill/ features/winter-at-anglesey-abbey

6  For an excellent summary of Britain's surviving wartime defences, see Mike Osborne, *Defending Britain: Twentieth-Century Military Structures in the Landscape* (Tempus Publishing, Stroud, 2004).

7  www.rhs.org.uk/plants/76666/geranium-pyrenaicum-bill-wallis/ details

8  https://en.wikipedia.org/wiki/Rosa_rugosa

9  www.rbge.org.uk/visit/dawyck-botanic-garden/

10 www.hillier.co.uk/trees/our-trees/alnus-glutinosa-laciniata/

11 D. G. Coombs, '10 Metalwork', in Francis Pryor, *The Flag Fen Basin: Archaeology and environment of a Fenland landscape* (English Heritage, Swindon, 2001), pp. 255–317.

## Chapter 12

1  www.painshill.co.uk/attractions/the-crystal-grotto/

2  https://eastrustonoldvicarage.co.uk/

3  https://happisburgh.org.uk/lighthouse/

4  See, for example: https://youtu.be/bW7j3cYnDmY

## Chapter 13

1  https://sussexpast.co.uk/attraction/fishbourne-roman-palace/

2  Barry Cunliffe, *Fishbourne: A Roman Palace and Its Garden* (Thames and Hudson, London, 1971).

3  The remains of ridge-and-furrow, or rig-and-furrow, fields can still be seen widely across East Anglia and the Midlands. For a succinct account of how they were used, see Richard Muir, *Landscape Encyclopaedia: A Reference Guide to the Historic Landscape* (Windgather Press, Macclesfield, 2004), pp. 219–221.

4  Laxton has an excellent Visitor Centre: http://www.laxton visitorcentre.org.uk/

5  Information from Prof. Susan Oosthuizen.

6  https://www.english-heritage.org.uk/visit/places/mount-grace- priory/

7  Quote from inside the front cover of the guidebook by Glyn Coppack and Mark Douglas, *Mount Grace Priory* (English Heritage Guidebooks).

## Chapter 14

1  https://rousham.org/
2  For an excellent account of Rousham Hall and Gardens, see A. Brooks and J. Sherwood, *Oxfordshire: North and West* (The Buildings of England, Yale University Press, 2017), pp. 442–9.
3  Rabbit bones have been found at Fishbourne Roman Palace, West Sussex.
4  www.woodlandtrust.org.uk/trees-woods-and-wildlife/animals/mammals/grey-squirrel/
5  www.theguardian.com/environment/2019/feb/10/plummeting-insect-numbers-threaten-collapse-of-nature
6  www.nationaltrust.org.uk/features/saving-our-native-black-poplars
7  www.greatbarns.org.uk/museums/cholstrey_court_barn.html
8  www.nytimes.com/2001/06/08/world/moscow-journal-take-cover-everybody-spring-alas-is-in-the-air.html
9  www.rhs.org.uk/plants/11394/i-narcissus-pseudonarcissus-i-subsp-i-pseudonarcissus-i-(13)/details
10 https://botanicgarden.wales/living-attractions/cenhinen-bedr-dinbych/

## Chapter 15

1  www.themorgan.org/collection/Humphry-Reptons-Red-Books
2  https://en.wikipedia.org/wiki/Elsie_Wagg
3  The NGS website has an excellent history page: https://ngs.org.uk/who-we-are/who-we-are-and-what-we-do/
4  https://en.wikipedia.org/wiki/Victory_garden

# Index

Page numbers in *italic* refer to illustrations

*Acanthus spinosus* (spiny bear's breeches) 186
aconites 90, 92, 93, 95, 138, 285
*Aeonium arboreum* var. *atropurpureum* 'Zwartkop' 70–1
*Alchemilla mollis* 222
alder 39, 85, 119, 243, 250
  see also *Alnus*
allotments 156
*Alnus* (alder)
  A. *glutinosa* 243
    A. *g.* 'Laciniata' 250
  A. *incana* 'Aurea' 243
Angel of the North sculpture, Northumbria 226
Anglesey Abbey, Cambridgeshire 240
Anglian Water 20
antiques centres 124
apples/apple orchards 125–34
  apple blossom 128
  apple varieties 127–31
  *The Book of Apples* (Morgan and Richards) 128, 132
  Bramley orchards 29, 49, 64–5, 67, 125, 126, 127
  cider orchards 126
  espaliers *135*, 136, 163–4
  harvesting and storage 132–3, 163
  Inley Drove Farm 125, 126, 127–33, 163

public taste preferences 134
rootstocks 29, 126, 129
tree pruning 29, 65, 125, 136, 163
windbreaks 125
windfalls 64–5, 125, 129, 132
archaeological ground inspection 45
arches
  hazel 138, 206
  wirework 206, *207*, 208
Arts and Crafts gardens 25, 189
ash 39, 63, 80, 81, 86, 87, 96, 119, 239, 271
ash dieback 82, 86, 96, 304–5
Ashton Wold, Northamptonshire 122
asparagus 157–61, *157*, 182
  asparagus beetle 160
  'Connover's Colossal' 158, 160
  crowns 158, 159
assarts 84
*Aster novae-angliae* 'Andenken an Alma Pötschke' 222
asters 222, 311
Aston, Mick 279
auriculas 185
Aylott, Joe 165–6, 167

Baldwin (Jack Russell) 88, 91, *107*, 229, 305
barns
  cruck barns 293
  timber 11–12, *13*, *15*, 78, 79
Beauty of Bath apples 129–30

bedding plants 235
beds and borders 53
  border edging 247, 310
  double borders 213, 214, 220
  hedges as backdrops 50, 220,
    276–7
  herbaceous borders 219–20
  Limetree Farm 51, 53
  Long Border (Inley Drove Farm)
    188, 209, 213–23, 216, 236,
    238, 241, 242, 243, 251, 254,
    256, 259, 262, 271, 272, 277,
    303
  mixed borders 50, 51, 95, 220
  plant heights 220
  raised beds 153–4, 182, 183
  seasonal interest 90
beech 50, 239
Beeching, Dr 153
bees 128, 163, 209
Betula (birch)
  B. nigra 250–1
  B. pendula 242
    B. p. 'Dalecarlica' 245
    B. p. 'Purpurea' 245
  B. utilis var. jacquemontii 250
bindweed (Convolvulus) 36, 166,
  228
biological diversity 40–1, 290
birch 87, 239, 249, 250
  Birch Grove (Inley Drove farm)
    240–6, 240, 248, 250, 251
  see also Betula
birdlife 131, 163, 177, 209, 223,
  271, 291–2
birds of prey 131
black poplar (Populus nigra) 218,
  229, 262, 292–3
  Black Poplar Walk (Inley Drove
    Farm) 292, 293–4, 296, 297
  catkins 296, 297
  dioecious 295–6
  planting 294, 295
blackberry 87
blackthorn 85, 289
bluebells 96–7, 138, 204
  see also Hyacinthoides

'borrowed' views 37–8, 238, 260–1,
  262–3
boundaries 80
  see also fences; hedges; walls
box 237
Bramley apples 29, 49, 64–5, 67,
  125, 126, 127, 129
brassica club root 37, 146, 155, 167
Brickell, Christopher 136
Bridgeman, Charles 283
Brogdale Horticultural Trust 128
Bronze Age 18–19, 150–1
  see also Flag Fen
Brown, Lancelot 'Capability' 20–1,
  37, 51, 52, 112–13, 189, 301
Brussels sprouts 149, 153, 166, 235
builders' rubble 181–2, 197, 201,
  217
Burnham Market 225
buttercups see creeping buttercup;
  meadow buttercup
butterflies 209, 229
buying plants 223, 224–6

cabbages 166
Calke Abbey, Derbyshire 185
Cambridge 61, 108
Cambridge University Botanic
  Garden 44, 45, 46–7, 72fn, 284
Canada 14, 92–3, 145, 188–9, 287
carpentry 14
carpet bedding schemes 234–5
Carthusians 279–80
Catalpa (Indian bean tree)
  C. bignonioides 221
    C.b. 'Aurea' 221
  C. x erubescens 221
  C. speciosa 'Pulverenta' 221
catkins 90–1, 296, 297
cauliflowers 157
Celtic art 52
chainsaws 64
Chatteris 29
cheap food 133
Chelsea Flower Show 70, 110
chemicals in the garden 40, 119,
  166, 286

cherry 86
wild cherry 85, 86, 107, *107*
Chicken Lane (Inley Drove Farm)
115, 288, 289, *289*, 290–1, 292,
294–5
chickens 287–8
churches, medieval 68, 79, 199
Churchill, Winston 313
cider 126–7
clematis 208, 236
clematis wilt 73
climate change 40, 48, 56, 72, 82,
93, 202, 210, 233–4, 297
clover 41
red 100
white 100, 101
club root 37, 146, 155, 167
cobnuts 139, 141–3, 285
gathering 141–2
*see also Corylus*
Collinson, William 109, 110, 143
Collyweston slates 255
continental climates 93
Coombs, Dr Dave 251
coppicing 85, 109, 142, 143
*Cornus* (dogwood) 45–6, 246
*Cortaderia* (pampas grass)
*C. richardii* 186
*C. selloana* var. 'Sunningdale
Silver' 112, 115–16, 118, 119,
120, 121, *121*
*Corylus* (hazel)
*C. avellana* 'Pearson's Prolific'
143
*C. maxima* 'Kentish Cob' 142–3
cottage gardens 190, 191
couch grass (*Elymus repens*) 36,
39–40, 166, 229
courgettes 161
Covid-19 pandemic 70, 112, 160,
223, 259, 264, 308, 312–13
cowslips 104, 105, 106–7, 109, 110,
112, 122, 238
*Crataegus monogyna* 86
*see also* hawthorn
creeping buttercup (*Ranunculus
repens*) 41, 60, 104, 110–11

crocus 95
cropmarks 150–1
Crown Imperial lilies 184
cruck barns 293
cucumbers 161
Cunliffe, Barry 267
cut flowers 209
cyclamen 249

daffodils 43, 80, 81, 93, 204, 244,
296
hybridised 296
*see also Narcissus*
daisies 104
dark mullein (*Verbascum nigrum*)
186
Darwin, Charles 40, 89
Darwin's Sandwalk, Bromley 89
dawn redwood (*Metasequoia
glyptostroboides* 'Gold Rush')
216
Dawyck Botanic Garden, Scottish
Borders 250
day length 92
dead nettle 104
desalination 31
Dickens, Charles 130
Dig for Victory campaigns 314
dioecious plants 295–6
dog kennels 180, 181
dog walking 68, 88, 89, 91, 98, 107,
305
Dog-in-a-Doublet sluice,
Peterborough 42
dogwood (*Cornus*) 45–6, 246
Dome Garden (Inley Drove Farm)
206–8, *207*, 270–3, 277–8, *278*,
280, 303
Down House, Bromley 89
droveways 23, 24, 26, *26*, 30, 78
dry weather and drought 49, 55,
230, 234, 237
drystone walls 288
Dumas, Alexandre 43
dumpy level 148
Dutch elm disease 82
dykes 9, 39, 106–7, 274, 276

brinks 106–7, *107*
IDB-maintained 72
dyling ditches 276, 277

earthworms 16, 167, 169, 177
Elgood's Brewery 195
elm 63, 82, 239
Ely 29, 261
Ely Cathedral 279
*Elymus repens* (couch grass) 36,
    39–40, 166, 229
*Encyclopaedia of Practical
    Gardening* (RHS) 136
English Brothers 11–12
English country gardens 20–1, 41,
    123–4
  'borrowed' landscapes 37–8
  views 37–8, 41, 113, 124, 238
  *see also individual gardens*
environmental degradation 16–17,
    82, 133, 290
*Eryngium giganteum* (sea holly)
    186–7

Farm Woodland Scheme 81, 83, 85,
    87, 285
farming
  farm machinery 82
  intensive cultivation 16–17, 81–2,
    133, 288, 290, 291
  medieval field system 275, 276
  prehistoric farming practices 26,
    139–40, 141, 143
fastigiate trees 87, 293
Felco 178
fences
  fence posts 204
  hurdle fences 202, 203, 204, 207
  mesh fences 149
  stock-wire fences 204, 288
Fengate 140
Fens 1, 6, 9, 11, 17, 27, 29, 32, 68,
    72, 78, 104, 125, 194, 233, 274,
    290, 297
  *see also individual fens*
*Ficus carica* 'Brown Turkey' (fig)
    174

field maple 85
fieldwalking 45
figs 173, 174
Fishbourne Roman Palace, West
    Sussex 267
Flag Fen 17–27, 136–7, 197, 224,
    251
  banks and ditches 23, 24, 26
  charitable trust 20, 22
  droveway 23, 24, 26
  funding 66
  Mere 56, 57
  name 217
  prehistoric carpentry 14
  reconstructed Bronze Age
    landscape 19, 21, 23–5, 26–7
  visitor attraction 17, 18–19,
    136–7
flooding 72, 77, 78
  flood-defence banks 49
  Inley Drove Farm 219, 242, 248,
    310
  Limetree Farm 43
forks and spades 169, 170
foxes 179
Fred (local farmer) 8–9, 10, 100
French marigold (*Tagetes patula*)
    161–2
*Fritillaria imperialis* 'Aurora' 184
Front Garden (Inley Drove Farm)
    173, 191–2, 197–9, 200–10,
    201, 271
frost
  air frost 164, 165
  ground frost 164
  hoar frost 164, 289
fuchsias 208

galanthophiles 94, 96
*Galanthus nivalis* (snowdrop) 94,
    95, 96, 307
  *G.n.* 'Flore Pleno' 183
garden centres 223, 224–5
garden design
  'borrowed' views 37–8, 238,
    260–1, 262–3
  borrowing ideas 44

bought-in plants 71
'destination' features 89–90, 115,
    117
differing types of garden use
    51–2, 88, 215
evolving design 181, 300
garden privacy 88, 192
garden 'rooms' 124, 267, 268,
    270
'historical' reconstructions 21
inspiration 116–17
integration of formal and
    informal 303–4
integration of house and garden
    187–8, 189
light touch 110
'no turning back' principle 118,
    119, 254, 269
off-the-shelf designs 181
pattern and purpose 51–3, 60, 63
regional distinctiveness 60
secret places and surprises 253,
    259–60
views, limiting 261
garden waste heaps 179
*Gardeners' World* (BBC) 60
gardening snobbery 299–300
garlic 162
The Gate Hangs High (Lincolnshire
    pub) 194–5
gazebo 206–7, 207, 208
Georgian gardens 25, 88, 163, 189
*Geranium*
    G. 'Johnson's Blue' 222
    G. *palustre* 244
    G. *psilostemon* 244
    G. *pyrenaicum* 'Bill Wallis' 243–4
The Glade (Inley Drove Farm) 244,
    246, 249, 265, 266, 271
global warming *see* climate change
glyphosate 40
Godmanchester 61
golden orfe 59
goldfish 59
'good taste' 190
Google Earth 195
Gormley, Antony 226

Grant, Sally 309–10
grape hyacinth (*Muscari
    armeniacum*) 184
grass 48–50, 100–1
    grazing seed mixes 100
    mowing 49–50, 230–1
    ornamental grasses 101, 234
    *see also* lawns; meadows
Graveley Howe, Hertfordshire 97
Great Dixter, East Sussex 43, 122
Great Ouse, River 32
greenhouses 38, 48
ground elder (*Aegopodium
    podagraria*) 166, 227–8
Guyhirn, Cambridgeshire 190

Happisburgh Lighthouse 263
hares 41, 98, 107, 179, 285, 286,
    288
Harry's Patch (growing ground)
    69–70, 71, 78, 104, 155
hawthorn 49, 62, 80, 85, 86, 289
hay
    cutting 102, 103, 112
    Hay Meadow (Inley Drove Farm)
        79, 84, 98, 102–3, 103, 105–6,
        109, 110–12, 120, 121, 219,
        238, 272
    ryegrass 100, 103
hazel 85, 90–1, 138, 139, 142–3,
    202–3
    arches 138, 206
    catkins 90–1
    coppicing 143
    rods and poles 109, 142, 143,
        206, 293
    *see also Corylus*
hazelnuts *see* cobnuts
heatwave (2022) 72fn, 233, 236
hedgehogs 41, 98, 179
hedges 85–6, 246–7
    arches and gaps in 120, 213, 257,
        258, 259–60, 265, 266, 278
    backdrops to borders 50, 220,
        276–7
    beech 50
    blackthorn 289

box 237
cutting and trimming 49, 256–7, 263–6
enclosure hedges 86
hawthorn 49, 62, 80, 86, 289
hornbeam 50, 120, 148, 149–50, 218, 220, 241, 242, 249, 265, 272, 276–7, 278, 310
leaf retention 50
Leylandii 61
local plant species 86
*Lonicera* 257
yew 255–7, 258, 259
*Hemerocallis* 244
'Golden Chimes' 222
'Hornby Castle' 222
'Marion Vaughan' 222
herons 59
Hindringham Hall, Norfolk 138
Holbeach 108, 276
Holbeach Fen 8
Holbeach St Johns 6, 8
Holkham Hall, Norfolk 59–60, 127, 189, 224
Holme Fen Nature Reserve 239–40, 242, 243
honeysuckle 94, 180
  *see also Lonicera*
hornbeam (*Carpinus betulus*) 50, 120, 148, 149–50, 218, 220, 241, 242, 249, 265, 272, 276–7, 278, 310
horses 129
Hoskins, W.G. 84
Hot Garden (Inley Drove Farm) 182, 184, 185, 186, 187
hunter-gatherer way of life 141
Huntingdon 61
hurdles 202, 203, 207
Hy-Mac excavators 21, 22–3, 24, 27, 217
*Hyacinthoides* (bluebell)
  H. *hispanica* 97
  H. *non-scripta* 97

Indian bean tree (*Catalpa bignonioides*) 221

Inley Drove 125, 192, 194, 196, 228
Inley Drove Farm
  acreage 238
  archaeological remains 274–5, 276
  Birch Grove 240–6, 240, 248, 250, 251
  Black Poplar Walk 292, 293–4, 296, 297
  charity plant sales 70, 186, 311
  Chicken Lane 115, 288, 289, 289, 290–1, 292, 294–5
  Dome Garden 206–8, 207, 270–3, 277–8, 278, 280, 303
  driveway 125, 126, 127, 191–2
  dykes and dylings 9, 106–7, 276, 277
  Front Garden 173, 191–2, 197–9, 200–10, 201, 271
  The Glade 244, 246, 249, 265, 266, 271
  Hay Meadow 79, 84, 98, 102–3, 103, 105–6, 109, 110–12, 120, 121, 219, 238, 272
  Hot Garden 182, 184, 185, 186, 187
  house siting and construction 14, 15, 77, 78, 193, 196–7, 209–10
  lawns 41, 113, 121, 217, 230
  Long Border 188, 209, 213–23, 216, 236, 238, 241, 242, 243, 251, 254, 256, 259, 262, 271, 272, 277, 303
  Long Walk 250
  'moat' 203–4
  National Garden Scheme openings 124, 185, 186, 246–8, 251, 262, 266, 272, 309–13, 312, 315–16, 316
  Nut Walk 127, 137–9, 142–3, 204, 284–5
  orchard 125, 126, 127–33, 163
  pasture 79, 100–1
  planning permission 11, 77, 78, 79, 102, 195–6
  Pond Garden 200, 217, 257
  Poop Deck (pergola) 187–8, 215, 218–19, 262, 303, 316

Rose Garden 95, 112, 236, 250, 277
Round Garden 249, 266
seats 249, 254, 256, 272
Serpentine Walk 239, 240, 241, 244, 245, 248–9, 250, 251, 303
sheep farming 11, 68, 79, 100, 101, 102, 167, 173–4, 179–80, 202, 289, 297–8
shelter belt 80, 81, 83, 98, 246, 271
soil 103, 152
spring meadow 109
'the Squint' 213, 266
Tea Shed 112
timber barn 11–12, 13, 15, 78, 79
Tup Field 218, 289, 291, 294, 313
Vegetable Garden 135, 136, 146–64, 167–70, 177, 214, 219
viewing and buying the land 5, 6, 7–10, 67, 68
weeds 99–100, 228–30
woodland 81, 83–8, 94–8, 113–14, 119, 274–5
workshops 12
yard 184–5, 186, 187, 196, 287–8
inosculation 176
insect species, decline in 290
Internal Drainage Board (IDB) 72, 106, 153
International B414 tractor 167
Iris
  I. ochroleuca 223
  I. pseudacorus 217
  I. sibirica 223
Irish Peach apples 130
ivy 229, 271

Jasminum beesianum 206
Jason (gardener) 264, 265–6
Jekyll, Gertrude 51, 189–90, 221, 301
Juniperus
  J. chinensis 'Blauuw's Variety' 221
  J. scopulorum 'Skyrocket' 221

Kent, William 283
King's Lynn 225

Knebworth House, Hertfordshire 20
Kniphofia (red hot poker) 186
  K. 'Prince Igor' 187

ladders 177–8, 264
land drains 242–3, 275, 310fn
landscape evolution 81–2, 199–200
Lane, Miriam 122
lawns 41, 113, 121, 217, 230
  mowing 230–1, 236–7
Laxton, Northamptonshire 275–6
Leylandii 61, 190
lilac 186
lime trees 60–3, 113
  lime avenues 113
  lime-tree stickiness 62
  pleached 60–3, 62, 136, 164, 175–9, 175
  pruning 164, 177–8, 179
  see also Tilia
Limetree Farm 29–53, 55–66
  borders 51, 53
  burglary at 65–6
  flooding 43
  grass 48–9
  greenhouses 38, 48
  Harry's Patch (growing ground) 69–70, 71, 78, 104, 155
  house 30
  location 31–2
  paths 55–6
  plant propagation 71–2
  pleached lime trees 60–3, 62
  pond 56–9, 57, 208
  purchase of 31
  sale of 11, 12, 67, 78–9
  shelterbelt 39, 39, 41–3, 81
  soil 30, 31, 33, 35, 55
  strawberry field 30, 33, 37, 38, 39–40, 48
  vegetable garden 146, 167
  views 29, 37, 41, 263
  weeds and weed control 36, 39–40, 228
Lloyd, Christopher 43, 47, 115, 122, 215
Lombardy poplar 125, 293

Long Border (Inley Drove Farm)
    188, 209, 213–23, 216, 236, 238,
    241, 242, 243, 251, 254, 256,
    259, 262, 271, 272, 277, 303
  colour scheme 221–2
  pergola 218–19, 262, 303
  planting 220–2
Lonicera (honeysuckle)
  L. fragrantissima 94fn
  L. japonica var. 'Halliana' 180
  L. nitida 'Baggesen's Gold' 257
lupins 222
Lychnis chalcedonica 222

Macmillan Nurses 314
Major (Labrador) 13, 69
The Major (plantsman) 59–60, 127,
    224, 225
The Making of the English
    Landscape (W.G. Hoskins) 84
manure 167–9
  digging in 167–9
mapmaking 194, 195
March, Cambridgeshire 29
Marie Curie Cancer Care 314
marsh samphire (Salicornia
    europaea) 277
Marshland 32
Maynard, Arne 109, 110, 143
meadow bindweed (Convolvulus
    arvensis) 228
meadow buttercup (Ranunculus
    acris) 60, 111, 112, 238
meadows 100–6, 122
  flowers 102, 104, 105, 109,
    110–11, 112, 122
  grazing seed mixes 100
  Hay Meadow (Inley Drove Farm)
    79, 84, 98, 102–3, 103, 105–6,
    109, 110–12, 120, 121, 219,
    238, 272
  modern recreations of 101–2
  mown paths 111–12, 120
  pasture 100–1
  soil fertility 102–3
  see also hay
Mesolithic Age 140, 141

mini-digger 182, 197–8, 203, 284
Miss Willmott's Ghost see sea holly
    (Eryngium giganteum)
moles 16, 288
Molinia 223
monastic life 279–81
Morgan, Joan 128
Mount Grace Priory, North
    Yorkshire 279–80
mowing 49–50, 230–1
  mulch mowers 49
  side-discharge mowers 60
  stripy effect 49–50
muntjac deer 107, 135, 219, 262
Muscari armeniacum (grape
    hyacinth) 184

Narcissus
  N. 'Hawera' 244
  N. jonquilla 244
  N. obvallaris (Tenby daffodil)
    296–7
  N. pseudonarcissus 296
National Garden Scheme 124, 185,
    186, 246–8, 251, 262, 266, 272,
    309–16, 312, 316
neighbours
  communal relations 19, 25
  trade and exchange 19, 160
Nene, River 31–2
Nene Washes 42
Neolithic Age 140
nettles see stinging nettles
New Fen Dyke 125, 194
Nicolson, Harold 268, 269
Norfolk Biffin apples 130–1
North Creek, Norfolk 225
North Level Internal Drainage
    Board (NLIDB) 72
numinous experience 278, 279,
    280–1
nurseries, local 223, 224, 225–6
nuts
  cobnuts 139, 141–3, 285
  Nut Walk (Inley Drove Farm)
    127, 137–9, 142–3, 204, 284–5
  squirrel predation 285, 286

oak 80, 81, 85, 87, 96, 119, 142, 227, 239, 271
  red oak 87
  standards 142
oilseed rape 99
Old Fen Dyke 125, 195
Old Vicarage Garden, East Ruston 262–3
onions 162
Ordnance Survey (OS) 194
Orkney 273
Oudolf, Piet 101, 110

Painshill, Surrey 253
pampas grass 186
  see also Cortaderia
Parkinson's UK 314
Parson Drove, Cambridgeshire 199
paths 89–90, 180–1, 200–1, 201, 207–8, 207, 239
  border edging 247
  character and appeal of 89, 90
  garden framework 89
  mown 89, 98, 111–12, 120, 121
Pattern and Purpose (C. Fox) 52
pears 125, 163, 164
  see also Pyrus communis
Pen (Labrador cross) 88, 91, 107, 129, 229, 305
peonies 73, 209
pergola 187–8, 215, 218–19, 262, 303, 316
Peterborough 17, 19, 26, 27, 30, 108, 140, 196
pheasants 286
philadelphus 221
Phorpres bricks 30
Physocarpus opulifolius 'Dart's Gold' 213, 221
pigmyweed (Crassula helmsii) 217
Pinus sylvestris (Scots pine) 262
Pitt Rivers Museum 290
planning departments 195–7
planning permission 11, 77, 78, 79, 102
plant breeding 133–4
plant diseases, spread of 63

Planting the Natural Garden (Piet Oudolf) 101
plastic pollution 113–14
pleaching 60, 61–3, 62, 136, 175–6, 175, 178
pollarding 42, 284
pollen records 94, 234, 239
ponds
  digging out 57–8
  escape ramp for wildlife 59
  filling 58, 58
  fish 59
  Inley Drove Farm 200, 217, 257
  Limetree Farmhouse 208
  liners 56–7
  pond plants 58–9, 217
poop decks 188
  Poop Deck (Inley Drove Farm) 187–8, 215, 218–19, 262, 303, 316
Populus nigra
  P. n. (black poplar) 218, 229, 262, 292–4
  P.n. 'Italica' (Lombardy poplar) 125, 293
potatoes 162
  potato cyst eelworm 156
pottery, Neolithic 140
Primula
  P. veris see cowslips
  P. vulgaris (primrose) 106, 122, 138
propagation 71
  plant division 104–5
property market, inflated 66–7
Pruning (Christopher Brickell) 136
Prunus avium (wild cherry) 85, 86, 107, 107
Pryor, Maisie 1, 6, 13, 57, 61, 87, 104–5, 115, 131, 178, 257, 259–60, 290, 302–3, 306
  colour sense 221–2, 235–6, 302
  family background 10
  and Flag Fen 17, 136–7
  love of flowering plants 48, 51, 59, 147, 187, 209, 221, 273, 302, 311

notebooks 46, 47, 137, 256
pruning skills 134, 135
specialist in ancient timbers 12,
    14, 66
vegetable growing 146
Pryor, Dr Mark 44
pyracantha 271
*Pyrus communis* (pear)
    *P.c.* 'Doyenné du Comice 164
    *P.c.* 'Onward' 164

rabbits 286
railway sleepers 153–4
rainfall 72, 248, 310
    rainwater harvesting 237
    *see also* flooding
*Ranunculus* (buttercup)
    *R. acris* 60, 111, 112, 238
    *R. repens* 41, 60, 104, 110–11
raspberries 161, 162
red clover 100
red orach (*Atriplex hortensis*) 216
red-hot poker (*Kniphofia*) 186, 187
Repton, Humphry 20–1, 51,
    112–13, 189, 301
Ribston Pippin apples 127, 131,
    132, 133
Richards, Alison 128
ridge-and-furrow field system 275,
    276
robins 177
roddons 9, 31, 32, 33, 34, 35, 77,
    80, 146
roe deer 107, 262
Rogues Alley 35
*Rosa* (rose)
    *R.* 'Daybreak' 206
    *R.* 'Kathleen Harrop' 59
    *R.* 'Morletti' 245
    *R. moyesii* 245–6
        *R.m.* 'Geranium' 209
    *R. mundi* 'Fair Rosamund' 209
    *R.* 'Prosperity' 209
    *R. rugosa* 135, 246
        *R.r.* 'Alba' 249
        *R.r.* 'Blanc Double de Coubert'
        249

*R. suffulta* 204–5
*R.* 'The Fairy' 209
roses 94–5, 145, 240
    pruning 134–6
    repeat flowering 311
    Rose Garden (Inley Drove Farm)
        95, 112, 236, 250, 277
Rotavator 168, 247
Rothschild, Charles 122
Roundup® 40, 119, 292
Rousham, Oxfordshire 261, 283–4
Royal Horticultural Society 128,
    136
*Rudbeckia fulgida* var. *sullivantii*
    'Goldsturm' 222
runner beans 161
rural landscape, changing 81–2,
    199–200
ryegrass 100, 103

Sackville-West, Vita 268, 269, 271,
    313
*Salix* (willow)
    *S. alba* 46
        *S.a.* var. 'Kermesina' 46, 47, 284
    *S. gracilistyla* 'Melanostachys' 44
    *S. udensis* 'Golden Sunshine' 221
salt 31
samphire 277
sandbanks 77
scent in the garden 210, 273
Scots pine (*Pinus sylvestris*) 262
Scott, Walter 25
sea holly (*Eryngium giganteum*)
    186–7
seasons, meteorological 93fn
secateurs 178
Second World War
    Dig for Victory campaign 314
    invasion defences 241–2
seedheads 187, 223, 304
septic tank 183
Serpentine Walk (Inley Drove Farm)
    239, 240, 241, 244, 245, 248–9,
    250, 251, 303
shade 72–3
sheep farming 11, 68, 79, 100, 101,

102, 167, 173–4, 179–80, 289, 297–8
lambing 102
shearing 202
sheep pneumonia 174
silt deposition 32
Sissinghurst Castle, Kent 268–9
Skara Brae 273
sloes 291, 292
snake's-head fritillaries 104, 107, 109, 110, 112, 238, 286
snow 72, 93
snowdrops 90, 91, 92, 93, 94, 95–6, 138, 183–4, 229, 285, 304–5
clumps 96
galanthophiles 94, 96
hybrids 95, 96
thefts of 305–9
transplanting 'in the green' 96
see also Galanthus
soakaway beds 15
sodium chlorate 166
soils
clay-silt 30, 31, 103
drainage 153, 167, 217, 218, 310
fertility 16–17, 152
silty 9, 16, 31, 32, 33, 151–2
South Creek, Norfolk 225
South Holland Internal Drainage Board (SHIDB) 72
Spalding 108, 196
spiny bear's breeches (Acanthus spinosus) 186
squirrels
black 287
grey 132, 143, 285, 286–7, 291, 304, 305
Stamford 202
statues, garden 50–1, 218
stinging nettle (Urtica dioica) 227, 228, 229
Stowe, Buckinghamshire 37–8, 52, 237–8
strawberries 37, 161, 162–3
strawberry fields 30, 33, 37, 38, 39–40, 48
Sturmer Pippin apples 132

Sutton Fen 8
Suzuki four-wheel drive 113, 192–3
Swiss Garden, Bedfordshire 138
Symphyotrichum laeve 'Calliope' 222

Tagetes patula (French marigold) 161–2
temples, garden 253
Thames Estuary 32
Thuja
T. orientalis 'Aurea Nana' 272, 278
T. plicata 262
Tilia (lime)
T. cordata 61
T. platyphyllos 62
timber barns 11–12, 13, 15, 78, 79
timber-frame houses 14
Time Team (Channel 4) 18, 158, 279
Tinker's Drove 35
tomatoes 48, 161–2
traveller and Romany population 35
Trifolium repens (white clover) 100, 101
Tudor gardens 25
tulips 183
Tup Field (Inley Drove Farm) 218, 289, 291, 294, 313
Twink (Border Collie) 135
twitch see couch grass

vegetable garden 145–70
boundaries 147, 214
companion planting 147, 161–2
crop rotation 152, 155–6
cut flowers 209
digging 152, 164–5, 169–70, 177
drainage 153, 167
Inley Drove Farm 135, 136, 146–64, 167–70, 177, 214, 219
laying out 148, 166
Limetree Farm 146, 167
netting 162–3
no-dig gardening 168
paths 147, 152

*potager* 161–2
raised beds 153–4, 182, 183
siting 146–7, 148
surplus produce 159–60
*Verbascum nigrum* (dark mullein)
    186
*Verbena bonariensis* 43–4
*Viburnum* 94
    V. x *bodnantense* 69, 94fn, 139
    V. x *b*. 'Dawn' 284
    V. *opulus* 139
    V. *sargentii* 'Onondaga' 221
Victorian gardens 25, 88, 163, 189
visiting other gardens 123–4, 137,
    247
    *see also* National Garden Scheme;
    *and specific gardens*
voles 59

Wagg, Elsie 313
walls 80, 172–3, 175, 200, 288
Walpole, Robert 130
Walsingham Abbey, Norfolk 95–6
Warley Place, Essex 186
the Wash 16, 32, 77, 158, 172, 276,
    277
washing line 182
watering 73, 235, 237
weeds and weed control 36, 39–40,
    99–100, 166, 227–9
Welland, River 32
*The Well-Tempered Garden*
    (Christopher Lloyd) 115
West Acre, Norfolk 225–7
western red cedar (*Thuja plicata*)
    262
Weston, Hertfordshire 165
white clover 100, 101
Whittlesey causeway,
    Cambridgeshire 42

Wicken Fen, Cambridgeshire 122
wild cherry 85, 86, 107, *107*
wild pear 85
wild plum 290–1
Wildlife and Countryside Act 97
Willmott, Ellen 186–7
willow 38, 39, 41–3, 44, 45, 46, 51,
    81, 221
    pollarded 42, 284
    propagation 47
    pruning 46
    rods 142
    *see also Salix*
winds 38, 39, 41, 149, 172, 175,
    204, 205, 241, 271, 297
winter
    gardens in 188–9
    winter jobs 61, 164–5, 177
    winter solstice 92
Wisbech 10, 11, 29, 30, 37, 108, 125
*Wisteria* 254
    *Wisteria sinensis* 188, 190
woodland (Inley Drove Farm) 81,
    83–8, 94–8, 113–14, 119, 274–5
    access routes 113–14, 115, 119,
    287
    'assart' curve 84–5, 86–7, *103*,
    115, 119
    grant-aided 83, 85, 87
    native hardwoods 85
    protective plastic tree tubes
    113–14
    spring bulbs 94, 96–7
woodpeckers 131
Worcester Pearmain apples 129, 131
Wrest Park, Bedfordshire 20, 238

Yellow Book *see* National Garden
    Scheme
yew 227, 255–7, 258, 259, 309, 314

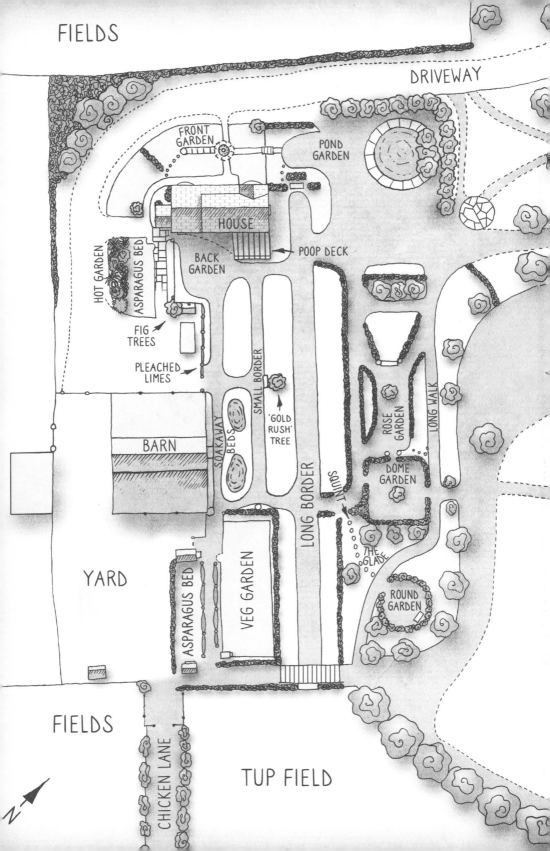